Miss Lizzie's War

The Double Life of Southern Belle Spy

Elizabeth Van Lew

Rosemary Agonito

Guilford, Connecticut

gpp®

Copyright © 2012 by Rosemary Agonito

Map by Trailhead Graphics, Inc. © Morris Book Publishing, LLC
Project editor: Meredith Dias
Layout: Kirsten Livingston

Agonito, Rosemary.
  Miss Lizzie's war : the double life of southern belle spy Elizabeth Van Lew / Rosemary Agonito.
    pages cm
  Includes bibliographical references.
  ISBN 978-0-7627-8012-9
  1. Van Lew, Elizabeth L., 1818–1900. 2. United States—History—Civil War, 1861–1865—Secret service. 3. Women spies—Virginia—Richmond. 4. Spies—Virginia—Richmond. 5. Unionists (United States Civil War)—Virginia—Richmond. 6. Richmond (Va.)—History—Civil War, 1861–1865. I. Title.
  E608.V34A36 2012
  973.7'85—dc23

                    2011048051

Printed in the United States of America

10 9 8 7 6 5 4 3 2 1

Contents

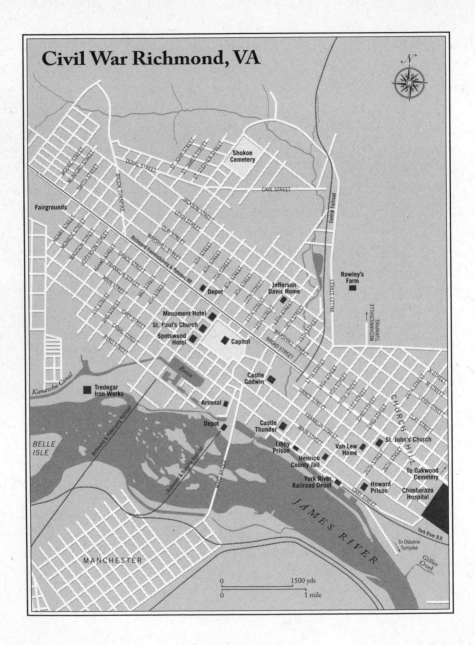

Civil War Richmond, VA

Shokoe Cemetery

Fairgrounds

MOORE STREET
M'AEORD STREET
SMITH STREET
DUVAL STREET
ST. JOHN STREET
ST. JAMES STREET
ST. STEPHEN STREET
BROCK TURNPIKE
CAVE STREET

JACKSON STREET
HENRY STREET
MONROE STREET
MADISON STREET
JEFFERSON STREET
ADAMS STREET
LEIGH STREET
CLAY STREET
MARSHALL STREET
5TH STREET
6TH STREET
7TH STREET

Richmond Fredericksburg & Potomac RR
Central Railroad
VALLEY STREET

Rowley's Farm

GRACE STREET
FRANKLIN STREET
3RD STREET
4TH STREET
8TH STREET
9TH STREET
10TH STREET
11TH STREET
12TH STREET
13TH STREET
14TH STREET
15TH STREET

Jefferson Davis Home

MAIN STREET
CARY STREET
1ST STREET
2ND STREET
CANAL STREET
BYRD STREET

Depot

Monument Hotel
St. Paul's Church
Spotswood Hotel
Capitol
Basin

MECHANICSVILLE TURNPIKE

Castle Godwin

Kanawha Canal

Tredegar Iron Works

Arsenal

BROAD STREET
MARSHALL STREET

11TH STREET
8TH STREET
9TH STREET
XTH STREET
21ST STREET
2ND STREET
23RD STREET
24TH STREET
25TH STREET
26TH STREET
CLAY STREET
LEIGH STREET
M STREET
N STREET

CHURCH HILL

Depot

BELLE ISLE

Richmond & Danville Railroad

Mayo Bridge

Castle Thunder

Libby Prison

Henrico County Jail

York River Railroad Depot

GRACE STREET
FRANKLIN STREET
MAIN STREET

Van Lew Home

St. John's Church

To Oakwood Cemetery

Howard Prison

Chimborazo Hospital

CARY STREET

J A M E S   R I V E R

Richmond & Danville Railroad

MANCHESTER

York River R.R.

To Osborne Turnpike

Gillies Creek

0   1500 yds
0   1 mile

February 1862

As she stepped reluctantly into the dark corridor, a burly guard slammed the massive oak door shut behind her and thrust the rusty metal latch into its bolt. The cell door quickly dissolved behind a watery film while the guard walked down the hallway. Elizabeth stood fixed to the spot. Overwhelmed by grief, she reached out her hand and touched the splintered door.

For months she had passed through that doorway, bringing food and supplies to doomed prisoners under order to be hanged. With each visit to that cramped and musty cell, the bond between her and Allen deepened. But in the dank cell crowded with men, their love never extended beyond hand-holding—never, until today. Today they tearfully embraced for the first time—and, she feared, the last. Tomorrow the cold, stone room would be empty.

"Miss," a voice bellowed from the hallway.

Elizabeth wiped her eyes and pulled herself away from the cell. A stale smell of decay and death filled the windowless corridor. Memory ghosts crowding her on all sides turned the passageway claustrophobic.

As she slowly moved down the hallway in its half-light, a jumble of thoughts thrashed about in her mind and she struggled to make sense of the tangle. This long nightmare . . . years in the making.

When the prison gate opened, blinding sunlight and frigid air swept against her, pushing her back. She grasped the doorframe to steady herself before stepping into the yard and moving toward the waiting carriage.

CHAPTER 1

A LEADEN MIST COVERED THE MOUNTAIN AS ELIZABETH CAREFULLY stepped over the rock-strewn trail. Moisture hung heavy in the air and she strained to see in the thick morning fog. All around, in the haunted groves and tangle of life, rot covered the forest floor. A chill ran up her spine as she pulled the shawl tightly around her shoulders.

In the summer of 1860, her father dead and her siblings married, only Elizabeth and her mother traveled to the mountain spa, hoping for relief from the country's sectional struggles. But the quiet peace of the cool hills had fled. Secession fever hovered over the mountain retreat like winged predators.

Alarmed and angered by the divisive talk at the springs, Elizabeth sought to escape by wandering off the garden paths and onto trails snaking through the dense mountain woods. As she moved aimlessly, ghosts from the past took shape in the fog, following her, clinging to her. In truth she welcomed them and felt comforted to drift back, to be enveloped by them.

A nostalgia swept over her as shadowy figures emerged. How her father loved the lush grandeur of these mountains. Every summer John Van Lew, a Northern transplant who made a fortune in the hardware business, led his family from their magnificent mansion on Church Hill in Richmond to the great estate at White Sulfur Springs. The excitement of those trips together, riding by carriage through the green countryside, rushed through her mind.

Elizabeth stopped and sat on a boulder. In the debris surrounding her, clumps of brightly colored mushrooms poked through the ground—red, blue, yellow, orange—strewn about like broken pieces of a rainbow. Bird songs and exotic scents covered her as she remembered a happier time with her brother and sister running along these same trails, poking about in the dense brush, imagining themselves explorers of the wild. She smiled, recalling her parents' gentle scolding when they returned scuffed, scraped, and stained.

As Elizabeth peered at the fog ghosts, her mother took shape—Eliza, who left behind her prominent Philadelphia family, politicians and early abolitionists, to marry John. Thinking back, Elizabeth marveled at how her slave-owning family moved so easily between conservative Richmond's powerful upper-crust and progressive Philadelphia's radical movements. She remembered with pleasure that Northern city, where they sent her to be educated, happily surrounded by books and chatter and girl giggles, and Richmond, where her parents filled their home with vibrant discussions and artists, writers, politicians, and dignitaries.

Those warm memories flooded Elizabeth's thoughts, filling her with longing as she sat staring at the mist-covered trees. But that wide-eyed, invincible girl with the mop of curly blond ringlets had vanished. She bent over and picked up a dry leaf, fragile and brown, lying among piles of dead leaves covering the forest floor. A sudden sadness overtook her as her thoughts wandered through the dark, slippery tunnels of her heart. Gone. All gone. Elizabeth dropped the crumbling leaf, rose, and made her way past the fog ghosts back to the grand hotel.

That evening Elizabeth Van Lew found herself in one of the estate's great parlors with overstuffed furniture, lush carpets, and glistening chandeliers, caught in the tirade of a man she roundly disliked, Edmund Ruffin. The prosperous Virginia farmer boasted of having traveled to witness John Brown's hanging and raved on about the Northern conspiracy to deprive them of their god-given right to own slaves. The old man's fierce words clashed with his fragile appearance—grizzled face, thin hair that fell to his shoulders, gray beard, and short stature.

"I tell you an invasion is coming. Virginia must join in seceding from the Union if we are to defend ourselves," Ruffin urged as his outburst wound down.

"Surely," Elizabeth boldly ventured at that point, "these conspiracies are overblown. What evidence . . . ?"

"Evidence?" the man snapped before she could finish. "John Brown is the evidence! The capture of Harper's Ferry is the evidence!"

"But he captured a Federal armory and the government put down the rebellion," Elizabeth persisted.

Blood poured into the man's thin face as he glared at the impudent woman, then turned his back and spoke to the men. "If Lincoln wins the election, we are finished, I tell you. We cannot wait."

As Ruffin spoke and a sharp anger rose in her throat, Elizabeth felt a gentle tug at her sleeve. Her friend, Eliza Carrington, pulled her away from the animated group.

"Please, Bet, be careful," her young friend whispered. "You can't argue with a man like that. It's dangerous."

"It's intolerable, Eliza! How *can* we be quiet?"

But Elizabeth knew her friend was right. To express pro-Union sentiment amounted to treason for these "fire-eaters." Seething inside, she held her tongue as black clouds swept through her mind and bitterness poisoned the beauty and tranquillity of the magnificent mountain retreat.

Those dark days in the brilliant summer sun of the mountain springs oppressed Elizabeth and her mother, who had secretly freed their slaves after John Van Lew died, despite the legal prohibition in his will. Their wealth and status, their inner circle of connections among Richmond's most prominent citizens, had provided cover and a safe middle ground. Enjoying a life of privilege among the aristocracy, they convinced themselves they were somehow above and apart from it.

Now a plague of fear infected everyone. That summer of madness made clear what they tried not to see at home. Their middle ground was shifting beneath their feet and sinking fast.

———

All night, smoking locomotives dragging noisy, jerking boxcars full of human cargo pulled into the rail station at the corner of Broad and Eighth. Torrential rains soaked the bloody warriors as they stepped, or were carried, onto the wooden platform in the eerie darkness where uneasy relatives stood watch. Here and there lanterns, buffeted by the downpour, threw a garish, snaky light over the figures moving anxiously about in the shadow of the capitol, searching the faces of the wounded. Muffled by the heavy rain, sounds of moaning and weeping, cries of recognition and distress, crept over the drenched platform and onto the flooded streets. All night the creaking rail cars came and went, belching sooty smoke and acrid smells, and expelling hundreds of wounded and dead.

That very day a joyous city had danced and cheered, celebrated in the streets, and shouted cries of victory. News of the triumphant battle near a mere trickle of a stream named Bull Run, north of Richmond, flew over the city, gripping it in an orgy of elation. Now the North would have to recognize an independent Confederacy. Lincoln and his cowardly army would have no choice, they argued.

Some, like Elizabeth Van Lew, saw things differently. She had watched in disgust from the great portico of her home with her friend Eliza Carrington as crowds spilled over the streets in a spasm of joy.

"Fools," she muttered, as Eliza stood silently frowning.

"What will these cheering women do, Bet, when their sons and husbands come home wounded or dead?" the younger woman asked.

"They know nothing of war, Eliza, but that will soon end," Elizabeth responded somberly in the breezeless summer afternoon.

Just then Mary, her sister-in-law, emerged from the house breathless. "It's wonderful! We've won!" The bubbly, dark-haired, dark-eyed beauty waved her arm across the great lawn, pointing to the swarming crowd below. "I should wake the children from their naps to see this glorious celebration."

"And what have we won, Mary?" Elizabeth gravely asked the young woman who had married her brother six years earlier and come to live in the mansion. She thought sadly how little she had in common with this woman, sixteen years younger than her brother.

"It means the Confederacy will triumph, of course," Mary responded testily, her eyes narrowed and her brow knit. "I don't understand why you can't be happy, Bet. Truly, I don't. You and your brother!" Averting her eyes from Elizabeth, she added contemptuously, "You'll see. Secession is the best thing that's happened to the South." With a swirl of her great rustling skirt, Mary turned and walked away, disappearing into the house as quickly as she had appeared.

Elizabeth exchanged glances with her friend as the door slammed. A black and white person—a girl really—she thought. No shades of gray, no nuances. How her thoughtful, serious brother had linked with Mary puzzled her. At the same time she understood how Mary's beauty overwhelmed those who met her. When she appeared, men stared and did not listen.

As the crowds below grew, the two women walked uneasily to the bottom of the garden to watch the demonstrations in the streets. Women, children, men snaked past, whooping, surging, singing in the sticky heat. Protesters carried the new Confederate flag with its palmetto tree, waving it defiantly. As their imaginations embellished the victory, the people of Richmond grew more jubilant and raucous.

"I can't watch any more of this," Elizabeth groaned after awhile.

Her friend, grim faced, nodded in agreement. "I need to get back. Let's hope this all passes quickly." With a wave of her hand, Eliza walked across the street to her home, weaving a path through the erratic revelers.

Sadly, Elizabeth turned and made her way back through the garden and into the house. Behind her the celebrating crowds grew louder under the blazing sun. The shouting and laughter continued until afternoon slipped away and rain began to fall. Then, like a group of children, the giddy partiers ran for shelter.

Her brother John came home from work late that night looking tired and dispirited. His clothes dripped from the steady rain that still fell. The hardware business consumed much of his time since his father died and his family saw too little of him. Mary and their children had already turned in, but his mother and sister sat together reading in the great parlor bathed by a soft gaslight.

Eliza hurried to get a towel from the kitchen. "John, you're soaked," she scolded him gently. "Where's your umbrella?"

"I left it with some people at the rail station. They needed it more than I did," he answered wearily.

"What's happened?" Elizabeth peered at his downcast face.

"There was such a commotion downtown that I went to look after I closed the store. The troops are coming back." He shook his head. "It's awful. So many wounded and dead . . . They're coming back in boxcars. People are frantic everywhere, searching for loved ones."

The two women sat grimly, taking in the news.

Shoulders slumped, John sank into an armchair, overwhelmed and disheartened by the sights following him, crowding his thoughts. "I can't believe it, but it truly has come to war."

"So many people are going North," Eliza said hesitantly. "Maybe we . . ." Her voice trailed off.

"What are you saying, Mother?" John asked, a nervous edge to his voice.

"My family would help, take us in if necessary. We could rebuild our roots there." Memories swept over her. "Your father and I had strong ties to the North."

"Move to Philadelphia?" Elizabeth, her own nerves frayed, had never seen her mother so worried.

"Mary would *never* agree," John said emphatically of his wife. "She detests anything Yankee. And I have to think of the girls. Uprooting Annie and little Eliza would be hard."

"All our friends are here—our ties," Elizabeth added. A note of sadness touched her voice. "Our dead are here."

"If we left, it would be seen as disloyalty. They could confiscate our property." John's thoughts raced in alarm. "So much of what we have is tied up in property."

"We could sell the property," Eliza's desperate voice had become a half whisper.

"That's not likely with so many leaving," her daughter said gently.

"What of the business?" her son added, his voice becoming more agitated. "How would we replace the income? It could take years to build a business in the North."

Eliza sighed and fell silent.

"If we stay and fight . . ." John hesitated.

"So many have been arrested already," Elizabeth finished his thought. A pall fell over the room. "Do we just withdraw to the mansion . . . bury our feelings?" she asked gloomily.

John shook his head in despair.

A frightening stillness spread over them and they retreated into the chaos of their thoughts. Overhead the eerie gaslight cast a somber glow around the parlor as a strange paralysis took hold of them. Through an open window topped by rich velvet draperies, a warm gust tousled the sheer lace curtains beneath.

A sense of terrible foreboding enveloped Elizabeth. "I fear in war there is no sanctuary."

Throughout that long night, the South's fighting men, the wounded and dead at least, poured into Richmond. The day's euphoria quickly faded as the first real taste of war seeped into people's consciousness. With hospitals overflowing, Richmond's citizens took the wounded into their homes and its women began ministering as best they could to the broken bodies.

——

Early the next morning, after an agitated and sleepless night, Elizabeth ventured downtown, anxious for news. The rain had stopped but heavy clouds still covered Richmond, pushing back the sun as she made her way around the puddles and mud holes left by the night's drenching rain. The sound of distant shouts grew louder as she approached and a light-headedness gripped her when she spotted Confederate soldiers herding uneven columns of Union prisoners into the city at bayonet point. All around, Elizabeth's countrymen lined the streets, hurling angry shouts and threats at the blue-coated men who shuffled past. The weary, tattered, dejected procession seemed endless as she anxiously watched.

For a long time Elizabeth stared as the rumpled Union troops walked by. When at last she turned and retraced her steps, a sad fury took hold of her. Her determined pace quickened as she hurried home.

On and on they came as an unprepared city scrambled to open prison space. No room existed in the crowded jails, so Brigadier General John Winder, Provost Marshal of Richmond, appropriated several tobacco factories and warehouses. Into these crude, makeshift penitentiaries a strange collection of hundreds of Union prisoners came—soldiers, but also civilians caught in a ferocious Union rout. They soon found themselves in crowded, dirty warehouse rooms without basic sanitation, little medical care, one or two meager meals a day, and bare floors for bedding.

——

That night, after watching the spectacle in the street, a stew of emotions welled up in Elizabeth—fear, anger, contempt, regret . . . Sleepless in her bed, she felt a specter in the room and sighed wearily.

"War has started, Poppa," she said without words, shaking her head dejectedly. "Over slavery . . ."

John Van Lew silently hovered in the room, bracing himself.

"Why did you need slaves?" she castigated him. "To fit in with Richmond's elite?"

This again! He flinched and looked around the room for a place to hide. *Why does it always come back to me? Dead men don't own slaves.* Wisps of air shifted.

"Even after you died . . ." Her silent voice grew sharper. "Forcing mother to keep slaves. Putting it in your will that she couldn't free them."

Her father frowned. *I'm trying to remember why you were my favorite,* he thought.

"You read, traveled, filled our heads with progressive ideas. That was *your* word, 'progressive.'"

And now you're the progressive? Please! When did you reject Richmond's elite? A slight gust of wind moved over her bed.

"Twenty-one human beings. And we had to figure out how to get around your will with every one of them. Making secret arrangements. Getting the ones who wanted to go North out of Richmond. Buying kinfolks so they could go together. Paying those who wanted to stay a decent wage."

The snaking in the room grew more agitated.

"And now we live this lie. Everybody thinks the Negroes are still our slaves. Whether they're in the mansion with us or on our farm."

My fault you live a lie . . .?

An audible sigh passed her lips. "Remember," she digressed, "when we were little and you took us to the farm?" He could see her blue eyes begin to sparkle in the dark. "We thought it was the biggest farm in the world when we roamed those thirty-six acres. How we loved that ride into the country south of Richmond, having the James River pop up again next to the farm."

Her voice softened a bit and she lay quietly for awhile. A wisp of sadness spread over the room.

"What would you do now, Poppa?"

He refused to answer.

Elizabeth turned her face from him. "The real question is what do *I* do." She lay, staring at the ceiling for a long time. A shard of fear pierced her heart, the kind of fear that peeks and hides, comes and goes. The kind it's easy to ignore in the midst of bravado.

Like so many ladies of her class she filled her life with charitable works among Richmond's poor. Elizabeth knew instinctively they would bear the burden of war more than her own class. She thought about Emmie, frail and weak, at one of the almshouses, and the others who had grown to be like family in the dingy recesses of the city's most run-down areas. What would war do to them?

—◦—

The next afternoon Elizabeth made her way to the office of General Winder. The silver-haired, heavyset man sat alone behind an immense table in his temporary quarters, papers piled high. He rose when she entered, bowing slightly.

"Miss Van Lew," he said, surprised to see her and motioning to a chair. "I had not expected ladies to be calling."

"So kind of you to see me," Elizabeth replied warmly. Drawing on that well of Southern feminine charm, the province of manipulative aristocratic ladies, she smiled coyly. "What lady would not want to call on so handsome a gentleman?"

"And how is your mother?" He asked, staring at the petite, well-dressed woman with her blond hair pulled back from the sides of her face and curls tumbling over her forehead accenting her clear, ivory skin. An animated face, high cheekbones, and sharp features gave her an aura of passion and intensity that belied her poised, ladylike demeanor. Her slender, well-proportioned figure, her strangely alluring throat and neck, naked above the lacy, form-fitting bodice that covered her firm breasts, could draw the eye of any man. But mostly he noticed her brilliant blue eyes that sparkled and glowed like a sunlit, bottomless ocean. The deep green silk dress she wore shimmered as Elizabeth shifted slightly in her seat. Still attractive, he thought, though her youth has fled.

"As well as can be expected in these difficult times. And Mrs. Winder?"

"Fine, fine," he answered, still wondering why she had come.

"I won't take much of your time, General, but I have a favor to ask." Elizabeth thought she saw the old man's back straighten a bit. "I'd like your permission to visit Union prisoners and bring them a few supplies."

A deep frown spread over Winder's face. "That's quite impossible," he said disapprovingly. "Whatever could you be thinking? Those men are not worthy of a lady's time and attention."

"I think, General, you'll agree that it is our Christian duty as good Southern women to practice charity to those undeserving. I've heard many a sermon exhorting us to be kind to our enemies as our Lord was."

Winder's puzzled face softened a bit.

"We all agree the Confederacy is on a moral path to protect our precious way of life. It can only strengthen the rightness of our position to be generous in our time of victory," Elizabeth pressed on. "We would want the Union to do no less for our soldiers."

The old man ran his fingers through his thick, disheveled gray hair, pondering the appeal for what seemed like a long time to Elizabeth. His craggy face had an aura of strength with its Roman nose, wide mouth, and cool gray eyes set deep under bushy white eyebrows. She knew she had touched a nerve. His own son fought on the Union side.

Finally he shrugged. "Well, this is unexpected, very unexpected. But . . ." he hesitated, "if you feel it is your Christian duty . . ."

"I *do*, General," Elizabeth smiled, her heart quickening.

"Then I ask that you limit your visits to officers and civilians. A lady should not associate with common rabble."

Elizabeth stifled the protest rising in her throat. "Well, then, that's a start," she said instead, another smile spreading across her face. "Today you prove yourself a true Christian gentleman."

"You'll need an authorization," Winder replied as he picked up pen and paper and scrawled a message on the sheet: *Miss Van Lew has permission to visit the prisoners and to send them books, luxuries, delicacies, and what she may please. John Henry Winder.* "That should do it, Miss Van Lew. Please give your mother my best."

Thanking the general, a determined Elizabeth left the makeshift office on Bank Street feeling her first bit of pleasure in many weeks. When she arrived home, two finely dressed ladies from the neighborhood sat in the parlor with her mother in animated conversation. Mary Bowser, the Van Lew's former slave, moved about serving tea. The women had come, Eliza informed her, to request their help with the war effort by sewing clothing for Confederate troops. Elizabeth instinctively glanced at Mary and caught the corner of her eye.

"I've told them," Eliza said solemnly, "that we are quite occupied with household matters at this time."

The ladies looked at each other, sharing their disapproval. "Surely we are all busy," one said stiffly.

"Many of us are nursing wounded soldiers in our homes," the other added pointedly. "I do hope you will reconsider."

"As soon as we're able," Eliza said evasively.

After the women left, an energized Elizabeth showed her mother the note from General Winder. "We'll be able to visit with Union soldiers in prison."

"How wonderful, Bet," the older woman exclaimed. "However did you manage this?"

"Feminine wiles, flattery, Christian duty . . ."

"You lied!" Eliza exclaimed.

"I prefer to call it 'dissembling.'" A roguish smile of delight broke across her face.

Eliza watched her daughter enjoying the thought of having deceived Winder. It was so like Elizabeth, who from childhood took a perverse pleasure in deception, especially when it got her what she wanted. "Tricks" young Bet called her manipulative lies when caught, refusing to see her dishonesty as anything more than a game. When her lies caused problems, she took her punishment stoically, like a competitor losing this or that parlor game. But this . . . lying to Winder . . . mucking about in war. A twinge of fear seized Eliza's heart.

Elizabeth turned to the tall, slender young black woman putting away the cups. "Mary, I hope you'll help."

Mary nodded. "You know I'll help, Miss Lizzie. And so will the others."

Eliza quickly added, "We'll have to be careful. More arrests."

"I know," Elizabeth frowned.

"And so many have slipped over to the Confederate side out of fear. Being labeled a 'traitor' is terrifying people, Bet."

"And why not? Imprisonment, having your property seized, facing the hangman's noose." Elizabeth scowled indignantly, her fists clenched in anger. "Traitor! Those rebelling against the Union commit treason, *not* those who remain loyal."

❦

As Elizabeth approached the three-story, flat-roofed brick building on Main and Twenty-sixth Streets, she spotted prisoners at all the windows, staring intently through the iron bars. Her heart sobbed for them, so far from home, so young, so unjustly imprisoned. Accompanied by Peter Roane, a servant and former slave who carried two large kettles, Elizabeth nervously entered Howard Prison, unsure what she would find.

Inside the dark corridor, a wave of second thoughts and fear suddenly swept over her. Hesitating momentarily, Elizabeth asked herself what she was doing here. The converted warehouse reeked of tobacco and a mustiness hung in the hot, still air. Resisting the urge to turn and flee, Elizabeth pushed herself forward in the dim light and showed her note to the guard. Scrutinizing the message, he escorted her to the commandant's office.

Lieutenant David Todd, Director of Prisons, who had the morning before refused Elizabeth entrance, glared at Winder's note, furious that she had gone over his head. Exasperated, he seemed not to know what to say and in the silence she thought of his special betrayal, this man, the brother of Mary Todd Lincoln.

Composing himself, Lieutenant Todd spoke, his tone sardonic and cutting. "And *who* exactly do you wish to see?"

Mindful of Winder's admonishment, Elizabeth asked to visit with the officers.

Todd mumbled something to the guard, who motioned Elizabeth to the door. After thanking the officer, she followed the young man into the gloomy hallway while Lieutenant Todd's piercing eyes fixed on her back.

The darkened, narrow corridor led past a series of closed doors, their secrets hidden from view. At last the guard lifted a latch on a large oak door and pushed it open. With Peter in tow, Elizabeth nervously stepped into the dirty, pungent-smelling room, squinting in the half-light at a group of men crowded into the large space, some standing, some sitting on the floor. She noticed a few men lying along the walls on the bare floor and quickly realized from their bandaged bodies that they were wounded. Only a rough wooden table and a few benches furnished the room, she observed as the guard slammed the creaking door shut behind her, noting that he would be just outside.

Startled by the sudden presence of a lady in their midst, the men rose quickly and awkwardly. One man, distinguished looking even in his wrinkled, dirty suit, stepped forward. Elizabeth immediately extended her hand and introduced herself and Peter as he placed the kettles on the table.

"Congressman Alfred Ely," the man said, bowing.

"Congressman?" Elizabeth said, surprised.

"From New York," the man added, offering her a seat on a bench. "And this is my good friend, Calvin Huson, a lawyer from Rochester, New York."

16

One by one, those who could stand moved forward to greet Elizabeth, an odd assortment of officers and civilians, all the while glancing hungrily at the kettles on the table.

"Please," Elizabeth told the men, motioning toward the kettles. "Help yourselves. It isn't much. And please see that the wounded get a bit," she added as they moved forward, tin cups in hand.

Her chicken soup and cornmeal porridge, and her lively conversation, buoyed the spirits of the hungry men. Eager for news, the men listened intently as Elizabeth told them what she knew. She took care not to betray her pro-Union sentiments but tried to find out as much as she could about conditions inside the prison and what had happened at Bull Run. She quickly learned that these Northern soldiers and civilians, like their Southern counterparts, had expected a swift defeat of the other side.

Before leaving, Elizabeth moved to the walls where the wounded lay, offering words of encouragement. One young man in particular caught her eye. His leg had been amputated and he weakly introduced himself as Lewis Francis. Fighting back tears, Elizabeth promised the hollow-eyed, pale youth who could barely extend his arm to her that she would send a servant every day to tend to his wants. When she asked the men what they needed, she was astonished at the lack of fresh bandages, the paucity of food, and the fact that only those who could pay got personal necessities.

"I'll do what I can," she assured the men before leaving.

Almost every day, with Peter or other servants, occasionally with her mother, Elizabeth made her way to the various prisons, bringing food, bandages, clothing, books, and whatever they could carry to Union prisoners. When she could not visit, Elizabeth sent servants with supplies, and a day did not pass without someone tending to Lewis Francis.

As Elizabeth grew to know the men, attachments formed and trust developed. She and Congressman Ely became friends and began to share confidences. Ely quickly learned of her antisecession, antislavery sentiments and her desire to serve the Union cause. Elizabeth in turn discovered more about Northern feelings regarding the war—that keeping the Union together was the prime motivation, not the abolition of slavery. She also visited frequently with Major Paul Joseph Revere, grandson of Revolutionary War hero Paul Revere, and Colonel William Raymond Lee, both of Massachusetts.

But one man in particular attracted Elizabeth's attention, Major Allen Lee Rockwell. A soft-spoken, pleasant, handsome gentleman, Rockwell always stepped forward to greet her when she stopped by Howard Prison. The man towered over petite Elizabeth and bowed slightly when he shook her hand. From the first day they met, he gazed intently into her crystal-clear blue eyes, so animated and full of life, as if he were trying to understand a mystery hidden deep in their recesses. At first, Major Rockwell's attentions embarrassed Elizabeth, but soon she found his interest flattering.

At forty-four, the dark-haired, brown-eyed Rockwell was a few years older than Elizabeth. His steady, calm demeanor reflected a stoic acceptance of his lot. The two spoke often, at first about ordinary things—the prison routine, the weather, a book she offered him. But soon they began sharing stories of their childhood, their parents and siblings.

On one of her visits, Rockwell asked, "And your husband, Elizabeth. What does he do?"

"I am not married," she responded simply. She thought she detected the slightest of smiles pass across his lips. "And your wife?" she inquired.

"My wife is dead," he answered, his face suddenly somber.

"I am so sorry," Elizabeth replied.

"It's been years," he said softly. "I can talk about it now. That wasn't always true."

He paused.

"My wife died in childbirth ... and ..." He spoke haltingly. "My child died shortly after. He was a fine boy, my son."

"That is more than anyone should bear," Elizabeth said, touching his hand gently. Tears flooded her heart for the man as he spoke heavily of his loss. "I think I understand . . ." She stopped and her gaze dropped to the floor.

Rockwell looked at her, seeing her sadness.

Elizabeth struggled to speak of something unspoken and buried for years in the labyrinth of her memory. "I too have suffered a loss—not as great as yours."

"Every loss is great," he said.

"I've not spoken of this since it happened," Elizabeth hesitated again. Her thoughts twisted through the dark caverns of the past. "I was to be married. My beloved fiancé, David, died on the eve of our wedding . . . a riding accident." A sob caught in her throat as the long-buried loss erupted to the surface.

At the revelations, a rush of emotions welled up between them. Although they sat on a wooden bench in a musty, shabby cell surrounded by other prisoners as they spoke, Rockwell gently touched her hand when she finished and the two suddenly felt completely alone.

"You have never married?" he asked quietly as they sat.

"No," Elizabeth answered. Then a small smile slowly began to curl across her mouth. "I'm told by my family that my expectations are too high. That I need to temper my unrealistic attitude because the perfect man doesn't exist." She broke into a laugh and a broad grin crossed his face.

"I can attest to that," he said with a chuckle.

"I'm not exactly the sort of woman Southern men want for a wife," she joked. "Strong-willed."

"Spunky!" Rockwell interrupted, laughing.

"Stubborn, some would say," she added with a mischievous smirk. "Truth is, I'm happy. My days are full and marriage has not been something I seek."

"You know, Elizabeth," he said, looking into her blue eyes, "not all men are Southern men . . ."

—◆—

To all the prisoners, Elizabeth and her mother became angels of mercy in their cruel, barren lives. But in Richmond they began to attract attention with their visits to the enemy. Neighbors whispered about the two women who refused to sew clothing for Confederate soldiers but ministered to the devils threatening them all. One day someone left an anonymous note on their doorstep warning the "Lincoln lovers" of "a fire," an incident that reduced John's wife, Mary, to near hysteria.

One morning Elizabeth sat pensively at the breakfast table drinking her coffee while Eliza arranged some flowers from the garden in a large crystal vase. Suddenly her sister-in-law burst in, waving a newspaper in the air.

"Now you've done it! Have you seen this? You'll destroy us yet." With that, Mary tossed the paper on the table in front of Elizabeth. "Now maybe John will come to his senses," she said angrily as she stormed out of the room.

To her great dismay, Elizabeth opened the *Richmond Enquirer* to find an article about their visits with Union prisoners. Although the paper did not identify them by name, its reference to "*two ladies, mother and daughter, living on Church Hill*" was unmistakable. The article excoriated Elizabeth and her mother for "*expending their opulent means in aiding and giving comfort to the miscreants who have invaded our sacred soil, bent on raping and murder, the desolation of our homes and sacred places, and the ruin and dishonor of our families.*" The article ended by asserting that the women's conduct affirmed their sympathy for the cause of the "*Northern Vandals.*"

"What is it, Bet?" Eliza asked apprehensively, watching her daughter stare silently at the newspaper, her face blanched and grave, her brow knit in alarm.

Elizabeth nervously handed her mother the paper.

As Eliza scanned the page, her face darkened. "This is not good, Bet."

For a long while the two women sat uneasily, considering their plight.

"We can't just ignore this," Eliza said, breaking the oppressive silence and fear that hung over them. "We have to do something." She stood and began fretfully pacing the floor.

Her mind churning, Elizabeth looked at her. "Well then," she spoke at last, shaking off her fear. "They suspect we are pro-Union. We have to convince them we are pro-Confederate. It's the only way."

Eliza stopped pacing, marveling again at her daughter's readiness to deceive. Her mind tumbled over the possibilities until an idea occurred to her. "The hospital . . ."

For the rest of the morning, Elizabeth and her mother gathered books, writing paper, pens, and flowers. By afternoon they set out with Peter by carriage for Chimborazo Hospital set on a hilly slope at the eastern edge of town not far from Church Hill.

At the sprawling, newly created military hospital, Eliza and her daughter, along with Peter, visited the wounded Confederate troops in its fever-ridden wards. Women, most without any medical training, cared for the soldiers. The cavernous rooms reeked of fetid human and medicinal smells. Beds lined the walls filled with sick and injured men, many of them amputees.

Elizabeth's heart ached for them and she fought back tears as she realized that the young men filling these beds belonged to the humblest classes. When offered writing paper so they might jot messages to their families, the men sheepishly admitted, one after another, that they could not write and asked their visitors to compose a few words for them.

Several were anxious to affirm their loyalty to the Cause. When one young man told Elizabeth that he had come from South Carolina to fight, she asked him why.

"Because Mr. Lincoln is coming south," the soldier replied earnestly, "to take all our Negroes and set them free." After a pause, he added,

"You needn't fear. We will protect you ladies." As he spoke, the young man seemed not to notice the black man standing stiffly next to the two women, his face impassive.

"It's appalling," Elizabeth fumed as they made their way home. "They are deplorably ignorant. Our own fine gentlemen are not fighting. Instead they send the poor and illiterate to fight for slavery. Young men who will never own a slave are dying for slavery!"

For days, Elizabeth and her mother visited wounded Confederate soldiers in Richmond's makeshift hospitals. Their simple gestures and flowers, seen by the two women as providing no measurable help to the Confederate cause, nonetheless aided their own cause immensely by reassuring their neighbors and the press of their intentions.

At the same time, Elizabeth and her mother continued their visits to Union prisoners even as suspicions against them lingered in some quarters. They made the case at every turn that their Christian duty required them to forgive their enemies and help those in need. They kept their primary reasons to themselves. But even as she made these arguments, it pained Elizabeth that so many clergy cheered on the Confederacy for its "divinely sanctioned" mission, spoke in favor of slavery, and railed against the Yankee devils.

—⋅—

In early September, Elizabeth approached Howard Prison with Peter, carrying their usual supplies and food, only to find the place in a stir. Congressman Ely told Elizabeth that someone had escaped from adjoining Ligon Prison the night before—he didn't know how—but Lieutenant Todd had doubled the guard.

Major Rockwell urged caution. "I worry for you, Elizabeth. Your visits displease Todd and he needs a scapegoat."

Within days word spread of the fugitive's capture. He had not even managed to make it out of the neighborhood and was found hiding in a wooded lot not far from the prison, starving and dehydrated. As a message to all would-be escapees, the young man was thrown into solitary confine-ment in a dank, windowless stone room with little space to move or stand.

The news of the unknown prisoner's capture greatly unsettled Eliza-beth. How had he gotten out? And where was he headed? He wasn't from the area. How could he know where to go? Who was there to help him? And if *he* had managed to escape, could others? The questions agonized her.

That evening a frustrated Elizabeth announced to her mother, "It's not enough."

Eliza looked puzzled, "What is not enough, Bet?"

"Bringing soup and porridge and bandages . . . I have to do more!" Elizabeth's delicate features and flashing blue eyes brimmed with passion beneath a crown of thick curls.

Her short, elegant-looking mother nervously stared at her without speaking.

"We have friends. We know people who support the Union cause. Something more has to be done to stop this death march." Elizabeth angrily pounded the palm of her hand on the table. "There has to be a way!"

"Do you realize what you're saying, Bet?" Eliza asked softly, her words so faint they evaporated into the still air.

Her daughter nodded silently.

"No, Bet. I mean do you *really* understand what you're proposing?" The older woman's voice rose and cracked. "People are sent to prison just for sympathy with the Union. People are dying for their beliefs." She paused. "It's your life you're talking about."

The younger woman took Eliza's hand in hers and searching her mother's eyes, she said, "And possibly your life as well."

For a long time they sat together, Elizabeth anxiously holding her mother's hand firmly in hers. Eliza said nothing.

"I can promise you I will be as careful with your life as my own." Eliz-abeth spoke at last. "I'm no hero. You know that. But it's *because* people are dying that I can't sit by."

Eliza looked at this daughter she loved so much and said, "You're right to want to do more, Bet. You're far braver than your mother." She paused again. With a weak smile, she added, "And far more clever at deception." Then, in a voice that had become almost a whisper, said, "I'll do whatever I can to help."

Elizabeth hugged her mother tightly, but could not speak because the tears sat too near.

That evening as Mary read to the girls in the parlor, Elizabeth pulled her brother into the library.

"John . . ." She hesitated. "I intend to do more for the Union cause."

Her younger brother started a bit. "You're already doing a lot, Bet. Bringing food and supplies to the prisoners."

"It's not enough," she said firmly. "The war is not going well for the Union."

"But what can you do? Anything more and . . ." His face suddenly looked alarmed and tense.

As the furrows in his forehead deepened, she quickly added, "I promise not to involve you in any way."

"That's not it, Bet. You know I feel the same. If it weren't for Mary and the children and running the business . . ."

Elizabeth gently pressed her fingers to his lips. "Stop. Running the business feeds all of us. You're already doing more than your share."

"But *what* do you want to do, Bet?" John pressed his sister.

Elizabeth nodded. "I'm not exactly sure. That young soldier who escaped . . . he had nowhere to go and no one to help. Perhaps if . . ." Her voice trailed off. Then she added firmly, "I'll find a way, John."

"Mary must not find out," he said sheepishly. "She doesn't agree with us and to be honest, I'm afraid she wouldn't hesitate to . . ." He caught himself and fell silent.

"Mary will know none of this." Then, probing her brother's eyes, Elizabeth asked, "Are things well between you two?"

John shrugged sadly and shook his head. "Not very. Her family doesn't help. You know how they feel about her marrying me. Me, part of the nouveau riche, and her a blueblood! And we argue so much about what's happening. She'll never understand how we feel about slavery and the Union. It's as though she thinks we're traitors. Lately I feel I'm married to a stranger."

"I'm sorry, John," Elizabeth said softly.

Just then the patter of feet and giggling came from the hallway. Annie and little Eliza burst into the library.

"Daddy, we were looking for you," Annie said breathlessly as the two girls leapt on their father. "Mommy finished the story and we have to go to bed."

"Then I'll come up with you, little ones," he said, standing as they grasped his legs.

"Goodnight, Aunt Lizzie." The girls rushed to Elizabeth, showering her with hugs and kisses.

Like a strong gust of wind they were suddenly gone.

CHAPTER 2

SUMMER PASSED INTO FALL AND THOUGHTS OF A QUICK VICTORY FOR either side faded. The wretched in Richmond's prisons languished in their sunless, foul-smelling cellblocks at the mercy of hunger, disease, dirt, and the occasional sadistic guard.

On one of her visits to Howard Prison in late September, Elizabeth learned from Congressman Ely that his friend Calvin Huson had fallen dreadfully ill. Wracked by fever, unable to eat, Huson languished without medical care as he lay on the stone floor of their cell. Elizabeth felt his burning head with alarm.

"We must do something," Ely exclaimed in frustration, rubbing his forehead. "I fear for his life!"

"We tried appealing to Lieutenant Todd," Rockwell said. "But he refuses to help."

Without hesitation, Elizabeth responded gravely, "Let me see what I can do." In an instant she disappeared through the great oak door.

Elizabeth went immediately to Edward Higginbotham, the physician in charge of prisons, to plead that Calvin Huson receive medical attention.

Higginbotham, unresponsive to her charming smiles and manipulative ploys, stood immobile as Elizabeth spoke. He stared at the woman, her intense blue eyes flashing. Sensing his cold hostility, she began anxiously fidgeting with the edge of a small purse in her lap.

"Have you any idea how shorthanded we are?" he scolded the presumptuous woman at last. "We can barely care for our own wounded troops."

Unmoved, Elizabeth persisted. "We cannot let him die."

"I'm sorry," he replied firmly, moving to the door. "We have other priorities." Opening the door he bid her good day.

She remained seated. "Then let me take him to my home where medical care is available."

"That's out of the question!" Higginbotham snapped. "He is a prisoner."

"He's a civilian, caught up in the fighting. What harm can it do?" Elizabeth stood her ground.

"I must ask you to leave now," the furious man insisted, his voice rising.

Elizabeth wanted to scream at the man, to pummel some sense into him. Instead she rose stiffly. Looking into the man's angry eyes, she walked out of the room.

She went directly to General Winder's office and found Philip Cashmeyer in the office. One of Winder's detectives, Cashmeyer had come from Baltimore to join the Confederate cause. The tall, well-dressed, almost regal-looking man informed her that the general was out.

He's not at all someone you'd think of as a secretive snooper, Elizabeth thought as she studied the man's face.

"Can I be of service?" Cashmeyer asked the woman he knew only by reputation.

"I have an urgent request for the general," Elizabeth answered. "May I leave him a note?"

"Of course." Cashmeyer pointed to a seat and handed her paper and pen.

As she scrawled her note to the general, Elizabeth became uncomfortably aware of the man's gaze fixed on her. When she handed him the paper, his eyes glanced across the page. It struck her as odd that the message elicited no reaction. Cashmeyer's face remained immobile, as though she had asked for nothing more than a weather report.

"Please see that General Winder gets my message. I'll be back this afternoon," Elizabeth said with her best Southern smile spread across her face as Cashmeyer bowed slightly.

Later that day, she returned and Cashmeyer escorted her to Winder's door. She found the general not very receptive to her request.

"Miss Van Lew, you continue to amaze me," the older man said, shaking his head. "I take it your Christian responsibility brings you here again."

"Of course, General," Elizabeth responded with a smile, ignoring the hint of sarcasm in his voice. With that, she launched into a long and passionate plea for the release of Calvin Huson to her care. She went out of her way to emphasize that Edward Higgenbotham had refused permission, knowing of the animosity between Winder and the doctor. For every objection the general raised, she presented a compelling response.

Exasperated, Winder finally declared, "Miss Van Lew, you ask me to simply release a prisoner to you!"

"But I assure you, sir, as soon as he is well, you will have him back. You have my word."

"I can see you will not let this go." Running his fingers through his great shock of gray hair, the old man smiled slightly. "It seems I must agree if I am to get any work done today!"

With that he issued a directive that allowed Elizabeth to take Calvin Huson to her home for medical care.

Peter Roane and another servant, "Uncle" Nelson, carried the fevered man by carriage from the prison to the Van Lew home, where the women put him in a guest room and tried to make him comfortable as they tended to his needs.

But not everyone was pleased. When Mary Van Lew returned home from shopping to find Huson, she raged against the move. "How can you allow this?" she asked her husband. "People will find out and what will they think? You put us all in jeopardy. I will not stay in a house with a Yankee," she fumed.

Her husband tried in vain to calm her. Elizabeth reasoned with her. Eliza appealed to her Christian sense. Even little Annie asked her mother why she didn't want to help the sick man. Nothing worked. Within days, Mary's family had arranged for her to move with the children to a house they owned not far from the Van Lew mansion. John refused his wife's demand that he too leave his mother's home.

The move pained Elizabeth, who felt responsible for the breakup. But John wearily assured his sister it was not her fault.

"This has been coming for a long time," he told the two women. "It would have happened in time anyway. It's the children I can't bear to see gone." He shook his head in despair. "But how can I keep them from their mother?"

Losing the children greatly upset Elizabeth and her mother as well. The two had grown very attached to the little ones. They also worried that Mary's lack of parenting skills and negligible sense of responsibility would not serve the girls well.

Unfortunately, in the Huson matter, Mary Van Lew was not alone in her censure. The idea of a Union prisoner being cared for in a Southern home angered many. Word spread quickly and the move provoked neighbors and strangers alike, and Elizabeth and her family endured open hostility. Some customers boycotted John's hardware business.

For a while the ailing man languished, barely recognizing his surroundings. At last the fever broke and Huson rallied. After a few days he even felt well enough to pen a note to his friend, Alfred Ely. "*I would give a great deal of money,*" he wrote, "*if only my family could see how well the Van Lew ladies and their servants care for me.*" But the recovery proved short-lived and Calvin Huson's health rapidly deteriorated. He slipped in and out of consciousness and his breathing became labored, alarming his caregivers. By the time Eliza could summon a doctor, the New Yorker lay dead.

A distraught Elizabeth hurried by carriage to Howard Prison and the officers' cell. With tears welling in her eyes, she reported the death of his friend to Alfred Ely, who sat slumped on a wooden bench. Rockwell and the others stood by helplessly as Elizabeth described Huson's last hours. As she spoke, a twinge of self-recrimination swirled in her mind and she kept asking herself what more she could have done.

As she was leaving the cell, Rockwell took her hand and tried to console her, "You did everything you could, dear Elizabeth." As though reading her mind, he added, "Don't blame yourself. It's better he died in your home than in this wretched place."

Elizabeth wanted to sob out loud and throw herself into the arms of the gentle man she had grown so attached to. Instead, she nodded sadly and left the room as the great oak door slammed shut behind her.

The next day, in mid-October, a quiet ceremony at Shockhoe Cemetery laid Calvin Huson to rest in the Van Lew plot. A cold wind blew phantoms across the graveyard filled with granite memories. Under a gray, cloud-filled sky, a small group paid their last respects. When the service ended, Elizabeth tearfully placed a bunch of blood-red roses on Huson's coffin as it descended into the damp, chilled earth. Sobs rose in her breast as piles of dirt splashed on the coffin in the dark pit and her heart bid the man farewell. As she stood paralyzed by the sight, a terrible tremor swept over her as her own dead loved ones suddenly came to life before her eyes—and died again.

Anger against the Van Lew family grew. Huson's death did not quell the animosity against them for having given aid and comfort to the enemy. In response to continuing threats, a desperate Elizabeth went to the office of President Jefferson Davis himself to seek protection. As members of one of Richmond's most prominent families, Elizabeth and her mother had accepted invitations to meet Davis and his wife, Varina, several times at social gatherings welcoming the family to the capital. Elizabeth also made it a point to attend as many sessions of Congress as possible when they deliberated, to track the political machinery of the Confederacy. Her frequent presence had attracted Davis's attention for what he saw as her devotion to the workings of the Confederacy.

The tall, thin, ascetic-looking president of the Confederacy, dressed in a gray Prince Albert coat, vest, and pants, received Elizabeth in his aloof but cordial way and listened patiently as she began by praising the Confederate cause and his leadership. She explained her family's plight and need for protection, insisting that her motivations in the Huson case rose from a Southern benevolence completely appropriate for a Christian lady and a member of her social class. As she spoke, stressing General Winder's approval, his face retained its characteristically impenetrable mask and his erect, stately figure seemed not to move a muscle.

When Elizabeth finished speaking, Davis said simply and without emotion, "I understand." Then, taking her completely unaware, he added, "Perhaps you can do something for us now."

"Of course," Elizabeth quickly replied.

"We have a new man taking over as director of the prisons, Captain George Gibbs. Lieutenant Todd is moving to a new assignment. Gibbs will be arriving in a few days with his family and has not yet found a place to stay. Could you and Eliza take them into your home as boarders for a month or two?"

Surprised by the request, but quickly recognizing the political advantage of having a Confederate commandant staying at their home, Elizabeth immediately agreed. Better protection could not be had. It would be hard for her neighbors and others to believe the Van Lews disloyal in such a circumstance, her racing mind assumed.

The Gibbs family proved a great shield to the Van Lews. Although Elizabeth found Captain Gibbs wanting in intellect and most untidy in his habits, his presence in the household helped dispel any doubts lingering over the Huson affair. Best of all, with Gibbs's approval, Elizabeth moved more freely than ever among the prisons of Richmond.

<center>~~~•~~~</center>

"Must you hound me?" Elizabeth snapped as she sat alone in the library shortly after her visit with Jefferson Davis.

Her father did a double take. *Me hound you,* he wanted to say.

"You think I'm a hypocrite—asking Davis for protection."

You said it, not me.

"I want to undermine the Confederacy, yet I ask for its protection. You think that's wrong, don't you?"

She spoke without words, but he heard the aggression in her voice.

"Would you feel better if I were arrested . . . or worse?"

Are we discussing how I feel about it, or how you feel, he thought indignantly. He could see through her rants.

"*You,* of course. I'm fine with this." Elizabeth paused and grappled. In her mind an accusation swirled and jabbed. "Alright! Maybe I'm not completely fine with going to Davis and asking for his help. Maybe I *am* a hypocrite. Or dishonest. Or a coward." She became agitated.

The dead are so much calmer . . .

"What exactly are you asking me to do?" she demanded.

When did I ask you to do anything?

"These conversations are so unhelpful—and annoying."

Tell me about it. I died and haven't gotten a time-out yet.

<center>~~~•~~~</center>

Barely three weeks after Huson's death, a grim situation unfolded at Howard Prison. Congressman Ely was forced to draw lots among the names of imprisoned Federal officers to identify fourteen men for execution. To her horror, Elizabeth learned that Jefferson Davis had ordered the executions in retaliation for the death sentences of fourteen Confederate officers and seaman captured on the high seas by the Union. Since the sovereignty of the Confederacy could not be acknowledged, the Lincoln administration had ordered the men tried as civilian criminals guilty of piracy, a capital

32

offense. Under the Davis ploy, the imprisoned Union officers selected by lots would also be considered civilian felons and executed along with their Southern counterparts in the North.

As hoped, news of Davis's order reached Federal authorities in time to halt the executions temporarily. But Lincoln was furious and refused to relent formally. So a standoff began. The Union officers chosen by lot were ordered transferred to the Henrico County Jail in Richmond on November 9. There they would remain as hostages until Lincoln acted.

On the day of the transfer from Howard Prison, Elizabeth anxiously hurried to the Henrico County Jail with Mary Bowser. The two women carried large baskets of hot rolls as a guard escorted them to the newly prepared cell after examining the baskets. The prisoners had not yet arrived, so they left the steaming rolls covered with white linens on a bench in the cramped and dingy room. Elizabeth squinted to see in a grimy darkness relieved only by a small, double-barred window set in a thick stone wall. The room had no source of heat, no cots, no bedding of any kind, and only two wooden benches. A fetid mustiness so familiar in all the prisons hung about the room and the cold dampness of the cell sent a shiver through her body.

Before she left, Elizabeth tucked a sealed envelope addressed to Major Allen Lee Rockwell on the bench under the baskets. Her fingers lingered on the fine paper before Mary said gently, "Come, Miss Lizzie."

The two women had barely gone when the condemned men arrived at the jail and entered the stuffy cell. Startled by a wonderful aroma, the men quickly discovered the rolls, still warm under a blanket of fine linens. As the men hungrily took the rolls, one of them, Colonel William Raymond Lee, spotted a corner of the envelope.

"What's that?" he asked pointing to it.

Major Paul Joseph Revere moved the basket and picked up the envelope. Peering through the dimness, he saw Rockwell's name and handed it to his friend. "For you," he said simply.

Rockwell instantly guessed who had written the note. He moved the short distance to the dirty window with its sad light and stared at the fine paper. The elegant handwriting spread across the envelope as a hint of perfume touched his nose. He held it for a long time before he broke the seal and carefully pulled out the note with its gilded border.

Dearest Allen,

My thoughts have not left you since I learned of the unkind predicament you and the others find yourselves in. If there were any way to save you from the hateful situation that robs you of a human life, I would gladly risk all. Please, dear friend, keep yourself safe. I will come as often as possible and I pray our Lord will protect you from harm.

I have come to need you.

Most Affectionately,

E.

Rockwell held the paper to the fading light and reread the words again and again. His heart filled with joy and sadness. Could he dare hope . . .? He folded the note and tucked it deep into his pants pocket, concerned that if it fell into Confederate hands, Elizabeth would pay a terrible price.

The next day, after a sleepless night and again accompanied by Mary Bowser, Elizabeth arrived at the Henrico County Jail with a steaming kettle of stew, fresh bread, and books. As she entered the cramped eleven-by-seventeen-foot cell housing the men, Rockwell immediately stepped forward and took her hand, squeezing it tightly and pulling it against his heart. In the half-light, their eyes locked in silence as the men came forward to greet their angel of mercy and ask for news, while Mary heaped the stew onto their tin plates. When Allen and Elizabeth were at last able to find a small corner, he told her in a hushed voice how much her note meant to him.

"I cannot think of leaving you," he said, "now that we have found each other."

Elizabeth smiled and held his hand tightly as they spoke of their feelings for each other. At last she sighed, "How strange that this hateful war has brought us together."

He smiled weakly and only a cliché came to mind. "The silver lining in the cloud . . .?"

She laughed. "A very dark cloud."

When the time came, Elizabeth found it harder than ever to leave. Her worry over Allen's plight left her emotionally drained and struggling to find words.

"I feel so helpless, Allen," she said as they moved toward the door.

"You have given me a reason to live, dear Elizabeth."

She gently touched his cheek.

Taking her hand, he kissed it. "I wait for nothing but your return."

So days passed into weeks and weeks into months with no sign of a resolution to the standoff. November passed, then December. Every day, a worried Elizabeth visited the Henrico County Jail and the bond between her and Rockwell deepened. The men somehow found ways in the crowded, small cell to give the two a tiny bit of space. Although they were never alone, Elizabeth and Allen felt, in their love for each other, secluded from the world. But the Lincoln–Davis standoff heightened the uncertainly and fear and cast a pall over everyone. The longer it continued, the more hopeless things looked.

That first winter of war lashed Richmond with a bitter cold not seen in years. Inmates scattered throughout the city's makeshift prisons suffered greatly from a paucity of food, medicine, clothing, and sanitary facilities. The frigid temperatures added to the misery of those confined in dank, often unheated cells without adequate bedding. Numerous captives died during the terrible winter of 1861–62, despite the efforts of Unionists like Elizabeth Van Lew to bring food and supplies.

Conditions for Richmonders themselves also deteriorated over the months after war erupted. The rebellious capital armed itself for battle at home and away. The quiet, slow, gentle pace of Richmond gave way to shrieking train whistles signaling the comings and goings of military personnel and hardware. Artillery practice pierced the air, and mounted cavalry tramped through city streets. Troops from other Southern states poured into Richmond.

In church basements, public buildings, and hotel meeting rooms, women sewed furiously for the troops. On lampposts, walls, and fences, hand-scrawled and printed notices appeared urging volunteers to join this or that fighting unit. Bugles blew reveille, waking babies and adults alike from their sleep. The acrid smell of gunpowder overcame the scent of tobacco. Funerals snaked through the streets accompanied by the mournful strains of Handel's *Dead March*.

A Union blockade of Southern ports cut off the arrival of needed food and supplies. Shops curtailed their hours because employees drilled with their units late in the afternoon or made bandages and clothing for the troops. When stores were open, the cost of goods edged up while some things, like real coffee, vanished altogether. The shortage of fuel in the winter cold kept many shivering under thick shawls in their homes.

Commodities necessary for industry in the Confederate capital, along with workers, slowly began to disappear. Textile mills and ironworks ran desperately short of fuel.

Still, as the shortages increased, so did Richmond's population. People swarmed into the city—troops, wounded fighters, prisoners, and displaced individuals fleeing the battles of war. Others poured in as well—deserters, drifters, prostitutes, war profiteers, criminals looking for a quick dollar in the confusion of war. The streets of the capital grew more dangerous by the day.

One thing did not change. Richmond's elite continued to enjoy their social life at parties, receptions, and stage productions. Insulated from the worst suffering and ever confident that the Confederacy would prevail, they carried on largely as they always had.

Occasionally bits of good news reached Elizabeth. Congressman Ely and a few others who had grown close to her were traded to the North in exchange for Southern officers held by the Federals.

But Allen Rockwell still sat in prison, his fate in limbo.

⌐⌐

The suffering of Richmond's poor, worse now than ever, spurred Elizabeth to redouble her charitable efforts. As she worked the prisons, she visited the homeless in and out of the almshouses and charity homes, treading along the dingy streets and alleyways of the downtrodden living beyond the margins of society. One almshouse, a stark brick building located behind one of the city's arsenals, housed mostly elderly poor, many of them bedridden, with nowhere else to go. In the musty wooden rooms and corridors of the building she befriended and ministered to its inhabitants. One woman in particular had long held her special affection.

"Emmie," Elizabeth said warmly as she hugged the frail woman in her eighties who was at once like a grandmother and daughter to her.

A wide grin broke across Emmie Crum's weathered face on seeing her friend. "Dear Lizzie!"

"And how do I find you today, Emmie?" Elizabeth looked at the small, gray-haired woman, her face lined with the trouble of ages, sitting in the rocker she had given her years before.

"With a mind working well enough in this here feeble body," the elderly woman answered, still smiling.

"And a fine mind it is," Elizabeth affirmed.

Hungry for news, Emmie asked about the world beyond her door, especially the war, as she did every time Elizabeth visited.

"Still no sign of an end, I'm afraid. There's dreadful suffering, so many wounded and dead, families torn apart. Men on both sides languishing in prison."

"I'd thought it'd be over by now," Emmie said, shaking her head. "How's the South hanging on with the good Lord siding with the North?"

Elizabeth smiled. Like many of Richmond's poor, Emmie had no vested interest in slavery and her sharp mind saw the connection between the exploitation of slaves and the laboring poor. "You best keep that opinion to yourself, my friend."

"What they gonna do to me, Lizzie?" Emmie scoffed. "I'm in prison already."

Elizabeth broke into laughter at the spunky woman's quickness.

"I expect they ain't many rich folks fighting in this war," the elderly woman continued.

"You're right about that, Emmie. They're talking about conscription in the Confederate Congress. They'll likely pass a law soon. But there's also talk of exemptions, of being able to buy your way out by paying someone to go in your place," Elizabeth said.

Emmie grunted in disgust. "Ain't no ordinary folks gonna buy their way out."

Elizabeth nodded in agreement.

"Makin' war is a coward's game," the old woman said derisively. "Yes, sir, a game played with other folk's lives!" Then she said abruptly, "Lizzie, you got time for a game of whist?"

"Always time for you, Emmie."

⁂

Through that long winter, small groups of Unionists met covertly in each other's homes. John Minor Botts, Charles Palmer, Franklin Stearns, and William Fay formed a tightly knit group with the Van Lews.

A prominent former congressman, John Minor Botts, although a slave owner, strongly supported the Union. A barrel-chested man known for his aggressive—some would say pompous—rhetoric remained steadfast in his belief that the Union would prevail.

Blustery and intense, Charles Palmer, a slave owner and prosperous import-export merchant in shipping, remained outspoken in his scorn for the Confederacy, bravely making no attempt to hide his Union sentiments.

"Scoundrels, braggarts," the elderly Palmer sputtered in contempt whenever they spoke of it. His visceral scorn intensified with the pain of seeing his son, a medical doctor, join in championing the Confederate cause and watching the split in his family widen. The war, especially the blockade by sea, took a serious toll on his shipping business.

William Fay, soft-spoken in contrast, passionately supported the Union. A carpenter and business associate of Elizabeth's brother in the hardware business, the religious Fay taught his little daughters to reject slavery and to prefer the path of love for all God's creatures.

Liquor distiller and merchant, Franklin Stearns lived at Tree Hill plantation, a splendid property on a hill at the southeastern edge of town overlooking Richmond. A Northern transplant and slave owner, Stearns expressed his strong Union support at every turn. For that he attracted the notice of the *Richmond Examiner*, which referred to his home as a "rendezvous for Lincoln sympathizers."

The group shared news of the war, of victories and defeats on both sides. They tracked the movement of Confederate troops through the city and speculated about what it meant. Elizabeth, ever the activist, disclosed what she saw of conditions in prison and spoke of what needed to be done. Eliza worried out loud about Confederate spies in their midst. The intellectual John Botts theorized about politics after the war ended and how the restored Union would look. William Fay, a practical realist, expected a long war. Charles Palmer, loud-talking cynic, railed against Confederate elites willing to destroy lives and the South's economy for slavery. Franklin Stearns, moderate and rational, spoke optimistically. But mostly they bolstered each other's morale and felt less alone in a Richmond turned alien and harsh.

Meanwhile Captain Gibbs's tenure as director of prisons proved short-lived and his family left the Van Lew household. His departure—and with it his protection—ushered in new difficulties for the angels of mercy.

In late January, as Elizabeth, her friend Eliza Carrington, and her mother sat at lunch, Mary Bowser entered the room with a letter from the Assistant Surgeon of prisons. Elizabeth quickly opened the envelope and read the disquieting message out loud.

Dear Miss Van Lew,

Dr. Edward Higginbotham, surgeon in charge of prison hospitals, has asked me to inform you that he is revoking your permission to bring food to wounded and sick prisoners. I am personally sorry that you will have to stop helping the prisoners for I believe your charity has served them well. However, I am powerless to do anything about this.

Sincerely,
Owen Hill
Assistant Surgeon

"That horrible man!" Elizabeth fumed, tossing the letter on the table.

"The good doctor is getting even with you for going over his head to Winder about Calvin Huson," her mother said.

"Then he'll have *more* cause to be angry with me," Elizabeth seethed. "I can't accept this!"

"Another appeal, Bet?" her friend Eliza asked.

"This time I'll go higher up," Elizabeth said defiantly. "I will appeal to Mr. Benjamin, if necessary."

"The Secretary of War for the Confederacy, no less!" Eliza Carrington said with a smile, then added, "I'll join you when you go."

Elizabeth looked startled for a moment. Though her heart was with the Union, Eliza had been hesitant about openly helping. Some members of her prominent family sat in the Confederacy's highest corridors of power.

"I know I haven't been much help, Bet," Eliza continued, noting her friend's surprise. "But I want to do something. You know that Judah Benjamin is a close friend of my family."

"Then let's be off," Elizabeth said impatiently.

"Wait," her mother interjected. "Why not take an offering to soften his resistance—some of my custard, perhaps?"

"It can't hurt, Bet," Eliza laughed as she placed her broad brimmed hat on her head.

When Elizabeth and her friend arrived at the office of Judah Benjamin, they met Albert Bledsoe, Assistant Secretary of War. He immediately noticed the bowl Elizabeth carried and asked about it.

"Why, it's my mother's wonderful custard," Elizabeth responded cheerfully. "Perhaps you'd like some?"

"Ladies bearing custard!" Bledsoe grinned. "Of course I'd like some."

Just then Judah Benjamin walked out of his office. "Eliza! And Miss Van Lew," he said to the woman he knew only casually, kissing both their hands in turn. "What brings you ladies here?"

Before Eliza could answer, Bledsoe jumped in. "It seems the ladies have a request. They have brought custard."

"Ahh, custard," said the portly Benjamin. "My favorite!"

"I thought you'd like to taste some of the dangerous contraband I have been smuggling into the prisons for Union soldiers," Elizabeth joked.

"Dr. Higginbotham has forbidden my friend Elizabeth from bringing food to sick prisoners. It's a small Christian gesture and I do hope you'll agree that no harm can come of it, Judah."

"Well, let's taste this contraband," Benjamin urged, smiling broadly, while Bledsoe scurried off to find spoons.

As the two dug into the sweet treat, Benjamin repeated more than once, "Wonderful custard, my dear." In obvious good spirits he added, "Are you sure a saw is not hidden in this tasty custard?" With that, he dug deep into the custard as a hearty laugh broke from his lips.

"You've been bringing food into the prisons right along, have you, Miss Van Lew?" Bledsoe asked between mouthfuls.

"Yes. General Winder kindly granted me permission months ago."

"In that case Higginbotham had no right to countermand that permission," Benjamin responded.

"Then you'll help?" Elizabeth smiled.

"Of course, my dear. I'll send a note to Winder right away. He'll not be happy to hear that Higginbotham disobeyed his directive." Then he added, "Our Confederate prisoners in Washington are allowed to receive food and supplies from civilians—though I doubt any of it tastes this good! We should do no less."

"How very kind you are, sir. I'll leave the rest of the custard and tomorrow a servant will pick up the bowl."

"If we are to lose this war, it will take more than your custard, Miss Van Lew," Benjamin said lightheartedly.

As the two women left, Benjamin called after them, "Give your parents my best, Eliza."

<hr />

The next day word arrived from General Winder that Elizabeth's permission had been restored. But more surprising came the news that Winder, in a gesture revealing his intense dislike for the man, had ordered Higginbotham arrested for "taking precedence in rank."

"You've made an enemy for life, Miss Lizzie," noted Mary after she brought the message.

Elizabeth smiled. "Mary, I need your help."

"Anything, Miss Lizzie," the black woman replied.

"Follow me," Elizabeth said, moving toward the great staircase leading upstairs and motioning to Mary.

Puzzled, Mary followed. They climbed to the third story where the servants' quarters were and down the long corridor to the attic entrance at the back of the house. Elizabeth opened the attic door and stepped up the stairs into the dim room. The small windows in the gables spread their meager light across the cavernous space with its huge wooden beams and peaked roof. Dust nipped at their feet as they moved across the grimy wooden planks. Apart from a row of large soot covered boxes and a few odd pieces of furniture long forgotten, the vast room had remained empty all these years. At both ends a partition completely enclosed an area around each chimney. Pointing to the partitioned space closest to the attic entrance, Elizabeth turned to Mary.

"This is where we will hide our fugitives," she said simply.

Mary immediately understood and began studying the area, wondering what exactly lay behind the partition. "We need an opening. Not too large. I'll get Peter."

When Mary and Peter returned they found Elizabeth lost in thought. A fantasy had taken her to the Henrico County Jail where she was busily spiriting Allen away from his cell, down the dark corridors and out the prison door as guards slept at their posts.

"Miss Lizzie . . ."

Elizabeth turned and saw the two. Peter carried a chisel and a saw.

"Where you want the hole, Miss Lizzie?" Peter asked, studying the partition and tapping the wood to find the beams.

"Use your judgment, Peter. Keep the opening small, but large enough for a man to get through."

Peter kept tapping lightly until he was confident he could avoid the beams. He began chiseling a line up from the floor until he had a square roughed out. Then he inserted his saw in the narrow slot and began sawing, releasing streams of sawdust. At last a piece of panel fell away and Elizabeth poked her head in to inspect the space. She noticed with surprise that the space was not completely dark as expected. She stooped into the opening and spotted two small triangle shaped windows rising with the pitch of the roof at either side of the brick flue.

"But this is wonderful, my friends. Windows!" Elizabeth exclaimed in delight, swiping at the cobwebs as she reached up and ran her fingers over the dust covered glass panels. Although the panes did not open, they let in the sun.

"I'll get a broom and clean the place," Mary said, hurrying off.

"We'll need a mattress up here, Peter, maybe two. And a chair . . ." Elizabeth's mind raced at the possibilities. It was a good sized space.

By the time they had finished sweeping away the cobwebs and dust, polishing the small window panes, laying in the mattresses, blankets and a small carpet, and adding a chair and small table, the fugitive room glistened in Elizabeth's eyes. When they left the rejuvenated space, Mary pulled the panel back across the opening and together she and Peter pushed the largest box from across the room to conceal the cut-away board completely. Satisfied that the attic looked exactly as it had before they entered, Elizabeth hugged Mary and Peter with great pleasure and the three walked down the stairs, closing the attic door behind them.

In the notorious Libby Prison, Erasmus Ross prepared to feed Elizabeth's fugitive room. Ross, a nephew of Unionist Franklin Stearns, posed as a staunch, often brutal Confederate, holding a key post as clerk of the prison. Elizabeth had encouraged the young man early in the war to apply for a position at Libby where he might do a great deal to help the Union cause. Very much feared by Union prisoners because of his abusive language, rough treatment, and strident praise of the Confederate cause, no one suspected his strong ties to the Union network.

Shortly after the preparation of the fugitive room, Ross and Elizabeth schemed to test a prisoner escape. At Libby, Ross arbitrarily selected Captain William Lounsbury as his test case.

During roll call one evening, Ross poked the officer in his stomach and barked, "You blue-bellied Yankee, come down to my office. I have a matter to settle with you."

Filled with dread, Lounsbury followed the hated rebel. After the two men arrived in the office, Ross, without a word, motioned the Captain behind a counter. There Lounsbury found a neatly folded Confederate uniform. At that, Ross slipped silently from the room, closing the door behind him. Bewildered and fearful, Lounsbury undressed and put on the gray uniform. Opening the door a crack, he saw the empty corridor leading to a nearby exit door out of the prison. Quietly, with great trepidation, he crept to the door and walked past a guard outside into the dark night, a blast of cold air rushing against him. He crossed the street directly to a vacant, treed lot, hoping to pass unnoticed from the area.

Suddenly a black man stepped out from behind one of the trees and said in a low voice, "Come with me, sah. I know who you is."

Lounsbury anxiously followed the burly man for several blocks through the darkness until they arrived at a stately mansion on a hill. Quickly the black man ushered him into the house by the back door where Elizabeth waited.

"Welcome, Captain Lounsbury," she said warmly. Then seeing the confused look on his face, she added, "You are quite safe here. You are among friends."

"I am at a disadvantage," he said. "You know me, but I do not know you, Miss . . ."

"It's best if you don't know my name. I hope you understand."

He didn't.

"Come, let's get you some food," she motioned him into the kitchen.

As he ate hungrily, she spoke of plans to get him out of the city. They talked for a long while at the kitchen table as she answered his questions without betraying any secrets. When he was satisfied that he had not fallen into a trap, she escorted him upstairs to the hidden chamber in the attic, all the while assuring him he could make it to Union lines.

Over the next few days, Elizabeth provided Lounsbury with detailed information and maps showing the best route out of Richmond, woods to hide in, where to cross the countryside to the safety of Union lines. She told him how to avoid Confederate pickets and home guards. Together they pored over the maps.

When the time came, Elizabeth packed food, drink, and clothes. Nervously, the grateful fugitive from Libby Prison said goodbye to the mysterious lady who had offered safety and friendship for a brief time in the comfortable, secret attic room in the mansion.

"Peter will help you down past the river," she said, "But wearing that Confederate uniform is the best help."

Elizabeth watched anxiously from the back doorway as her escaped prisoner slipped into the shadowy darkness of the garden behind Peter. Overhead a sliver of moon and countless stars watched.

"There will be many more of you," she vowed.

———

On a blustery February day, news arrived at last that Elizabeth anxiously waited to hear. Lincoln had relented and would not execute the Confederate prisoners held as privateers.

An elated Elizabeth hurried to the Henrico County Jail. She found the men in a state of excitement.

"What will happen now, Allen? She asked.

"I'm not sure," Rockwell answered. "We may be transferred back to Howard." He looked at her intently and hesitated. "Or . . ."

"Or?" Elizabeth repeated.

"There is talk of a possible prisoner swap. We fourteen for their fourteen."

Without thinking, Elizabeth jumped up from the wooden bench. "That would be wonderful, Allen. It would mean your freedom!" With that she threw herself into his arms.

"Freedom without you means nothing," he whispered into her ear.

A sudden realization took hold of Elizabeth—the realization that Rockwell might not be there each day. That she might no longer look forward to their daily visits. That the touch of his hand on hers might end. She pulled back, embarrassed at her emotional display.

"This wretched war cannot go on forever," she quietly answered. "With the end of winter, the Union will surely move against Richmond. Why, news has arrived that General Grant has successfully invaded Tennessee. Fort Henry and Fort Donelson have fallen to Union troops. It can't be long now."

But even as she spoke, a wave of doubt washed over Elizabeth. In a few days, Jefferson Davis would be inaugurated as president of the Confederacy. Just a year ago he took office as president of the Provisional Government of the Confederacy. The South showed no intention of backing down.

"Your life has been spared. Nothing else matters," she continued softly, pushing back her doubts.

"Dearest Elizabeth . . ." Rockwell whispered and fell silent in a surge of emotion.

"This is a time for celebration," Elizabeth proclaimed, raising her voice and turning to the men. "I'm overjoyed for all of you. I pray you quickly reunite with your families."

That night Elizabeth sobbed herself to sleep as a torrent of conflicting sentiments racked her heart. After a fitful night of ambivalence, she rose early, anxious for word from the Henrico County Jail. Half afraid of what news she might hear, Elizabeth made her way to the prison on Main Street. She found the men talking eagerly in small groups.

The news was good and the news was bad.

"Union authorities have arranged a prisoner swap," Rockwell told her as soon as she arrived. "In a matter of days, we will be shipped north."

A long, strained silence passed between them.

"I can't bear to leave you," Rockwell said at last, taking her hands in his.

"You must and you will," Elizabeth said firmly, without hesitation. "How can either of us want to keep you here under these conditions?

"I would ask you to come with me," Rockwell said earnestly. "But I am not going home. We will be rejoining our regiments."

"Then we both have our work for the Union and . . ."

"I want to marry you, Elizabeth," he interrupted.

Her breath caught and the words in her heart could not find a way out.

"I have dared all these months to hope that you feel the same," Rockwell continued, his voice eager and solemn.

She stared, taking in the words. Mistaking her silence, he nervously persisted. "I am being presumptuous. I have offended you . . ."

Elizabeth smiled at his intensity and confusion and the words found their way. "No, no. You have not offended me. I am struggling for words to express my happiness."

An audible sigh of relief escaped Rockwell's lips. "Then you consent to marry me?"

"Yes," Elizabeth replied emphatically. Then she paused, knowing as she spoke how unlikely that was to happen any time soon. With that realization, threads of sadness wove their way through her heart and tightened around her pleasure in the moment.

As if reading her mind, he whispered, "This hideous war *will* end."

She nodded weakly.

"I fear it will not help if your neighbors know you are to marry a Union devil," Rockwell added with a smile. Then turning serious again, "I worry for you, Elizabeth—that you will pay a price for all the help you give us."

"Only my family will know, Allen. And you must not worry for me. I am quite safe here in Richmond. You must take care of yourself when you return to your regiment and . . ." Her voice caught and a hint of tears welled up in her blue eyes.

"Then we shall *both* keep ourselves safe," Rockwell affirmed.

When Eliza heard the news, she was ecstatic for her daughter. "Your father would be so happy, Bet." But, growing a bit stern, she added, "I've wanted to say for a long time that you have mourned for David far too long. Clinging to the past as you have."

Her brother too expressed joy at the revelation, but teasingly added, "I will set my spies to determine whether this Rockwell is good enough for my sister!"

They all agreed the engagement would be kept secret.

The next day Eliza and John accompanied Elizabeth to the Henrico County Jail to meet with Major Rockwell. The meeting proved emotional, but the four spoke in earnest, not of the present, but of the future.

On her last visit before his departure Elizabeth gave Allen a brooch with her picture in it. "So you do not forget me," she smiled.

"I would have to suffer amnesia to forget you." He shook his head sadly. Then he removed the gold ring he wore and offered it to Elizabeth. "It belonged to my father," he told her softly.

"You must write me as often as possible," she urged. "And I will do the same."

"If the war drags on much longer, we'll try to meet somewhere in the North." His voice took on an urgency. "I cannot bear the thought of this separation."

Elizabeth nodded, pushing back the tears and stroking his cheek.

In the end, there were not enough words to express their love for each other. When the time came to leave, they embraced tightly and kissed for the first time since they met and a tearful Elizabeth bid Major Rockwell and the others a safe farewell.

After she stepped reluctantly into the dark corridor, a burly guard slammed the massive oak door shut behind her and thrust the rusty metal latch into its bolt.

CHAPTER 3

A DRIVING, COLD RAIN BLANKETED CAPITOL SQUARE AS GEORGE Washington stood guard over the odd pair being sworn into office on his birthday. The crowd surrounding the canopy-covered, wooden platform huddled under dripping, black umbrellas and strained to hear the tall, thin man whose rambling speech evaporated into the noise of the drenching downpour. Next to the rather gaunt-looking man straining to be heard stood his strange bedfellow and second in control, a small, slightly built man, his posture somewhat stooped, older-looking than his forty-nine years. The former Georgia congressman had voted against secession, advocated peace, and wanted the North and South to settle their differences. He was no great ally of the man he stood with.

As the throng watched on that dismal, cold day in February, the Confederacy, no longer provisional, re-inaugurated Jefferson Davis as its president. And it inaugurated as vice president Alexander Stephens.

Throughout the speech, Varina Davis gazed at her husband intently, but her uneasy mind tumbled chaotically over the present and past.

"So many military defeats recently and so many lives lost," she thought to herself. "My Jeffie sacrificing so much and having to put up with all the carping and disapproval of him by ungrateful politicians and military leaders. And the press—they're the worst! Look at him. How terrible he looks, one debilitating illness after another. And how did I find him just before the speech? In a state of prostration, on his knees imploring for divine support."

She watched in dismay as the relentless downpour lashed at her pale and emaciated husband, driving onto the platform from the sides of the small canopy.

"Why did they have to do this outside? Look at that pathetic awning over that platform—it's temporary too. Temporary. Just like everything else."

The grayness of the scene, the wind, and the incessant rain threw Varina back to another dreadful day.

"Just like today. I can't bear to think of it. I wasn't ready when you died, Sammy. I would never have been ready, of course. Losing a firstborn child, so young, so sweet. To have you *only* two years . . . That horrible rain, drumming, drumming on the carriage, on the umbrella, so mournful. People should be sent off in sunshine, in hope, if they're going to a better place. But no. You got sent off, my little one, in a coffin descending into a cold, flooded grave to die all over again for me."

An audible sob broke free.

"The *permanent* Confederacy they say now. Why doesn't it seem so?" Thinking of their home on the Mississippi, she thought, "I swear our lives seem built on the Shaking Prairies of Louisiana, where the earth melts and water swallows everything in its path." A wistful notion flew into her head. "I wish I were the wife of a dry-goods clerk. Then we could dine in peace, go for a buggy ride on Sunday, live a simple, private life . . . Idle, silly thoughts! My only hope these days rests on the children." Her mind passed over them—her baby, little Billy, Margaret, Jeff, and Joe.

Her husband's speech wandered on interminably and the rain kept falling.

"Jeffie, be done with it!"

At last the talk drew to a close. Jefferson Davis flung his arm out and threw his head back. "To Thee, O God! I trustingly commit myself, and prayerfully invoke Thy blessing on my country and its cause." Then he kissed the Bible on which he had sworn his oath.

The sight greatly unsettled Varina. A cutting fear suddenly twisted through her as she watched in dread. Before her eyes an image flashed of her beloved Jeff walking as a willing victim onto a blazing funeral pyre. Stricken by the thought, she turned abruptly and rushed back to her carriage, the rain battering her black umbrella and rushing in rivulets down its channels. Around her shouts rose against the din of the downpour, "God bless our president."

At the back of the crowd on Capitol Square, Elizabeth Van Lew also watched the spectacle with dread and dismay. To her surprise, she saw Varina dash to her carriage when the president had barely finished speaking.

It was not a happy day, either, for the man charged with leading the now permanent Confederacy. The gloomiest shadows dogged a tired Davis as he greeted supporters at a reception in the executive mansion that evening. Desperate people fleeing war continued to pour into Richmond, swelling its population as vital supplies and food grew scarce. Union victories in Tennessee, Missouri, and Kentucky piled on. These Confederate losses in western battles had emboldened Unionists in Richmond and graffiti and brazen signs had begun appearing on buildings throughout the city that read, "Rally around the old flag," "God Bless the Stars and Stripes," and "Union men to the rescue!" More menacing, General George McClellan's huge Army of the Potomac stood waiting for winter's end to strike Richmond.

With these gloomy shadows in mind, Davis quickly took the extraordinary step of declaring martial law in Richmond and a ten-mile radius surrounding the city, effective March 1. He put the area under martial law, Davis claimed, to provide "an effective defense" against Yankee attacks, appointing John Henry Winder, Provost Marshal General, to oversee Richmond's martial law and establish a military police force to ferret out traitors and spies.

Winder lost no time after the declaration of martial law. The next day, his detective, Philip Cashmeyer, and a number of police broke into the home of former Virginia congressman John Minor Botts late at night, pulling him out of bed in front of his distraught family. Known to be an avowed Unionist who had fought against secession in the run-up to war, Botts's enemies continually fueled suspicion, writing letters to authorities accusing him of sedition against the Confederacy. While arresting Botts and hauling him off to prison, the patrician-looking Cashmeyer expressed his "deep regret" to the prisoner about the detention.

That same day, police went to Tree Hill and arrested Franklin Stearns. In addition to charges of treason, the wealthy liquor merchant was accused of undermining the war effort by providing liquor to the troops. Winder ordered a stop to all sales of alcoholic beverages in Richmond and confiscated the distilleries of Stearns and others. Taverns closed, or so it seemed. Many continued to operate through the back door. For working people, this back-door business posed some risks, but the city's elite, senior officers, and officials took their drink undisturbed in private homes and gambling parlors.

Winder had Botts and Stearns incarcerated in the notorious McDaniels Negro Jail, which shortly after took a new name, Castle Godwin. There they languished in vermin-infested cells in solitary confinement with only a dirty pile of straw to rest on.

During Botts's incarceration, Confederate Captain George Alexander, a sinister figure among Unionists, visited him in his cell. Having been imprisoned himself in the North, Alexander had escaped and fled back to Richmond. As one of Winder's prison directors, the devious officer acquired a particular reputation for cruelty.

Before Alexander could speak, Botts lashed out. "Do you know who I am?"

"Yes, yes, of course. What a pity that a distinguished gentleman such as yourself is here," the slippery Alexander commiserated. "But we can remedy that."

"You can remedy this by setting me free immediately. You do not have enough prisons to hold the South's Union men," Botts growled.

"I'm sure you exaggerate, sir," Alexander laughed. "But I have a proposition for you."

Botts eyed the man coldly.

"I can free you now, right now. I'm prepared to offer you a commission as brigadier general in the Confederate army. If you accept this commission . . ."

"If I accept your commission," Botts interrupted, "and have ten thousand men under my command, be assured, sir, that before sundown I would hang you and every traitorous scoundrel from Jeff Davis down."

"Such a pity. I had hoped you'd listen to reason," Alexander said moving toward the door.

Botts turned his back to the man and waited silently until the great, creaking door slammed shut and the iron bolt clanged into place.

Over the course of that month, twenty-eight men fell under Winder's dragnet—all accused of sedition against the Confederacy. Never had Elizabeth and her family more cause to worry. Included in the arrests were a number of Van Lew family friends—not only Botts and Stearns, but William Fay, John's business associate in the carpentry trade, and Charles Palmer, their close friend. Palmer fell under suspicion when he insisted on visiting Botts in prison and blustered about, arguing vigorously against his friend's arrest. Winder's tentacles also stretched into the church, despite the Southern clergy's wide support of the Confederacy. Pastor of the Universalist Church in Richmond, the Reverend Alden Bosserman landed in prison after he prayed publicly for the defeat of the Confederacy's "unholy rebellion."

The roundup filled Richmond Unionists with dread. Images of arrest in the middle of the night plagued their restless sleep and dogged their days. But in Elizabeth's anxious heart alarm also mingled with fury. In this upside-down world of the Confederacy, loyalists had become traitors and traitors loyalists.

The Van Lews huddled often during this time of fear, scanning the newspapers for any bit of news.

"So many names here we've not been aware of," Elizabeth noted as she read.

"Who, Bet?" her brother asked.

"There's mention here of a Burnham Wardwell who's been arrested for sedition. He's an ice dealer." She read on. "And they've arrested a man who runs a small grocery, a John Higgins." She paused, looking a bit alarmed.

"What about him?" Eliza inquired nervously.

"Well," she hesitated, reluctant to alarm her family. "It seems he's brought suspicion on himself by helping Union prisoners."

Eliza's face blanched.

"These are working-class people," John noted with interest.

"If there's any good news here, it's that our small group is not alone," his sister added. "Every day, new names. There are lots of potential allies out there, it seems."

Despite the pervasive fear, Elizabeth felt oddly empowered by the news and less isolated. Extensive reports in the press of every detention informed Richmond's elite Unionists of working class loyalists, spinning invisible threads that would link them all together in time.

Eliza's thoughts raced in another direction. "I'll not sit by, waiting for the axe to fall here."

"What are you thinking, mother?" John asked.

"I'll open our home to wounded Confederate soldiers," she answered emphatically. "For a while, at least. That will divert suspicion from your prison work, Bet."

So Eliza, ever the protector of her family, quickly began to accommodate injured soldiers in her home. Again, the strategy provided Elizabeth a defense against suspicions that she too committed sedition.

At night, alone in her room in the great mansion, a visitor often came.

"Troublesome times, Poppa," Elizabeth whispered in her sleep.

It happens—when people do what you're doing.

"I knew you wouldn't approve."

Did I say that?

"My friends in prison . . . I feel so powerless."

Powerless Bet. An oxymoron, he thought.

"Why them? Why not me?" she wondered, over and over. "Why was I spared?"

Your connections? Your wealth? Your gender? How should I know?

"I have to do something to help my friends. But what . . . ?" She thrashed about in troubled sleep.

Please. These late-night conversations are the worst. I need my sleep, he wanted to tell her, but he kept quiet.

"Why not me?" she repeated.

Why me, he thought.

Shortly after his arrest, Botts wrote a note to Elizabeth asking her advice. In response, she organized a contingent of prominent women, including Botts's daughter, to argue for his release. They flooded the Secretary of War and other Confederate authorities with letters protesting the arrest of such a distinguished Virginian. After Botts's court-martial almost two months later, he was paroled for lack of evidence, but placed under house arrest at his country estate outside Richmond for the rest of the war.

The wealthy Franklin Stearns, who hired a team of lawyers, won his release in late April as well. Charles Palmer gained his freedom in a matter of days after his son, a captain in the Confederate army, vouched for him. Less well connected, working class Unionists like Wardwell, Fay, and Higgins suffered for months in wretched conditions before their release.

As the arrests provided new names to Elizabeth and her Unionist friends, so too did it offer an opportunity for working-class Unionists to identify them. Two men in particular sought out Botts, Stearns, and Palmer after their release—William Rowley, a farmer and native of New York, and Frederick Lohmann, a German immigrant and owner of a small eatery. Both men were abolitionists and anxious to help the Union cause.

Ironically, martial law and the wave of arrests, intended to weaken Unionist power, actually expanded their connections. The network grew in strength and numbers over the months following the arrests, emboldening loyalists and setting then on a path of ever stronger resistance.

My Dear Elizabeth,

The days away from you are endless and empty. I think always of our time together and these memories bring me great joy and comfort. At night my dreams are of you.

The world is a hard place. But the sound of your voice, the blueness of your eyes, the sweetness of your smile, and the softness of your touch brighten the world immeasurably for me. Because of you, dearest Elizabeth, I can see a future.

I long for this war to end so we can be together again.

Yours,
With all my love and affection,
Allen

In his many letters Rockwell never wrote of his army service, where he was, or what his regiment was doing for fear the letters might be read, despite their transport under a flag of truce. She, in turn, never wrote of her Unionist work for the same reason. But she worried for him and he worried for her.

How strange, Elizabeth thought, that these pieces of papers and their sentiments can mean so much. But in the end, all the notes in the world were no substitute for Allen. She longed to see him, to embrace him, to kiss him again . . .

~ ~

Unknown to Richmond Unionists at this time, charges of espionage during those fearful days were not limited to them. At the trendy, five-story Spotswood Hotel on the corner of Main and Eighth, another spy drama unfolded after the Davis inauguration that would soon lead to Elizabeth's door. The famed hotel with its lovely, high-ceilinged rooms, reputed to be as fine as any on Fifth Avenue in New York, had long served as the home of Richmond's transient elite—foreign dignitaries, politicians, press corps, and others passing through. It had provided a temporary home for the Davis family when they arrived in the city. Union spies also favored the Spotswood, situated in the shadow of the capitol.

On a bitterly cold day in Washington, far from the Spotswood, two men wearing new suits, hiding Colt revolvers, and carrying baggage with a sack of gold buried in each, listened as Allan Pinkerton bid them a safe passage through enemy lines. Pinkerton, head of the Union intelligence service, pressed a note into Pryce Lewis's hand granting him and John Scully permission to cross Union camps and the Potomac River on their way to Richmond.

The two men made their way through Union lines without incident. But the Potomac River balked as a violent winter storm descended, kicking at their boat and dumping the two into its frigid waters. Somehow Lewis and Scully survived and crawled ashore. Days later, after eluding rebel forces, they entered Richmond posing as smugglers for the Confederacy. Their real mission: to find Pinkerton operative Timothy Webster, one of the agency's most effective spies, whose regular information feed from the Spotswood Hotel had mysteriously stopped.

Acting as a courier for Confederate authorities, double agent Webster had secured the confidence of General Winder by bringing letters to and from his son in Washington, who remained loyal to the Union, much to his family's dismay. An imposing figure with a thick moustache and beard, a high forehead, and thoughtful, penetrating eyes, Webster easily ingratiated himself with Richmond authorities, including Secretary of War, Judah Benjamin. A magical aura surrounded the charismatic forty-year-old man that seduced good will.

When Lewis and Scully did not find Webster in his usual haunt, the Spotswood Hotel, they followed his trail to the nearby Monument Hotel where they found him seriously ill. Years of narrow escapes, midnight rescues, nights hiding in the damp cold, and flights in icy streams and rivers left him suffering from severe rheumatoid inflammation. Weak and emaciated, the once vigorous man could not leave his bed. Posing as his wife, Hattie Lawton, his lover and herself a Pinkerton agent, tended their friend. When Lewis and Scully entered the hotel room, they found a Confederate officer visiting Webster. Unable to speak freely, they left, determined to get the sick man's report before returning to Washington.

While calling on their bedridden friend the next afternoon, one of Winder's detectives unexpectedly appeared to wish Webster a speedy recovery. Calm and quiet, Scully and Lewis watched as Detective McCubbin chatted with the sick man, who nervously glanced at his two friends.

A few minutes later, with the detective still in the room, the son of former Senator Jackson Morton also came calling. Scully and Lewis froze. The young man was none other than the person they had guarded in Washington after police detained the Morton family and placed them under house arrest. Terrified, the two men turned from Morton's son in an effort to hide their faces. Within minutes the young man began whispering in McCubbin's ear. Scully and Lewis quickly excused themselves and hurriedly walked out into the hallway. Too late, for the detective rushed after them and together with two other officers in the hotel lobby, detained them on the spot.

Scully and Lewis soon found themselves in General Winder's office being questioned by the general and McCubbin. Who were they? What were they doing in Richmond? Why had they visited Timothy Webster? How did they explain Morton's accusation? In the end, the testimony of the young man and other members of the Morton family, hastily brought to Winder's office, overcame the prisoners' claims of mistaken identity. Winder had them arrested and thrown into the Henrico County Jail.

Throughout the spring of 1862, Elizabeth defiantly continued her visits to Union soldiers, bringing food, books, and other supplies, despite the arrests of her friends. Buoyed by the growing strength of the Unionist network, she worked at solidifying and expanding operations.

Shortly after authorities shipped her beloved Rockwell north, Elizabeth met two new inmates at the Henrico County Jail, John Scully, a short, down-to-earth Irishman with a nervous look about him, and Pryce Lewis, a well-educated, distinguished-looking gentleman, both charged with espionage. She met them in the same musty room recently vacated by her fiancé and the others. The two tight-lipped men accepted her offerings cordially but shared nothing about their arrest or their mission.

From his first hour in the dingy prison, Lewis resolved to escape. His plan proved nothing more elaborate than sawing through the window bars with a sharp knife stolen from the kitchen. For two weeks Lewis sawed throughout the night. By day he covered the thin opening at the base of the bars with a concoction of brown soap and sawdust until at last he completely chiseled through. Along with Scully and eight other prisoners, Lewis escaped during the night of March 16 while a group of black inmates sang to conceal the fleeing footsteps.

News that ten Union men had escaped greatly unsettled the capital. Where were they hiding? What threat did they pose to Richmonders? A frantic search began as the city's newspapers fanned fear with incendiary articles.

For two horrifying days the men slid through the cold darkness at night and the bright sun by day, struggling to hide first in the city streets and alleys, then through a well-guarded countryside. In the knotted, foggy swamps along the Chickahominy River east of the city, the men inched their way by moonlight, falling into icy waters, scraping their arms and legs and stumbling over twisted roots. At the river they built a small fire in a deep pit to dry their wet clothes. Hungry, freezing, and weak from their imprisonment, some of the men could no longer continue on their own. The others took turns helping them. Lewis and another man carried an older comrade as they slowly crept forward, not sure where they were.

As a gray dawn slowly spread across the dark skies, Lewis and the men hid during the day and slept a fitful sleep. When he woke, Lewis could barely move. His clothes, still moist from the night's stumbles, had frozen and he felt covered as if in concrete. But with darkness again descending over the countryside, the men dragged themselves on through another night. Late on the second day a Confederate patrol spotted them on the banks of the Pamunkey River.

On hearing news of the capture, Elizabeth once again agonized over the fate of the escaped men, remembering that other young man who had failed to make his way home. "Intolerable," raced through her mind again and again as she vowed not to miss another chance to help. She had spoken to Pryce Lewis several times before the escape that he was no doubt planning. But she had failed to win his confidence. She asked herself again and again what more she could have done.

As wagons carried the captured Yankee prisoners back into Richmond, an anxious and angry crowd lined the streets, hurling curses at the miserable fugitives. Nerves and tempers stood at fever pitch and a panic had slowly taken hold with the approach of spring and a threatened Union assault on the city. Martial law had done nothing to stop the expected advance of General McClellan's forces toward Richmond.

Fearing the fall of the Confederate capital, many packed what they could carry and fled. An oppressive fear hung over those remaining behind. But in the mansion on Church Hill, Elizabeth and her family cheered on McClellan's march, expecting it would bring an end to the war.

General Winder ordered Pryce Lewis and the others put in leg irons and transferred to solitary confinement in Castle Godwin. The dilapidated prison appeared on the verge of collapse from the outside. Not long ago the structure had served as a holding pen for slaves. Once inside, the guards pushed Lewis into a small, dark room with rodents and vermin his only company. Straining to see in the dim light of a small window and a single lantern he saw a pile of smelly, dirty straw in one corner as the odor of mold filled his lungs.

Elizabeth wasted no time and hurried to the jail. When she saw the haggard, dirty man in leg irons, she gasped, hardly recognizing him. He hungrily ate the bread and jam she offered as she tried to reassure him. In a quiet whisper, as she uneasily glanced toward the wooden door with its small barred opening, Elizabeth shared her Union sentiments and told him he had friends in Richmond willing to help. As she spoke she tried to fathom the man's face in the faint light of the lantern. His eyes stared at her out of swollen red sockets. He saw the mop of curls around her face, the beautiful blue eyes, the ladylike manner, and the fine clothes, but he spoke no words.

"I understand," Elizabeth said at last. "You are right not to trust anyone. I will come again."

With that she gently touched the man's bruised hand. He felt it as a feather softly floating to earth. Then she rose to leave.

"Bless you," Lewis murmured, barely audible, as she passed through the heavy door and a light went out in the room where the dim lantern still burned.

On the first day of April, after a three-day trial, guards led Lewis to Scully's cell. There an officer of the court read the verdict to the two men: Guilty of spying. Sentence: On April 4, both men would be hanged.

Lewis turned to stone inside, but betrayed no emotion and did not look at his cellmate as the verdict was read. Neither spoke for a long time. During the night Scully twisted and turned on his bed of straw, moaning and crying out from his tormented sleep as Lewis paced the floor and rats dashed about the room.

The next morning, Lewis left the cell to meet with his lawyer. They concocted a strategy of sorts—a desperate attempt to claim that, as a British citizen, born in England, the Confederacy had no jurisdiction over him. Scully too left the cell later that morning, although a preoccupied Lewis paid little attention. Later, on Scully's return, Lewis become aware of sobbing. Going over to his friend to comfort him, he heard Scully reveal that he was going to meet Winder shortly to admit being a spy in exchange for a pardon. Lewis recoiled in disbelief.

The desperate words, "You cannot betray Webster!" had barely passed Lewis's lips when a guard appeared at the door and escorted the distraught Scully from the room. Another guard took a shaken Lewis back to his old cell where he found himself alone again. Immediately a commotion erupted outside his cell. Lewis peered through the barred opening in the door and saw General Winder and some other men rush down the hallway to Scully's cell. All afternoon men came and went as Lewis's fury at Scully grew.

The next afternoon, Lewis heard a carriage pull up to the prison and hurried to the tiny window. Two prisoners, a man and woman, stepped out of the carriage accompanied by the arresting detective, Philip Cashmeyer. Lewis gasped as he recognized Timothy Webster and Hattie Lawton. So haggard and weak had Webster become that he had to be helped from the carriage and into the building by Cashmeyer. Scully's betrayal was now certain.

～⌒～

By some miracle—the desire for more testimony against Webster, it turned out—Lewis received word on the morning of his scheduled execution that his sentence was postponed. As one wretched day after another passed, Lewis grew desperate to know what was happening. Elizabeth continued her visits to his cell, but other than asking for news of Webster, which she knew nothing about, the desolate man remained tight lipped. A judge came once and in a lengthy interview tried, unsuccessfully, to drag a confession from Lewis, who admitted only to delivering a letter to Webster from a friend in Baltimore.

Then, two weeks later a guard took him from his cell to the Richmond courthouse. Webster's trial had begun and Scully had already testified. Authorities expected Lewis to do the same. In the courtroom, Webster's appearance greatly distressed Lewis who deeply admired his friend. The once stout, impressive man sat shrunken in his chair, more skeleton than living human being. Try as the authorities might, Pryce Lewis would say nothing against his friend, sticking to his story. When he finished his testimony, Lewis passed by Webster's chair and the two men looked deeply into each other's eyes. A silent word of appreciation met Lewis when he nodded almost imperceptibly to his old friend.

As the trial dragged on, a troubled Elizabeth went daily to the prison cell of Hattie "Webster," as she called herself. The calm strength of the prisoner moved Elizabeth deeply and it was never quite clear who was comforting whom. In the end, word came that Hattie "Webster" was sentenced to one year in prison and Webster would be hanged on April 29.

Distraught over the death sentence, Hattie cast about in her mind for a source of help. She wanted to plead on Tim's behalf, but who would listen? In desperation it occurred to her that another woman would understand, a woman of power—President Davis's wife. She would plead with Varina to intervene on Tim's behalf that his life might be spared. But how could she get to Varina?

When Elizabeth visited the next day, Hattie implored her friend to carry a message to Varina asking her to intervene in sparing Timothy's life. A skeptical Elizabeth warned Hattie there was little chance of success. But in the end, she could not refuse the request and agreed to carry a letter to Varina.

Elizabeth approached the presidential mansion with considerable unease about her mission. The beautiful three-story brick mansion stood on a high hill just three blocks from Capitol Square. Varina received Elizabeth warmly although they had met only a few times at social functions since the First Family arrived. They chatted and worried together about the hard times in Richmond. As they spoke, little Joe burst into the parlor wanting to play with his mother. The two women showered attention on the energetic child and laughed together as the two-year-old babbled on.

Finally Varina sent the child away with his nanny. "Little Joe is Jeff's favorite and his greatest joy in life," she confided to Elizabeth.

"I can understand why, Varina," Elizabeth responded, smiling. "I won't keep you from the children any longer. I am the bearer of a message from Mrs. Hattie Webster." Elizabeth scrutinized Varina's face.

Varina looked puzzled. "I have heard the sad story of her imprisonment, but what has she to do with me?"

"Then you know her husband has been sentenced to death," Elizabeth continued, handing her the envelope from Hattie.

Varina appeared to read the letter a number of times before she spoke. "It is a cruelty of life that women must bear the consequences of their husband's actions." She paused. "I *am* sorry for her predicament, Elizabeth. But I cannot interfere in this in any way. I have made it a rule not to meddle in matters of state. Even if I wanted to, my wishes in these matters have no weight at all. None," she added for emphasis. "I regret I cannot help."

Varina looked again at the letter and Elizabeth thought she saw a sadness in her face.

"If my husband were imprisoned and threatened in this way, I would do exactly what Mrs. Webster has done." Again a powerful and unsettling premonition swept over Varina as she spoke. With a shaky hand she refolded the letter, placed it in the envelope and handed it back to Elizabeth. "Please convey my sympathy to her."

"You have been most gracious to entertain Hattie's plea," Elizabeth said, rising. "I will let you get back to your delightful son." After they said goodbye, Elizabeth walked through the door and across the path leading through the lawn and gardens, grateful that Varina had not pressed her to explain her own interest in the Webster matter.

As the end drew near for Timothy Webster, Hattie was present by his bedside. General Winder had been called in to hear the doomed man's last request, that he be shot instead of hanged like a common criminal. Hattie, too, delivered a passionate plea, urging the general to grant Timothy's dying wish. But Winder refused, citing the court's order.

On the morning of the execution, crowds made their way to the old fairgrounds as the first light of dawn crept across the dark sky. A cool mist rose from the ground, blanketing the area and lending a surreal look to the scene. Farmers drove their wagons and families into town. Laborers came on their way to work. Confederate soldiers flocked to the scene, boasting that the Yankee would beg for his life. Prostitutes and street hustlers appeared. Accompanied by gentlemen, Richmond's ladies, dressed in their finest, with silk shawls over their shoulders, stepped from their carriages onto the sweeping lawn, damp with morning dew. Young boys climbed into trees for a better view in the gathering haze. A spirited carnival atmosphere covered the grounds where the first Yankee spy was to hang in the name of the great cause.

That morning a sorrowful Elizabeth, accompanied by her friend Eliza Carrington, went to Hattie's prison cell in Castle Thunder to be with the grieving widow in her desperate time of need, only to find her gone. Captain George Alexander met the two women and informed them that

Hattie had left. The stout, villainous looking Alexander, feared for his cruelty and rumored to be corrupt in his financial dealings, had allowed Hattie one last visit with Webster in his cell before he left for the fairgrounds. He would not, however, allow her to attend the execution.

In their last moments together, Webster gently kissed Hattie as she sat on a chair, bent over his body on a stretcher. She pressed his hand to her heart and fought back the tears. The two silently clung to each other until a guard pulled her to her feet.

"Dearest Tim . . ."

"Don't fret for me, my love," Timothy said, his voice barely a whisper. "I believe in a just God. I will die with dignity."

As the guard dragged her from the room, Hattie held back a torrent of tears until the prison door slammed shut. Distraught and weeping violently, she was taken back to prison.

After a painful journey in a jostling carriage, Webster arrived at the fairgrounds so weak he had to be lifted to the ground. Supported by soldiers, the condemned man struggled to climb the steps of the wooden scaffold where his hands and feet were bound. Webster took a long look across the crowded grounds shrouded in an unearthly mist and slowly a quiet calm passed over him. As a hushed silence settled over the crowd, the executioner adjusted the noose around Webster's neck and a clergyman pleaded with God in a loud voice to forgive the sinner standing before them. Then a thunderous crash cut the silence as the wooden trapdoor opened. Instantly the noose slid off the doomed man's neck and he plunged to the ground, writhing in pain. A gasp rose from the crowd.

The soldiers rushed to Webster, groaning in agony. This time they carried the tormented man up the scaffold as the confused and inexperienced executioner examined and measured the noose. In what seemed like an eternity to the man without hope, the noose at last made its way around his neck again, tightly.

"I suffer a double death," Webster whispered to his killer just before the trapdoor fell for a second, lethal time.

As a lesson to would-be traitors, the body hung for a half hour on the scaffold for public viewing before guards cut it down and placed it in a wagon. As the corpse left the fairgrounds, people scrambled to grab a piece of the rope as soldiers cut it into bits.

Back at Castle Thunder, a slick Captain Alexander, pompous in his bright red and gray uniform, coldly informed Hattie of Webster's death. Elizabeth Van Lew and Eliza Carrington sat with the grief-stricken woman as Alexander brought the word. Later, with Elizabeth's help, Hattie appealed to General Winder for permission to see the body and send it north to his family for burial. He agreed that she could view the body, but Winder refused permission to send the corpse north.

Hattie asked Elizabeth to accompany her to the funeral parlor. There Elizabeth sorrowfully held onto the distraught woman as she said goodbye to the corpse of her dead lover. When Hattie's tearful visit ended and they returned to prison, Elizabeth pleaded with Captain Alexander to allow the grieving widow to stay with her on Church Hill, at least for a few days. He flatly refused. So Hattie returned to her dreary cell in the prison on the corner of Carey and Eighteenth Street, alone and friendless, except for Elizabeth Van Lew.

Outside the prison walls, on the order of General Winder, Timothy Webster's cold body made its way to an unmarked grave in a desolate pauper's field.

John Scully, informant and betrayer of his friend, escaped execution. But so did Pryce Lewis, who remained loyal to the end. To Scully's great dismay, he, who had helped convict Webster, as well as Lewis who had not, continued to languish in prison.

Chapter 4

A THICK, STICKY HEAT SQUEEZED THE HOMES ON CHURCH HILL IN THE early morning hours as the tiny hand pounded on the great door of the sleeping Van Lew mansion. Narrow streaks of light made ready to guide a tardy gray dawn across the cloud-filled sky. Shivering in the heat, the girls waited anxiously for someone to come. One of the children began knocking again.

In the kitchen at the back of the house, Mary Bowser stoked the oven's dying embers and put together a pile of twigs to restart the smoldering fire. Oliver Lewis, the butler, and Peter Roane came down from the servants' quarters, moving sluggishly and rubbing their eyes. Caroline Till, cook for the Van Lews, rolled two mounds of dough for biscuits on a great wooden table and stabbed a round cutter across the floury mass, placing the circles on a metal sheet.

Suddenly Peter stopped and listened as a sound, like a woodpecker's insistent tapping, softly made its way from the other side of the house. Everyone stopped and listened.

"Go see, Peter," Caroline said, gesturing with her sticky, flour-covered hand to the front of the house.

As the tall, bulky black man stiffly made his way to the front door, the tapping became louder. When he opened the ornate wooden door, he strained to see into the darkness.

Before he could speak, a pair of arms threw themselves around his legs.

"Peter. Peter," the girl shouted through her tears.

"Miz Annie! Miz Eliza . . ." he exclaimed in disbelief as he strained to see who had brought the girls to their door at such an hour. But he saw no one.

"Come in. Come in." He pulled the little ones into the house as Annie broke into a torrent of tears. It was then that he noticed little Eliza limply hanging back.

"Child, what's wrong?" Peter asked Eliza, who hung her head and rubbed her red eyes. "Annie, where is you mama?"

At that moment Caroline hurried to the front door, shaking the flour from her hands, followed by Mary.

"Mammy!" Annie cried out when she saw the cook, running to hug her.

"Lord, child . . ." Caroline exclaimed.

"I'll get their father," Mary said to Peter, but Annie had already left "mammy" and darted for the great staircase, loudly sobbing.

"Daddy, daddy! Aunt Lizzie! Granmama!"

Mary picked up little Eliza and carried the drooping child into the parlor, laying her gently on a sofa. She felt the child's burning forehead.

"Stay with her while I get a wet towel," she said to Caroline and Peter as she dashed from the room.

The commotion had roused the house. "Uncle" Nelson, Mary's father, entered the parlor. The girls' aunt, still in her night clothes, rushed into the room behind him.

"What is it?" Elizabeth asked Peter anxiously, as she hurried to the feverish child.

"She sick, Miz Lizzie. Mary is bringing da towel."

"Where's her mother?" Elizabeth asked looking about the room.

"They come alone, far as I kin see," Peter answered.

"Alone? At this hour? she said incredulously, as Mary ran up to the child holding a basin of water and a towel.

Just then John rushed into the room carrying Annie who continued to sob, followed by a confused Eliza.

"Mother, send for the doctor," Elizabeth said quickly.

As Mary dipped the towel into the cool water and spread it over the girl's forehead, John anxiously questioned Annie. As best they could determine, the girls' mother had left home with a gentleman the evening before, after putting the girls to bed and telling them she would return shortly. But she never came back.

"Was Eliza sick when mommy went out?" her father gently asked Annie.

"Yes, daddy," Annie sobbed. "We were scared alone in the house. Eliza kept calling for you, daddy," she sniffed. "So I brought her here."

"You did the right thing, Annie," John said, hugging the child. "You're safe now."

As the girls lay exhausted in their beds and Eliza sent for a doctor, John pulled Elizabeth aside and whispered to her, "I'll find her." Then he added emphatically, "The children are home to stay!"

At Mary's house, John waited. Dawn had barely broken when he spotted his wife approaching the house on the arm of a tall, well-dressed man. Laughing and talking, the pair stopped suddenly when they caught sight of John standing in the shadows on the porch. The man mumbled something to Mary and quickly left as John stepped forward.

Indignant at the sight of him, Mary Van Lew brushed past him into the house as John angrily confronted her. She would hear none of it and made a scene, demanding to know why he had come and loudly protesting that she had done nothing wrong.

"The girls are at the house. They showed up alone. How could . . ." he sputtered.

"How could I know they would leave home in the dark?" she interrupted in a huff. "The girls were tucked safely in their beds when I left. They can look after each other and . . ."

"Annie is barely six years old!" John shot back angrily. "Why was their nanny not with them?"

Mary responded defiantly. "She is no longer employed here. I can't seem to find any good help these days."

"You mean you can't *keep* good help—the way you treat servants!" He glared at her. "If there was no one to watch them, you should not have gone out."

"Am I to have no life of my own, then?" the young woman bitterly objected.

"Will you never grow up, Mary?" John snapped as she turned away from him. "You were not ready for motherhood when I married you and you are not ready now!" Then, pausing, he added, "Alright then, you shall have a life of your own. The girls will stay with me. I'll see our solicitor today." Then he abruptly left as the stunned woman stood speechless.

In the end, Mary did not contest the removal of her children; she could not. But she harbored a deep and abiding resentment against John, his mother, and his sister. Although she was allowed visitation of her daughters, Mary never again went to the Van Lew mansion. Instead the children were brought to her parents' home periodically to call on their mother.

From that day, Mary nursed her bitterness.

~

Meanwhile trouble called beyond the Van Lew home as well, as the noose tightened around Richmond through the spring of 1862. Convinced that Major General George McClellan would soon take the city and end the war, Eliza Van Lew prepared a room in the mansion for the soon-to-be-victorious general. She redecorated a lovely chamber with velvet drapes, fresh linens, a satin bedspread, and a new carpet. But weeks of waiting turned to months. Although Federal gunboats moved up the James River, Union observation balloons ominously floated above the city, and the sounds of battles reached Richmond, the expected assault on the city never seemed to materialize.

"Little Mac," his men fondly called him. A short man ~~~ rel chest and jet-black hair and moustache, McClellan plann~~~ the peninsula between the York and James Rivers and move fr~~~ there against the capital of the Confederacy. Handsome, intelligent, well-liked by his men, the thirty-five-year-old McClellan assembled a fighting force of over one hundred thousand men and fought his way up the neck of land from his base at Fort Monroe southeast of Richmond. Throughout April and May, he moved closer and closer to the capital.

As McClellan's forces advanced, especially after they took Yorktown and Williamsburg, more and more people panicked. General Winder found his office swamped with citizens seeking passports to leave Richmond. While people fled in fear, Confederate authorities grew more desperate and escalated their campaign against disloyalty and sedition. This time they cast a broader net, searching every corner of the capital, including prestigious Church Hill.

It was a lovely June day. The late morning sun climbed high in the sky as Elizabeth sat alone on the back portico of her home writing a letter to her beloved Allen. Engrossed in musings about the gentle man who had unexpectedly come into her life, a pile of his letters in front of her, Elizabeth did not notice the Confederate Lieutenant approaching stiffly from the street below. Only when Eliza nervously burst through the door onto the portico did she look up. Behind her mother a tall, rigid-looking young man in a spotless gray uniform carried a letter.

"He says he must give this directly to you," Eliza said haltingly.

"Elizabeth Van Lew?" he asked formally.

She nodded. The soldier handed her a sealed envelope, bowed, and excused himself, walking across the great portico and down the sloping lawn toward the street below.

"Open it, Bet," Eliza said anxiously.

Slowly, Elizabeth broke the seal, hesitated, then pulled out the note, reading it twice before speaking.

"Captain Alexander has summoned me to his office in Castle Godwin," she said ominously and handed the note to Eliza, who quickly scanned the paper.

Miss Van Lew,

There is talk about you and I am obliged to investigate. Come immediately to my office.

Captain Alexander
Castle Godwin

An alarmed Eliza did not want her daughter going to the prison alone, but Elizabeth would have none of it.

"We must treat this as a routine summons," she told her mother, stifling the wad of fear rising in her throat. "I cannot even hint that I feel threatened or that I need support. Any suggestion of fear on my part will make me appear guilty."

As calmly as she could, Elizabeth gathered Rockwell's letters, papers, and pen and rose from her chair as Eliza watched in alarm. Before leaving she firmly took her mother's arm and squeezed it tightly, as she smiled and kissed Eliza on her cheek.

"I'll be back shortly."

Peter took her by carriage to the prison on Franklin Street as she wrestled with the fear that had turned to a terrifying dread.

"Wait here, Peter," Elizabeth said as she turned and entered the guarded door of Castle Godwin and struggled to compose herself.

"Ah, Miss Van Lew," Captain Alexander greeted her as he might welcome an unexpected visitor. "Come in. Come in."

Elizabeth looked straight at the shifty man who always appeared so villainous to her.

"You sent for me?" she asked directly and coolly.

"Please, sit down." He motioned to a chair and sat across from her.

"I trust this won't take long, Captain. It's a very busy day—for *both* of us, I suspect." Her steely blue eyes unflinching, she showed no emotion, even as her inner defenses stood at a fever pitch.

Alexander shifted in his seat, his conniving eyes fixed on her. "We have a problem, Miss Van Lew."

"What kind of problem?"

"There is talk . . . Some have made charges against you." His oily voice became slippery.

Elizabeth waited silently.

"Your repeated visits to Union prisoners do not sit well with . . ."

"General Winder has approved my visits," she interrupted, her voice firm and even. "Are you suggesting that General Winder approves of disloyalty?"

"Of course not," a flustered Alexander shot back. "But many . . ."

"And the Secretary of War has no problem with my visits," she broke in again. "Both gentlemen understand that I act in the name of Christian charity. Who are these people who disagree with the Provost Marshal and the Secretary of War?"

Alexander looked stricken, but he quickly regained his composure.

"This is not about Winder and Benjamin. This is about you. You are giving aid and comfort to the enemy."

"With the support of John Winder and Judah Benjamin? I hardly think those two men would approve of me giving aid and comfort to the enemy." Elizabeth smiled, tossing her head slightly in distain as she wrestled inside to stay calm and betray no fear.

The frustrated interrogator measured his words. "General Winder has given me a free hand to investigate suspicious activity against the Confederacy. There are many complaints against you, Miss Van Lew. Many. And I am forced to act on them."

"In what way, sir?" she asked calmly.

"I intend to detain you as long as it takes to get to the bottom of these charges."

Elizabeth sat perfectly still.

"What was your business with Pryce Lewis, the spy? And Hattie Webster?" he demanded sardonically.

"My business with all men and women, whoever they are, is the same. I do what we are all exhorted to do by our Lord, forgive and care for all of God's people. It is my Christian duty as a good Southern women to practice charity. You, no doubt, have heard the same sermons exhorting us to be kind to our enemies, as our Lord was."

"We are at war, Miss Van Lew and . . ."

"All the more reason for generosity in our victories," Elizabeth interrupted yet again. Then, in a precise and measured tone, she said, "I should tell you that President Davis and I have spoken of my work in the prisons and he understands.

At the mention of Jefferson Davis, a startled look passed over Alexander's broad face and he suddenly looked less menacing. For the first time he fell speechless.

"I should also remind you," she pressed on, her piercing blue eyes narrowing, "that when Dr. Higgenbotham countermanded General Winder and forbade me from visiting wounded prisoners, he was relieved of his position."

Alexander turned pale.

"I understand you have a job to do," Elizabeth quickly added in a conciliatory tone. "But surely chasing Southern ladies because of a few malicious voices is a waste of your precious time."

The displeased captain struggled for words as he grasped his chin and a deep frown passed over his face. "Well, Miss Van Lew, I . . ." He paused.

Elizabeth waited as he rose and paced to his desk.

After a long silence he said simply, his voice uneven and strained, "Well, then. It seems the allegations against you have already been looked into." Then he added, as though forcing himself to speak, "I'm pleased we've been able to clear up these charges."

"Then I'm free to go?"

"Of course, of course." He gestured toward the door with a sweep of his hand. "I'm sorry to have interrupted your day."

Elizabeth felt a weakening in her knees and a breathlessness as she rose to leave, but she strained to maintain her self-control. Nodding and smiling slightly at the flustered officer, she strode out the door.

❦

That night, very late, a troubled sleep at last overtook Elizabeth.

This was just a warning shot over the bow, she thought she heard her father say.

He protested that he had not said anything and was in fact sleeping.

"It was a terribly scary experience, Poppa," she said, tossing in her bed.

Interrogations always are, he wanted to say, but he was too tired.

"They're not going to stop me, you know."

I know, he thought. *I raised you, remember?*

"It's infuriating. I'm accused of being a traitor by the likes of Alexander and people who have rebelled against their government!" She was indignant. "Everything is upside-down. Patriots are traitors and traitors are patriots."

He'd heard her make that point many, many times.

"Plucking solid citizens from their homes with wild accusations . . ." she huffed indignantly.

He marveled at her charade of innocence.

"They justify their war by the constitution, but they violate constitutional rights. It's the tyranny of war and of despots!"

He braced himself. *A philosophical discussion in the middle of the night? Whatever happened to crazy dreams?*

"But it won't work! McClellan will be in Richmond soon," she dreamed.

He let out a sigh of relief. She's changed the subject.

"It'll all be over soon. I'll see Allen again."

77

The war? Over soon? I don't think so . . . He yawned and went back to sleep.

⌒

By May, with McClellan's troops massed to strike Richmond, normality vanished everywhere in the capital. The Confederate Congress adjourned. Departments of government packed their paperwork in large boxes. The Treasury filled crates with its gold. On all of the boxes, the words "Columbia, South Carolina" appeared. In the press and on posters in shop windows, cartoons caricatured Confederate politicians running with baggage in hand, chased by various Union insects and animals.

At the president's mansion, Varina Davis tried to carry on as usual. In the middle of a reception a courier arrived with an urgent message, interrupting the entertainment and summoning the president out of the room. She thought little of this everyday occurrence until her husband re-emerged into the drawing room looking ashen and distracted.

After the guests left, Varina anxiously asked, "Jeffie, what is it?"

"Enemy gunboats are coming up the river, Winnie. We are being squeezed." After a pause he added, "You must take the children and leave Richmond."

"Leave? You know I'm not one to flee troubles," she said.

"I know, I know, Winnie. But you must take the children away. For them and for me. It would pain and distract me to worry about my family when I go to the front. I would be torn when I need to be focused on my work." Pulling her to him and stroking her thick, black hair, he said softly, "You must leave tomorrow."

"But who will look after you? You don't eat. You don't sleep. You're not well," she entreated, thinking of his long days in the office with only the food brought by her, his long nights pacing the floor, and his recurring bouts of illness. "I cannot bear to leave you."

"The one who stays behind has double pain when loved ones depart, Winnie. To him everything brings remembrance of the loss." He hugged her tightly and kissed her forehead. "But it must be done."

78

The next morning Varina and a maid packed up the necessities and she gathered her children to say goodbye to their father. Margaret protested that she didn't want to leave her daddy. Jeff, at five years, announced he was prepared to fight with his father, and little Joe clung to his father's legs. Varina carried her baby, William, barely a half-year old, in her arms. Looking immeasurably stricken, her husband hugged and kissed every child in turn, urging them to be strong and good for their mother. Then he hugged Varina, clinging to her for a long time. As his family tearfully pulled away in their carriage, bound for Raleigh, North Carolina, Jefferson Davis, pale and stooped, watched sadly from the portico until they disappeared from sight.

In late May, General McClellan's forces continued their relentless advance, capturing Mechanicsville, just seven miles northeast of Richmond. On the last day of May, at a small railroad station near Seven Pines and Fair Oaks, barely five miles east of Richmond, hellish battles erupted. In some of the most intense fighting of the war, General Joseph Johnston, ferocious Indian fighter and victor at Bull Run, stopped McClellan's advance. Thousands of casualties on both sides spilled into the North and South. In wagons of every kind, Confederate dead and wounded poured into a Richmond unable to care for the wounded it already had. Among the returning injured was General Johnston himself, badly hurt by gunshot.

Again the city's women opened their doors and took in the countless mangled bodies. Parlors, bedrooms, and basements turned into wards where the disabled lay on sofas, beds, and floors. Tents sprang up around the city where the severely wounded lay in desperate hopelessness. The largest stores on Main Street became hospitals where the sick languished in full view of people passing by. So fetid and oppressive were the smells of death and dying in the city that people, including the Van Lews, could not bear to sit outside. The military draw continued for some three weeks as both sides regrouped and nursed their injured.

Emboldened by her encounter with Captain Alexander and increasingly worried that an end to the war was not near, Elizabeth Van Lew set out by carriage on an oppressively hot day in late June with her friend Eliza Carrington to visit fellow Unionist John Minor Botts. An eerie calm hung about as they moved along the Mechanicsville Turnpike. Special passes in hand, the women wove past guards, soldiers on horses, and wagons of equipment rattling past. They found Botts, under house arrest, with his family at their farmhouse past the outskirts of Richmond.

The two women had barely arrived when the calm suddenly vanished and the terrible din of battle began in an onslaught of explosions that rattled the windows of the Botts home and shook the ground. They found out later that Major General "Stonewall" Jackson had thrown his forces against McClellan at Mechanicsville, a few miles from the farmhouse.

As the family and Eliza hovered anxiously in the parlor listening to the frightening crashes, Elizabeth and Botts conferred quietly in the library.

"John, I know you cannot help our cause," she said, referring to his house arrest. "But we need your advice."

"I was sorry to hear of your encounter with Alexander. Wretched man!" His own jail house encounter remained fresh in his mind.

"He's made me more determined than ever. If I was hesitant before, I'm not now." She leaned forward. "We need names . . . names of people who are strong Unionists."

"You read the names of those arrested in the newspapers?"

"Yes. But whom can we trust? Whom can we count on to help?"

"I'll tell you what I know, Elizabeth. Then you must use your own judgment. Two people have gone out of their way to offer help—John Rowley, a farmer, and Frederick Lohmann who owns a small working-class eatery. They sought me out after my release." With that, a list of names spilled from his lips—men, women, whites, blacks.

Unwilling to commit anything to paper, Elizabeth repeated every name several times, fixing them in her mind. She also conferred about other names that had come to her attention during Winder's dragnet. Together they carefully sorted through the list.

Elizabeth pressed on. "I need to know what each of these people can contribute in your view. Who can give money or use their homes for safe houses? Who can act as courier or guide, get information, work in the prisons . . . ?" Her animated voice eagerly ran on as her blue eyes sparkled.

Botts smiled at her energy and contagious excitement. He elaborated as best he could on every person, their means, location, and whatever insights he had. "But you must be careful, Elizabeth," he cautioned. "You need to be very sure whom you are dealing with. Alexander and the others will not remove their tentacles."

After a hurried lunch with the Botts family, Elizabeth and her friend, Eliza, climbed into their carriage surrounded by ear shattering explosions and clouds of dust rising from the direction of Mechanicsville. Cautiously, Peter directed the horse toward Richmond. Guards stopped them at a number of checkpoints as they slowly worked their way through the rush of troops and equipment clogging the road in the sticky heat.

For seven days the ferocious battle raged in temperatures hovering around 100 degrees at a dreadful human cost. Casualties numbered in the tens of thousands. When it ended, Robert E. Lee and his men had succeeded in driving George McClellan's forces from the area.

～～

While President Lincoln called off the peninsular campaign in despair at the carnage and replaced McClellan, Richmond's Unionist network came together and flourished. Throughout that summer, fall, and winter, Elizabeth organized a cadre of Unionists composed of wealthy elites, working-class men and women, freed blacks, and slaves into an elaborate underground. Safe houses sprang up for escaped prisoners, Confederate deserters, civilians wanting to flee north, and fugitive slaves. Guides ferried those fleeing through Confederate lines to the safety of Union strongholds. Money flowed to hire lawyers to defend those charged with sedition, to bribe Confederate guards in the prisons, to buy food and supplies for Union captives, and to reimburse people of limited means working for the network.

All of it grew under the cloak of respectability and connections enjoyed by the Van Lew family—connections that Elizabeth was determined to cement.

"It's time to invite the Winders to dinner, mother," she told Eliza one evening. "A visit is long overdue."

Eliza immediately understood. "It's done!"

Within days, the Winders joined the Van Lews for dinner at the mansion. During the meal, Elizabeth spoke sympathetically about the Confederacy and their recent victories against McClellan.

"Nothing good can come of this war," Mrs. Winder unexpectedly responded, much to the Van Lews' surprise.

After an awkward moment, John ventured vaguely, "War is hard on everyone."

"It's not natural—families torn apart," she continued.

"Hopefully it won't go on much longer," General Winder said to his wife soothingly.

"How is William Andrew doing?" Eliza asked, inquiring about their son in the Union army.

"Last we heard, he was well, Eliza," Winder answered.

"But it's a great worry," Mrs. Winder interjected. "Him in Washington on one side, the rest of his family here . . ."

"This is why we must be kind to our enemies. If anyone in our families were to be captured, we would want them treated kindly," Elizabeth said sympathetically, glancing at General Winder. "We were once a great family, North and South. When the war is over, we must be able to reconcile." Then, turning to Mrs. Winder, "Your husband understands so well the need for Christian charity in these difficult times. He's a great man."

Winder smiled at Elizabeth and nodded his head slightly.

"And John and Sidney?" Eliza asked of their other sons in the Confederate army. "And your daughter, Caroline?"

"All well," Mrs. Winder said. "But, Caroline can't forgive her brother for staying with the Union. You know how strongly she feels about secession."

We surely do, thought Elizabeth, very aware of Caroline's rabid pro-slavery, pro-Confederate stand.

"This dreadful war!" the troubled mother added in disgust. "So unnecessary!"

Eliza and her daughter exchanged curious glances.

The rest of the evening passed pleasantly. The Van Lews and the Winders shared a meal, chatted about memories, spoke of many things. Small talk really, all of it. But most revealing small talk . . .

CHAPTER 5

CARRYING AXES, PITCHFORKS, CLUBS, AND PISTOLS, HUNDREDS OF ANGRY
women descended on Capitol Square shouting, over and over, "Bread!
Bread! Bread!" Their leader, Mary Jackson, wife of a Richmond sign
painter and mother of a Confederate soldier, brandished a gun as she
loudly urged the women on.

"We will be heard," she thundered above the din of chants and rushing footsteps.

The enraged crowd made its way through the gentle breezes of an
early April warmth to government storehouses loaded with provisions.
With their axes and weapons, the women smashed into the locked doors,
sending them crashing to the ground in splinters. In an instant the
enraged throngs poured through the jagged openings. After a momentary jolt at seeing the large amounts of food stacked along the walls, the
women angrily grabbed what they could carry—sacks of flour, bacon,
slabs of dried meats, bags of beans, salt—and staggered back past those
still pushing into the broken doorway, dragging their loads. On and on
more women came, striking not only at the food storehouses but attack-
ing clothing stores as well.

Within minutes the mayor ordered out the guard who quickly surrounded the area. Trying to speak above the shouts and noise, Mayor
Joseph Mayo read the riot act to the women—to no avail.

Next Governor Letcher appeared and bellowed loudly at the women,
"You are a disgrace to the great Confederacy." Still the women paid no mind.

Finally, Jefferson Davis rode into the Square leading a detachment of Confederate troops on horseback. He fired a round of shots into the air, bringing the women to an abrupt stop.

Mary Jackson quickly pushed her way forward, still holding her pistol, until she stood before the tall figure neatly dressed in gray, stiffly seated on his horse. A hush fell over the crowd as the two glared at each other in the momentary calm.

"Disperse!" demanded Davis, brandishing his weapon and gesturing to the crowd.

"We will not disperse," Mary said. "We demand to be heard."

"The Confederacy will never listen to a mob," he answered.

"The Confederacy did not listen when we were peaceful petitioners. *When* will you listen? Our families are hungry and we cannot afford to feed them." Then she repeated the plea a committee of women had made to Governor Letcher the day before. "We only ask that the government sell us food at the same low prices it pays its citizens for the food it confiscates." Next, nodding at the governor, she said, "He would not listen to our just grievances."

"And so you choose to attack the Confederacy for a loaf of bread?" Davis responded with contempt.

"We choose to feed our hungry families. Yes, we take a loaf of bread. This is little enough for the government to give us after it has taken all our men," Jackson shot back defiantly.

"Disperse!" Davis shouted again at the crowd, turning from the insolent woman before him, his men lined up on horses behind him, weapons in hand.

No one moved.

"If you do not disperse, I will give my men the order to fire into this mob of insurrectionists."

Still no one moved.

At that point, Davis shouted to his men, "Ready . . ." The uneasy men raised their rifles. They were being asked to shoot their mothers and sisters, their neighbors.

"Aim . . ." The rifles lowered, their barrels fixed on the crowd.

With the weapons suddenly positioned on them, a panic swept over the women and they fell back in a wave.

"Disperse!" Davis shouted at them again.

Slowly, reluctantly, the women began to move away, dropping the food at their feet. But Mary Jackson stood her ground.

"Arrest her!" Davis ordered.

Two of his men rushed to the woman and wrenched the pistol from her hand, dragging her from the square.

Within days many others were arrested, as the press damned the Richmond matrons taking part in the riot as *"prostitutes, professional thieves, Irish and Yankee hags, and gallows birds from all lands."* Mary Jackson emerged in print as a *"forty-year-old Amazon, with the eye of the devil."*

Newspaper in hand, Elizabeth raged at the injustice. Near famine had descended on Richmond during the bitter winter of 1862–63, especially for the city's poor and working classes, as the Union blockade by sea tightened, the population swelled, and food was diverted to Confederate troops.

In court lawyers quickly emerged to defend Mary Jackson and the others. Bail money was posted. How could such riffraff afford these lawyers and bail, the press ruminated? Surely the North lurked behind these lawless riots and more could be expected, they wrote in conspiratorial tones.

Quietly, with the greatest care, Elizabeth's Unionist underground worked to help the incarcerated women with lawyers and bail money—without any aid from the North, despite the press's suspicions. Elizabeth huddled with Franklin Stearns and Charles Palmer after the bread riots.

"We are always putting out fires after they start," she worried.

"You're right, Elizabeth," Palmer agreed. "It's not a very effective way to fight."

"We're not connected in any serious way to the Union command," Elizabeth continued, frustrated. "That's the biggest problem. We fight our small fights here, but there's no coordination with Union authorities, whatever the press chooses to think."

"We don't know what Union officials need us to do that would most help the North," Palmer added, shaking his head.

"We need a way to connect," Elizabeth repeated.

"I agree." Stearns had been chewing over the same problem. "We can't use the mail. It's too risky." They all knew that although mail still passed between North and South under a flag of truce agreement, it seldom passed unread by censors.

The case of Mary Caroline Allan stood as a painful reminder of that fact to any Unionist who had once thought otherwise. Confederate authorities charged Allan with treasonable communications with the enemy. Originally from the North, she had written many letters to friends in the Union, including one to the brother of Union General John Dix. The arrest resulted, authorities alleged, from the passing of secret information about troop movements and other sensitive material. Ultimately, her legal team raised enough doubt in the judge's mind that she returned to her family plantation on bail to await a new trial.

"Sending what we know with our fugitives as we've been doing is too haphazard. We have to find a better way to send information North," Elizabeth urged.

"We never know who our valuable leaks reach or if they reach anyone at all," Palmer added. They had sent information on troop strength, positions, and movements from their sources in the War and Navy Departments, without any sense of what happened to that material.

Stearns nodded. "We have to find a way," he repeated.

While the network grappled with the communication problem, news from the various fronts through the spring and summer alternately dashed and raised their hopes—Chancellorsville, Gettysburg, Vicksburg . . .

Through it all, Elizabeth worried about Allen. Was he involved in any of these battles? The letters kept coming without a hint of combat. She hoped he had been spared the horrors written about in the press and that his regiment was stationed on the peninsula or near Washington where relative quiet prevailed. As long as the letters kept coming she could hope.

As Unionists worked for a breakthrough with some high-level Northern contact, a momentous opportunity presented itself to Elizabeth. Her friend Eliza Carrington mentioned in passing one day that Varina Davis, who had returned to Richmond after the defeat of McClellan, increasingly found herself overwhelmed by the many meetings and functions at the presidential mansion and was always looking for reliable help. An uncontrollable excitement swiftly spun through Elizabeth's head.

"Why, I can spare Mary to help at some of these events," she told Eliza.

Her friend looked quizzically at Elizabeth who betrayed no particular emotion and casually continued her work, all the while suppressing a sudden, mind-numbing exhilaration.

"You could offer Varina a chance to observe Mary working at a few gatherings." Then she added, "It would be a good opportunity for Mary to earn some extra money."

"Mary working for the Confederacy?" Eliza puzzled.

Elizabeth said nothing.

"Well, if you think it's a good idea . . ." Eliza shrugged at last. "I'll pass the word to Varina."

It *was* a good idea, a *very* good idea—the ultimate deception, Elizabeth thought to herself with delight over and over after Eliza left. Mary Bowser was no ordinary servant. She was special.

"You would have liked Mary, Poppa," Elizabeth reflected in the library as she conjured up her father, who endlessly hovered about in the mansion. "She was just a girl when you died."

He knew that.

"She's one of those slaves you forbade momma to free," she added in her usual accusatory tone when she spoke of the slaves.

Her father listened and groaned in anticipation of another tongue lashing over the slavery thing. But instead, Elizabeth reminisced warmly about Mary.

"Her name was Mary Jane Richards then. A remarkably intelligent girl. Anyone could see that. But we couldn't educate her here, so I sent her north. Used my own money—well, the money you left me." She smiled and her father heard the irony. "No one but the family knew, of course."

A good thing they didn't know, he wanted to say.

"Could I have done that if you were alive?" she asked him.

He sighed. He was not going to escape after all.

"Anyway . . ." Elizabeth quickly brushed that aside. "Every time I think of it, I'm amazed. School fired Mary up. When she finished her education, she spent time working in Liberia with repatriated Negroes. She stayed there for awhile."

The sequence of events that brought Mary back to them rolled through her mind. He had heard this story before, but he listened, grudgingly.

"She was unhappy there, and homesick. I got word that she wanted to come back. It was tricky. As *you* well know . . ."

A touch of annoyance passed over him as he listened. Why was she always bringing it back to him? *He* didn't make the laws.

". . . free Negroes who left Virginia could not return. If she was still a slave, that would be different. So the 'slave,' Mary Jane Richards, came back to us. Well, we couldn't live with that, so we had to create a new person—Mary Jones—a free Negro servant we 'hired.' That we made official, put it in the record." She turned to him. "Mary Jones was the only free Negro recorded as living in our household in the 1860 census." She paused. "Thanks to you and that will!"

He started to get really annoyed and agitated the air around her.

"To this day all the others are still 'slaves,' even though mother freed them. But what's the sense of dredging that up again?"

Exactly.

"Then Mary met William Bowser—he was a factory worker—and they wanted to marry." Elizabeth chuckled wickedly. "I caused quite a stir when I had them married in St. John's Episcopal Church—St. John's *White* Episcopal Church. That shocked even our progressive friends." She paused. "And you, Poppa? Would it have shocked you?"

Sometimes he wished she were still a child so he could send her to her room! Instead all he could do was listen and twist about the library.

"Sadly, the marriage ended in a few months when William died in a factory accident. Mary's heart broke." Elizabeth sat quietly for awhile. "She's been such a good force in this house. Like a sister to me . . ."

A quiet descended over the room. She stopped talking and he stopped listening.

⁓

That night Mary Bowser huddled with Elizabeth. Mary instantly understood the significance of Elizabeth's proposal. Given Lincoln's Emancipation Proclamation now in effect, the idea grabbed at her brain and an excitement rose in her breast at the thought that she might help her people's cause by hastening an end to the war.

When Varina Davis agreed to hire, on a trial basis, the servant highly recommended by a Carrington, Mary and Elizabeth excitedly whispered their plans.

"You must not appear intelligent in any way, Mary," Elizabeth cautioned. "They *must* not know that you can read and write."

Mary nodded in agreement.

After serving efficiently at three formal dinners at the presidential mansion, Mary Bowser, a free black, was asked to join the Davis household as a paid servant. Elizabeth felt light-headed with joy at the news.

The first thing she did was contact Unionist Thomas McNiven who ran a bakery on North Fifth Street. One of his customers was the Jefferson Davis family. They would bide their time while Mary settled into the presidential mansion, but a clear plan emerged. When McNiven delivered baked goods to the Davis home at an appointed time, Mary would emerge from the mansion to pick up the bread and delicacies and slip him whatever information she had learned.

In December of 1863, Elizabeth embarked on a daring plan. With Mary planted in the Davis home, it became more than ever essential to develop a means to send critical intelligence to the highest authorities in the Union. The underground must help a Union officer escape from prison, she decided. He would then be asked to carry a message to a high Union official and, with the help of the underground, cross over to Federal territory.

This meant a prison break from the notorious Libby Prison, which now held Union officers. But Elizabeth had never been allowed entrance into Libby, despite her charming requests to General Winder. While he had not revoked her previous privileges, the murmurings against her made it impossible for him to extend those privileges. And he himself repeatedly fell under criticism for being too lenient with those giving aid and comfort to the enemy. Another way had to be found.

In early December, Josephine Holmes, fifteen-year-old daughter of Unionist Arnold Holmes, made her way through the cold, windy streets of Richmond to the large, three-story brick building at Twentieth and Cary Streets. Situated in front of the James River abutting the Kanawha Canal, all the windows wore iron bars, even those on the first level, which held the prison offices and hospital. On entering, she showed the stern-looking man her pass. After examining the document, the guard made Josephine place her sack on the large wooden table inside the door and began pulling out the small packages within.

"Tobacco," Josephine said simply as he opened several and peered in.

At last the guard motioned her through and she carefully placed the small packs back into the sack. She walked down the long chilly corridor to the door marked INFIRMARY. A young guard smiled at the pretty girl and opened the door as she nodded pleasantly at him and passed through. In the cavernous, shabby room, cots lined two walls, most of them full of the sick and wounded. Slowly she made her way from bed to bed chatting softly with the men. She handed small packs to those able to receive them, scrutinizing the men as she moved from cot to cot.

When she came to the bed of a man who did not look very ill, Josephine paused and gazed at him intently. The man immediately introduced himself as John McCullough, assistant surgeon, First Wisconsin Infantry. As he spoke, she glanced down the rest of the row and quickly concluded that the others were very ill.

"I've brought you a little tobacco," she smiled, handing him a small pack.

McCullough seemed genuinely moved by the gesture.

Josephine glanced at the guard standing by the door, who was apparently distracted by some papers in his hands.

She whispered almost inaudibly to McCullough, "In the sack." Then she added, "I'll return tomorrow. Will you be here?"

Surprised, he nodded. With that she proceeded to walk down the remaining row of cots with her sack.

A puzzled McCullough watched the girl finish her round of the ward and leave by the door she had entered. His attention turned to the small sack, but he waited for the guard to leave the room. Quickly, his eyes glancing at the door the whole time, he moved his fingers around the tobacco inside the packet until he touched a small, folded piece of paper at the bottom. Carefully, he pulled the paper from the sack and thrust it under the edge of his blanket as he read the note. *Would you be free? Then be prepared to act.*

McCullough's heart raced as questions tumbled through his mind. Who was the girl? What did the note mean? What was he being asked to do? His uneasiness grew. Was it a trick? He spent a troubled night, sleeping in fits and starts, his thoughts churning. He woke long before dawn and waited.

At midmorning the girl emerged once again, smiling at the guard by the door and proceeding to stop at each of the beds. Again she carried a sack from which she drew small packets and gave them to the men able to receive them. But this time she spoke at length to the men, asking how they felt, encouraging each to get well and inquiring about their families. McCullough watched anxiously as she approached him and a shiver rushed through his body.

When at last she stood by his bed, the girl again spoke as she had to the others, but this time whispered a few words here and there. By the time she had finished, he understood that the next day, December 8, he was to escape from Libby by pretending to be dead. He could bring one comrade with him. He should leave right after dusk by the door closest to the morgue. She would be a block away in a certain direction carrying a white handkerchief. They were to follow her, remaining at a distance.

Suddenly she left his side, moving to the remaining beds. The arm of fear passed over McCullough as he watched the girl disappear for a second time, past the guard and through the door into the empty hallway. I am to die, he thought, the statement rolling over him like a question.

That afternoon, his friend, Captain Harry Howard, accompanied by a guard, came down from his cell above to visit his sick friend, as he did every afternoon. Harry's real name was Catlin and he served as a scout for General Benjamin Butler, though his Confederate captors knew nothing of his true identity. When the guard left, McCullough told his astonished friend what had happened, speaking in whispers.

"I will chance it," he said. "And I want you to come with me, if you want to risk it."

Captain Howard's face brightened at the prospect of fleeing the dismal, brutal conditions of Libby Prison and without hesitation he agreed. They quickly laid out a plan.

After Howard left, McCullough pretended to get worse. As guards walked the ward, McCullough moaned loudly and thrashed about in his bed. When his dinner of soaked hard bread and rancid meat appeared, he feigned a lot of pain and indicated to the guard that he was too sick to eat. He passed a second agitated night imagining in turn every terrible outcome of his coming escape.

The next morning he again pretended to be deathly ill. When the prison doctor made a cursory pass by his bed, he heard the guard nearby tell the physician what a lot of pain the sick man was in. The doctor shrugged, mumbled about the lack of medicine, and went on his rounds.

Captain Howard appeared in the sick ward later than usual that afternoon and tried to console his sick friend. When another visitor distracted the guard, Howard whispered that everything was arranged and he could "die" as planned. A thin smile passed across McCullough's face and within the hour he died, Howard at his side.

His friend gasped and made a show of attempting to revive him, shaking the corpse on the bed. A guard rushed to their side, demanding to know what happened.

"The poor wretch is dead," Howard said tearfully. "My friend is gone. His poor wife . . . His children . . ." While he spoke he pulled the blanket slowly over McCullough's face.

Death visited the Libby hospital ward almost daily, so the guard mechanically made ready to transport the body to the morgue. He motioned to two other prisoners visiting their sick comrades in the ward.

"Come," he ordered. "Carry the body and follow me."

Howard prepared to assist the men, wrapping the body in a blanket. After the three men took the body to the morgue and laid it on the cold floor, Howard's tears began to flow and he entreated the guard to give him a bit of time to say some prayers over his friend's corpse.

"It is my Christian duty," he pleaded with the guard.

The uniformed man nodded and motioned the others out of the room. As they left a glance passed between Howard and the men, who immediately returned to their cell. The guard paced impatiently outside the morgue door as Howard mumbled his prayers, exhorting the Lord to bring McCullough safely home. Within minutes a loud commotion erupted from the second floor cell. Shouts broke out in the hallway outside the morgue and Howard watched anxiously as the guard rushed away.

Quickly he shook his friend, unwrapping the blanket as the upper floors erupted into a fracas that grew thunderous. Howard peered into the empty hallway and motioned his friend. Instantly they unbolted the heavy wooden door leading outside and slipped into the gathering darkness. Within minutes they spotted the mysterious girl and her white handkerchief. Keeping a good distance behind her as directed, the two men followed her through the shadowy streets, taking care not to betray their agitation to the few passersby who huddled indifferently against the cold night.

At last they arrived at the home of Arnold Holmes. Safely behind drawn curtains, they entered the parlor and were happily greeted by Josephine and her father and a petite blond woman with the most striking blue eyes they had ever seen.

"Elizabeth Van Lew," the woman introduced herself, as Josephine's mother hurried into the room.

"Come, come," Elmira Holmes motioned to them. "First you get comfortable and eat. You must be hungry. Then we can all talk."

After the men had washed and changed into clean, warm clothes, she escorted them into the dining room where a large table stood, set with a linen tablecloth and napkins, fine silver, and real glasses. The two fugitives stared in disbelief. No banquet could ever again rival this simple supper for McCullough and Howard who had languished in a filthy cell, eaten from tin plates and dined mainly on moldy bread and rancid meat since their imprisonment.

"To the Union," Arnold Holmes toasted the meal.

"To the Union . . . and our saviors, who brought me back from the dead," McCullough responded as the others broke into laughter.

While the two men hungrily ate, the table burst with good cheer and conversation flew from one to the other. After they finished the meal, McCullough paused and asked, "How can we ever thank you enough?"

"I'm sure you will help us more than we have helped you," Elizabeth smiled enigmatically, as her mind savored this latest successful deception.

Around midnight, Burnham Wardwell, freed at last from prison, appeared at the Holmes house. Undeterred by his arrest, he had joined Elizabeth's network. After hurried introductions, he took the weary men part way by carriage and then by foot through the countryside to avoid Confederate checkpoints. Well before morning, the trio arrived at the farm of William Rowley. The tall, lanky farmer had a great beard that swept down to his chest but no mustache, as was the custom of his religious sect, the German Baptist Brethren Church. Like all his brethren in the church who followed the example of Jesus, the pacifist Rowley could not countenance the war. A simple, steady man, he dressed in functional black clothes, pants, shirt, and coat. With a kind face and thoughtful eyes set deep under his brows, he greeted the men warmly and hid them well.

❦

On the second day after their arrival at the Rowley farm, Elizabeth Van Lew came calling. She told them of her critical need to communicate with a high level Union official. Captain Howard volunteered the name of General Benjamin Butler as someone they could put her in touch with.

Delighted, Elizabeth smiled. "Would this be Benjamin 'the Beast' Butler?"

"One and the same," Howard laughed. "You know of him?"

"Everyone in the South knows of Order Number Twenty-Eight," she answered, emphasizing the words *Order Number Twenty-Eight.*

The infamous "Beast" had gained his reputation for treating rebel insurgents harshly and for advocating the recruitment of Negroes into the Union army, but most of all, because of his "slight" to the honor of Southern ladies. After the fall of New Orleans to the Union, Butler had been named commander of occupying troops. The ladies of that venerable city took it upon themselves to harass Union soldiers in a variety of creative ways, believing that their gender, respectability, and race rendered them immune from reprisals. They emptied putrid chamber pots on the heads of Union soldiers as they passed below windows, sneered at them, hurled insults their way, spat on them, and treated them as lepers by crossing the street to avoid any contact. To stop the demoralizing behavior, Butler issued Order No. Twenty-Eight, commonly known as the "Woman Order." The decree stated that any woman who spoke or acted in ways that insulted Union soldiers would be viewed as "a woman of the town plying her avocation," in short, a prostitute.

"For myself," Elizabeth continued, "I find it refreshing that Butler takes us ladies seriously enough to hold us accountable for our actions! The South sees women as helpless and what we do as of no consequence."

"Well, there will certainly be no political immunity for 'helpless women' from the general, although it has cost him a bounty on his head," McCullough added, smiling.

"Yes." Elizabeth spoke more somberly now, shaking her head. "Jefferson Davis has issued an order calling for Butler's immediate execution when captured. And for this—women's *honor.*" Then she asked, "Will you be my emissary to General Butler?"

"Of course," McCullough responded.

"We are at your service, Miss Van Lew," Howard echoed.

In the days that followed, as Elizabeth carefully prepared a communiqué to General Butler, Rowley sought the help of Samuel Ruth, influential superintendent of the Richmond, Fredericksburg, and Potomac Railroad—and a member of the Unionist underground. With the help of Ruth and $3,000 in Confederate bribe money, Rowley secured passes for Howard and McCullough to leave the area. Embarrassed prison officials had not let news of the men's escape leave the walls of Libby, although they quickly established a permanent guard in the morgue for the dead, who could no longer move about freely.

Early on the appointed day of Howard and McCullough's departure, Elizabeth visited the two for the last time. She handed them a small bouquet of dried flowers with a letter tucked inside the wrapping.

"For General Butler," she said simply.

The men took her bouquet and McCullough tucked it deep inside the gray shirt he wore, sewn by Unionist women from Confederate blankets.

"We will guard this with our lives," McCullough assured her, fearing that if the contents fell into enemy hands, Confederate authorities would quickly snatch Elizabeth from the company of the free.

After Elizabeth left, William Rowley took the men by carriage through Confederate checkpoints on the turnpike. Guards scrutinized their passes and let them move on. Then, leaving the carriage at a farm on the outskirts of Richmond, Rowley led Howard and McCullough northeast through the countryside to the banks of the Chickahominy River where they made their way across a shallow, narrow part of the icy stream to a spot north of Cold Harbor. From there Rowley guided them along the silent Richmond, Fredericksburg, and Potomac Railroad tracks for a short distance, then across farmland to the Pamunkey River where again they forded a rushing waterway, leaping across wet boulders as the torrent chased them, rising angrily to grab their legs.

All along the way, the uneasy men hid from and skirted around rebel forces moving about the area. At the Mattapony River they hid in an abandoned barn until dusk. Under a sliver of moon they carefully crossed at a shallow point and continued through the dark countryside to the mighty Rappahannock River, where Rowley located the small boat hidden in the brush by the underground. Swiftly the three men rowed across the rushing waters, struggling to keep from being dragged downstream by the current that swept beneath the boat. At the other shore, Rowley hid the boat deep in the rushes and urged them on till they reached the safety of the Union line near the Potomac River.

Learning that Butler was now headquartered at Fort Monroe, Howard and McCullough went quickly to the general by steamer down the Potomac River and along the Chesapeake. When they found the general, Howard and McCullough presented him with Elizabeth's bouquet. After reading her letter, Butler listened intently as they revealed the extent of the Richmond Unionist underground and their desire to establish a high-level link with Union authorities.

When they finished, the stocky, balding man slapped his hand across his thigh and exclaimed, "Wonderful news. Wonderful," his moustache dancing over his lips and his shirt with its double row of shining buttons straining against his girth and rippling over his chest. Then, pausing, his eyes peering over the thick bags hanging beneath, he asked, "But can we trust the lady, gentlemen?"

"Miss Van Lew proved herself true by arranging our escape. You cannot find a more trustworthy correspondent in the Confederate capital," Howard responded without hesitation. "But if you wish, contact Charles Boutelle, a good friend of the lady."

Butler immediately wrote to his friend Boutelle, an engineer and commander of the *Chancellor Bibb,* the ship that had escorted Butler's troops to New Orleans. He explained his great desire for an informant in Richmond and Elizabeth Van Lew's offer to serve in that capacity. "I am told by the bearer of her offer that she is a true Union woman with a heart as strong as iron. Is this true?" Boutelle lost no time in responding with the greatest praise of Elizabeth, her intelligence and her patriotism.

"It's done then," Butler told Howard when he summoned his scout back to his office. "I want you to return to Richmond to meet Miss Van Lew and bring my response."

In late January, Captain Howard made his way through enemy lines and slipped back into Richmond to the Rowley home. Elizabeth came quickly when summoned to the farm.

"Mr. Howard, you are safe!" she exclaimed when she saw him.

"Yes, yes, dear lady. And I bring the news you want to hear." With that he handed Elizabeth a letter for Eliza A. Jones from "James Ap. Jones" addressed to "Dear Aunt." A puzzled look crossed her face as she read the letter inquiring about her health and her family and chatting about himself, his family, and his ailing mother in Norfolk. A perplexed Elizabeth looked up at Howard who broke into a hearty laugh

"Come," he said, a wide grin on his face, as he led Elizabeth and Rowley into the kitchen. Howard asked Rowley for some milk and pulled a small brush and a bottle of clear liquid from his pocket. Taking the letter from Elizabeth, he placed it on the wooden table. Next he dipped the brush into the cup of milk set before him. With careful strokes he brushed the milk across the page, lightly covering it from top to bottom as Rowley and Elizabeth watched in earnest. Then he moved to the stove from which a steady warmth escaped, pushing away the winter chill. Holding the page over the heat, he waited. At last, smiling, he walked to Elizabeth and handed her the paper, now transformed into a second letter.

Elizabeth gasped at seeing yet another communiqué scrawled across the page.

"Invisible ink, dear aunt," Howard said.

The new letter was addressed to *My dear Miss.* It spoke of having received the thoughtful bouquet and of her kind willingness to serve as correspondent to aid the Union. It instructed her to write her information in invisible ink using the techniques Howard would demonstrate. Over the invisible letter she should write a "family" letter to her nephew in Norfolk, James Ap. Jones, and send routine letters under the Flag of Truce. Critical information would go by courier. For goods and people being spirited out of Richmond, a series of drop-off points should be established by the Union underground. The letter ended with an expression of great joy at hearing of the Union sentiment that still existed in Richmond. It was signed, *B.*

"So . . ." Elizabeth said mischievously, after a pause, her heart quickening, "I am now a spy." A spy! Never in her wildest childhood play-acting at deception could she have imagined this outcome. The excitement, the thrill, yes, even the danger of the game, exhilarated her.

Howard nodded. "Let me demonstrate how you must do it."

Butler's scout then produced a secret code on a very small piece of paper. The cipher consisted of a square diagram with six horizontal rows and six vertical rows overlapping. On the left side and along the bottom of each row, the numbers 1 through 6 were listed, but not in order. The rest of the boxes in the rows held the letters of the alphabet in a seemingly random fashion. The communications, written entirely in numbers and using invisible ink, would utilize the cipher so that, if discovered, they would appear incomprehensible. Howard also gave Elizabeth the bottle of clear liquid—the invisible ink—and the brush.

After a heartfelt goodbye and sincere wishes for Howard's safe return to Union lines, Elizabeth left the Rowley farm.

~

When Elizabeth arrived home, she immediately went to her room and took off her watch. After unscrewing its back plate, she folded the small paper containing the code until it had shrunk to the size of a child's fingertip. Pushing the cipher into the back of her watch, she screwed on the back plate and replaced the watch on her arm.

From there Elizabeth went to the library. As she stood alone in the middle of the room, her eyes rolled over the shelves, desk, chairs, draperies, floor—searching. When her sight landed on the fireplace she moved forward, running her hands over the mantel, across the metal screen, and up the columns at either side of the hearth. Her hand stopped suddenly as it slid over one of the bronze statues perched on top of the columns.

The smooth surface of the crouching lion held Elizabeth's hand as her fingers groped about the figure. When she felt a crack down the middle of the captive creature, her hand stopped moving. Her mind rushed back to her childhood when these lions had fled the jungle to come live in her home. She remembered the workers carrying the majestic animals into the great library in halves—half a face, half a mane, half a body. She had watched, entranced, as the workers brought the lions to life, a whole face, whole mane, whole body. They had let her touch the sticky glue as they fitted the wild animals together and allowed them to crouch on the columns so they could leap onto the library's visitors. Over the years the hardened glue on one of the lions' back had begun to erode, leaving an open crack down the creature's back.

Elizabeth rushed down to the basement and grabbed an awl from the tool bench. As the lion watched warily, the woman bored into his back with the tool, slowly pushing the halves apart just enough to reach her fingers into the animal's belly. Quickly she pressed the lion back together as he watched suspiciously from the corner of his piercing eye. Pleased with herself, Elizabeth winked at the lion, "Good as new!"

From the front of the house Elizabeth heard a commotion as a door slammed. The giggling voices of Annie and Little Eliza bounced through the house and into the library followed by the two girls.

"Aunt Lizzie!" a breathless Annie called out from her thick wool scarf and hat that almost hid her face. "It's snowing! Granmama says we can make snowballs."

"Will you play with us?" little Eliza asked, panting, as she tugged at her aunt's sleeve.

"Of course, little ones," Elizabeth laughed as her smiling mother caught up with the children. "Let me get my coat."

From the top of its perch, the lion watched disdainfully as the four bustled out of the room and thick white flakes floated past the library windows, tumbling out of a gray January sky.

That very evening, Harry Catlin, alias Captain Harry Howard, began his journey back to Fort Monroe through the falling snow. He got as far as the Chickahominy River before he fell into the hands of Confederate soldiers as the falling snow detailed his footsteps, betraying his latest escape attempt from Richmond. The notorious Castle Thunder, designated for the worst offenders and sporting its thick metal bars on the corner of Carey and Eighteenth Streets, swallowed the master of escape, plunging him into in its cold, dark, hungry belly.

———

The next morning Elizabeth visited Thomas McNiven at his bakery. While ordering bread, she told McNiven to alert Mary Bowser during his delivery to Jefferson Davis's home that an opening to the Union high command had at last been made.

"She'll know what to do," Elizabeth told him softly. They arranged for Peter to stop by the bakery each afternoon for any information Mary might have sent. As they spoke and she dug into her purse to pay for the bread, the bakery door opened and its bell clattered noisily.

A startled Elizabeth saw Detective Philip Cashmeyer enter the shop.

"Miss Van Lew," he said bowing slightly, a thin smile on his face and his eyes fixed squarely on hers. "Buying bread, I see."

Elizabeth quickly composed herself as McNiven appeared to go about his business indifferently. "And you, Mr. Cashmeyer? I can't imagine what brings a gentleman to the bakery," she said, as casually as her alarm could muster.

"Nor can I imagine what brings a lady to the bakery," he responded, his cool eyes still fixed on her. "Actually I was just walking past and I spotted you."

"Why, I'm flattered that you stopped, Mr. Cashmeyer," Elizabeth answered, ignoring his comment and putting on her sweetest smile. "So nice to see you. I trust General Winder is well."

They chatted briefly, although afterward Elizabeth could hardly remember what they spoke of, given her unease at the ominous meeting. Cashmeyer's eyes bored through her the whole time, searching for something, she felt. When at last she took her leave, she could not shake the cold eyes that followed her long after she left the bakery.

Shaken by her encounter with Cashmeyer, Elizabeth sat in the library as the lion and her father watched.

"Why does that man frighten me so, Poppa? She asked without words.

He's a detective. You're a spy.

"Do you think he knows something?"

How would I know, he wanted to say.

"It would be a disaster to get caught now—just when I'm about to really help the Union," Elizabeth fretted.

Delusions of grandeur, he muttered to himself.

"What did you say?"

Nothing.

"Didn't you raise me to make something of myself?"

Now it's my fault you've become a spy?

She sighed. "Could you *ever* have imagined you'd have a daughter who's a spy?"

Spy? No. Professional liar? Yes.

"A spy!" she repeated with great self-satisfaction, ignoring him.

Your sister had the good sense to get married and have babies, he thought, but he kept it to himself.

"Could *I* ever have imagined . . ."

He yawned and moved to the couch.

"I'm glad Allen doesn't know."

Allen? Be glad no one knows.

She left the room. He went back to sleep.

———

Within days the baker's deliveries to the presidential mansion paid off. As he pulled his wagon up to the servants' entrance at the Davis home, Mary walked out carrying a sack to hold the baked goods. As Mary watched silently, McNiven placed a loaf of bread into the bag and quickly felt along the bottom. A piece of paper folded very small lay in the sack. McNiven tucked it into his sleeve and continued to load the sack. When he finished Mary lifted the sack, thanked him and turned back to the house.

That afternoon Peter bought bread at the bakery and returned to the Van Lew mansion. Going directly to the library, he walked up to the lion peering curiously from the column next to the fireplace and, petting the disdainful creature, slipped a folded piece of paper into the crack along its back. From there he went into the parlor and told Elizabeth he had brought home the bread for dinner.

Thanking him, she rose and went to the library, closing the sliding doors behind her. Within moments she retrieved a piece of paper from the annoyed-looking lion and went to her desk. She gasped at the revelations as she read the note. Mary had detailed troop movements, the presence of new batteries on the road to Danville, the location of Confederate pickets in the Petersburg area south of Richmond, and preparations for a raid against Union forces. She also disclosed that a lack of horses forced Lee to disband three cavalry regiments. Most important, Mary revealed that Confederate authorities had decided to remove all Federal prisoners from Richmond to prisons in Georgia and that preparations had already begun.

Elizabeth immediately understood that the removal of Union captives would put them out of Federal reach and that freeing them, which Lincoln hoped to accomplish, would be infinitely more difficult. She unscrewed her watch, took out the code, got the invisible ink from her desk drawer, and began writing her first intelligence dispatch to General Benjamin Butler. Carefully, using the cipher code, she wrote the information on a sheet of paper as the page remained blank. To Mary's revelations she added her own advice on any attempt to storm Richmond and free the Federal prisoners before they could be moved south.

Beware of new and rash council. This I send you by direction of all your friends. No attempt should be made with less than 30,000 cavalry, from 10,000 to 15,000 infantry to support them, amounting in all to 40,000 or 45,000 troops. Do not underrate their strength and desperation.

When Elizabeth completed the blank page, she wrote a family note over it in black ink to her "Dear Uncle" from "Eliza A. Jones." She then brought the letter, dated January 30, 1864, to William Rowley. Entrusting the communication to his young son, Merritt, Rowley led the boy through Confederate lines to Union troops, who then escorted Merritt to General Butler.

Butler understood the gravity of Elizabeth's message, because it coincided with his own plan to free the thousands of Union troops held captive in Richmond. With these troops, the city could be taken, Jefferson Davis and his cabinet captured, and the war brought quickly to an end, he reasoned. In addition, public pressure to secure the release of Union prisoners stood at fever pitch in the North. From the war's beginning, fugitives and Richmond Unionists had leaked a steady torrent of information to Northern presses about the abject state of Federal captives and the horrific conditions inside prisons in their city.

With Elizabeth's letter in hand, Butler immediately contacted Secretary of War Edwin Stanton with an urgent communiqué of his own: "Now, or never, is the time to strike."

CHAPTER 6

IN THE CRAMPED DARKNESS RELIEVED ONLY BY THE FLICKERING FLAME of a small candle, the exhausted man chiseled at the packed dirt in the tunnel with only fearless rats as company. He alternated between a spoon, a broken chisel, and his hands as he hacked and scooped, hacked and scooped in a mindless effort powered only by hope. Slowly the wooden spittoon filled with dirt. When it could hold no more, he tugged at the rope tied to the vessel and watched it disappear down the black, narrow passageway. Moments later, after a tug of the rope from the other end, he pulled the empty spittoon back through the tunnel and began chiseling again.

As his breath became labored in the stifling air, and the heat in the coffinlike chamber rose, Colonel Thomas Rose signaled he would follow the cuspidor out of the tunnel. Moving with great difficulty, he slid backwards until he reached "rat hell," a musty, foul-smelling room in the east cellar of Libby Prison. Once a kitchen and now strewn with piles of straw, the east cellar had been sealed off from the rest of the prison and its door nailed shut.

Beyond the thick stone wall on the west side of the room, opposite the tunnel, lay a basement cell for the most difficult prisoners, and beyond that room sat the west cellar holding black prisoners. Above him the prison hospital on the first floor groaned with its cargo of wounded and sick. The hospital adjoined the prisoner kitchen and dining room, and to the west of that room lay the prison office and Confederate quarters. On the second and third levels prisoners languished in large open cells, formerly warehouse caverns, without furniture of any kind, pacing, sitting or lying on the floor, with only one washroom and troughs to relieve themselves. Their only movement consisted of access to the first-floor kitchen, where they could prepare food when they had any, water soup, gruel, or a bit of meat. Although forbidden from entering the kitchen at night, no one stood guard at the foot of the stairway adjoining the kitchen. There was nowhere to go, with the exterior doors heavily watched by sentries.

In rat hell, Rose's four comrades waited, Major Andrew Hamilton, who had organized the escape attempt with him, Lieutenant John Fislar, Major Bedan McDonald, and Captain Terrance Clark. Each had a function—one pulled the dirt-filled vessel from the tunnel and dumped it under the straw, another continually fanned the musty air into the tunnel, another waited to relieve his comrades, and the fifth kept watch. With a basement cell full of prisoners adjoining the huge east cellar, the diggers had to work silently, so silently that only the squealing of the rat hordes echoed through the room. In the darkness, the men gauged their movements in and out by the Confederate guards calling the hour and post in the room over their heads.

Working around the clock in three groups of five men, fifteen Union prisoners, unknown to other inmates, rotated the work of building the long escape tunnel underground to a point beyond the fence surrounding the perimeter of the prison. They entered and left the east cellar through a hole in the back of an unused fireplace in the kitchen where prisoners ate and prepared food on two large stoves that blocked a view of the fireplace.

The hole in the fireplace had been laboriously dug out. Under cover of night when no one used the kitchen, a handful of men had anxiously chipped at the mortar around the bricks in the fireplace wall, opening a cavity that could be closed with the bricks they removed. Then they slowly dug a diagonal hole through the massive floor to the east cellar, muffling their sounds while the prison slept. After two weeks of hard labor, their nocturnal venture had paid off as they descended into rat hell using a crude rope ladder.

Concealing the five diggers' absence each day proved the biggest challenge. Well over a thousand prisoners reported every morning and afternoon for the required count. To confound the Libby clerk taking the tally, five conspirators had to insure they were counted twice. They first stood at the head of the mass of bodies, then, once counted, they slipped behind the assembled men to the far end to be added again as someone else. Among themselves, they joked about the addle-headed clerk, Erasmus Ross, who never caught on. "Little Ross" they called the brutal guard because of his short stature.

This was not Rose and Hamilton's first attempt. Their original tunnel breached the canal wall running behind the prison, nearly drowning Rose. Their second passageway dug too close to a furnace over them that collapsed just enough to make the tunnel useless. On their third attempt the men tried to reach a small sewer line leading to the main sewer, through which they hoped to flee. But thick oak lumber lined the small sewer, not wide enough for a man's body to enter. After more than a month's hard labor and three attempts, Libby held them as tightly as ever. Undaunted, Rose had encouraged the disheartened men to try yet again.

In January, while the agonizing dig inched forward, a visitor called on Elizabeth at the Church Hill mansion. Unionist Abbey Green brought the startling news of the escape plans in process at Libby Prison.

"How do you know this?" a surprised Elizabeth asked.

"Josie spoke to Robert," she said of her servant who regularly brought supplies to the prison. "Robert sent a message from Colonel Rose that he wanted brought to you, Elizabeth."

Although she had never met Robert Ford, Elizabeth had been on the receiving end of information he sent from Libby. A Northern free black serving in the Union army and imprisoned after being captured in the Shenandoah fighting, Ford became the personal servant of Dick Turner, second-in-command at Libby. The brutal Turner, Libby's appointed "Negro-whipper," carried out his duty with relish, flogging blacks almost daily. Feared by Union soldiers and blacks alike, Turner gained special notoriety when he hauled six black women into Libby, stripped and brutally whipped them for the crime of offering bread to captured Union soldiers as Confederate troops escorted them through Richmond to Libby. As she thought of Turner's cruelty, Elizabeth marveled at Ford's extraordinary courage in communicating with Unionists.

"A tunnel is being dug from Libby," Abbey continued. "Josie didn't learn how, but Colonel Rose wants us to prepare for the escape. He expects there will be thirty men and they need precise information about how to get to our safe houses."

"Thirty men!" Elizabeth replied in amazement, since only one or two had escaped at any given time before this.

"We have to be careful where we send them, Bet," Abbey said. "So many!"

"How much time do we have, Abbey?"

"We don't know how far along they are with their digging. Maybe soon, maybe not."

"Then we have to move quickly. I'll draw up a plan and we'll have to send only two or three men to each house."

Abbey nodded. "It'll be complicated. Josie will have to remember all the details and somehow communicate it all to Robert. We can't risk writing any of it down."

"Does Erasmus know?" Elizabeth asked.

"I don't know." Abbey shook her head.

"If he does, he'll help," Elizabeth affirmed.

Among his many functions at Libby Prison, Erasmus Ross was to keep track of prisoners through counts and roll calls. As part of the

Unionist network, he frequently looked the other way when prisoners failed to appear for the counts, an omission the diggers mistakenly attributed to dull-wittedness in Ross.

In the days that followed, Elizabeth alerted safe houses nearest the prison to prepare for the great escape. Josie carried information to Ford for passing on to Rose, giving directions to safe houses in Richmond. At the prison, the relentless dig continued.

But an unforeseen event threatened the escape for a fourth time. In late January, Captain John Porter, a fellow Libby inmate, knowing nothing of the well-guarded secret dig, shaved his beard, darkened his eyebrows, and disguised himself as a clergyman using clothes smuggled into prison. His masquerade complete, he boldly strolled out of Libby, past the guards on duty, and up several streets to the home owned by Unionist John Quarles, not part of Elizabeth's network. Within days, Quarles spirited Porter to Union lines and joined the Union army himself.

Back at Libby Prison, an enraged Dick Turner discovered Captain Porter's absence and a hammer fell on the detainees. He immediately ordered a lengthy roll call and, from that point, these roll calls would replace the prisoner count. Now Erasmus Ross was to call out each name, and every man had to answer and step forward for scrutiny by the guards. In the confusion and milling about as the men gathered for the hastily ordered roll call, one of the conspirators was able to alert the lookout on duty at the fireplace. Three of the workers below quickly slipped up through the opening. But Isaac Johnston, digging deep in the black tunnel, could not get out in time.

For a long time the men stood waiting as the young, handsome clerk with his slick hair, fine features, and long sweeping moustache shouted each name in turn. When at last Erasmus Ross called out Isaac Johnston's name, no one stepped forward. Turner ordered the guards to search the prison and a frenzied hunt began.

As an apprehensive Johnston waited among the ever moving rats, a sudden hammering and clanging shook his body. The sealed door at the far end of the east cellar connecting to the hallway outside the prisoner cell was being stripped of the boards nailing it shut. He heard the bolt being lifted. Terrified, Isaac blew out his candle and scrambled in the darkness to hide, burying himself under a pile of vermin-infested straw as far from the door as he could get.

When the massive, creaking door opened at last, two shadowy figures stood in the doorway, outlined in the meager hall light. They thrust a candle into the opening as rats scurried about. For the longest time they peered into the black, cavernous room straining to see. They banged a stick against the door to frighten off the fearless rats, to no avail. Unwilling to step into the putrid smelling space, the guards mumbled to each other as Johnston lay breathless under the stinking straw at the far end, rodents gnawing at his clothes. In the distance he could hear the sounds of prisoners moving about their cell and talking. At last the figures retreated and the great door was sealed shut again.

As guards searched the prison and Turner paced the floor, fuming, Rose spread a rumor that Johnston had escaped. An uneasy day passed for the conspirators as they worried about whether guards had searched the east cellar. Late that afternoon Rose anxiously huddled with a few of the men in a corner of the dining room.

"Isaac cannot come up again," Rose whispered to Hamilton, Fislar, and McDonald.

"Then we'll bring him food and water," Fislar said in a barely audible voice, eying the guard at the door.

"We need to work faster. He can't stay down there with the vermin for long," McDonald anxiously interjected.

The others nodded.

"John, you see that our men are told what is happening," Rose said. "Andrew, you and I go down tonight. Bedan, you stand guard."

When at last the prison fell asleep, Hamilton and Rose furtively made their way to the kitchen and crept through the fireplace opening, down into the east cellar. As the flickering light of a single candle descended the rope ladder and spread its paltry glow, they found Johnston slumped on a pile of straw in the dark. No one spoke as he wolfed down the clumpy corn bread and morsels of pork fat. After quietly sharing what had happened above, they urgently resumed the dig.

With Erasmus Ross's rigid roll calls monitoring absences, the schemers abandoned their daytime digging. But every night they descended into hell and clawed their way deeper into the grave. After several days in the fetid air, the dank chill, and the endless darkness of the tunnel, Johnston's breathing became labored. Worried about his health, his comrades arranged for him to creep upstairs each night, sleep for a few hours, then slip back down before daybreak.

When at last they concluded that the tunnel reached beyond the fence, Rose crawled into the passageway to determine for certain if they had advanced far enough. At the farthest end, he broke up through the ground into the night darkness covered with tiny, jewel-like spots of exquisite light in the distant sky. As a rush of emotion flooded his chest and tears blinded his eyes at the sight, Rose shoved a shoe through the broken earth. Then he carefully refilled the small hole, packing the dirt firmly in place.

When he emerged, he told his comrades he would look out a window facing the tunnel in the morning to see if the shoe had escaped beyond the fence. "We must be sure."

Rose, Hamilton, and the others spent a troubled night. At the first hint of dawn, Rose began peering out an east window, straining to see. Slowly the open lot stole into view. His eyes anxiously searched the grassy yard as the grayness lifted. To his horror, he spotted it. The shoe lay waiting for rescue on the prison side of the fence. Slowly he motioned to Hamilton and Bedan, then John. One by one the workers learned they had fallen short. That night the shoe was retrieved and the dig began anew, more urgently than ever.

At last, certain the tunnel now passed beneath the fence, the five men in the basement spoke again of their original plan to secretly invite one friend each to escape Libby. They decided to leave the following night, fifty-two days after first breaking into the east cellar. The four men returned to their cells before morning, and spread the word among their teammates. This was to be the day.

The fifteen conspirators above ground spent an uneasy, endless day waiting for the cover of darkness. Toward evening, each man spoke in whispers to a bewildered friend. Hamilton arranged with General Hobart, who knew nothing of the dig, to follow them as they descended from the kitchen, seal the hole in the fireplace, give them one hour to escape and then allow other prisoners in small groups to exit the same way. A startled Hobart gladly gave his word.

At eight o'clock that night the fireplace opened for them one final time. One by one they climbed down the rope ladder into the putrid room, agitating the rats more than usual with their numbers. When the last man descended, Hobart sealed the fireplace. Below they quietly wished each other well. Armed with Elizabeth Van Lew's directions to their respective safe houses, they prepared to crawl for the last time through the long, narrow tunnel under the ground. They planned to walk away from the fence that shielded them from the peering eyes of Libby sentries, in twos or threes so as not to arouse attention.

Meanwhile, some days before the end of digging, as Rose, Hamilton, and the others worked feverishly to finish the tunnel in Libby, Elizabeth found herself caught in a family crisis. The Confederacy had conscripted her brother into the army.

As John had prepared to depart his home and family with great apprehension, Annie and little Eliza tearfully clung to their father. Distraught, Elizabeth and Eliza urged him to refuse, to flee.

"If I refuse, you know I'll be arrested. If I flee, what of the girls? And they will confiscate the business." The unhappy man shook his head, believing he had no choice.

"We can survive without the business," Elizabeth said earnestly, though she understood differently.

"But for how long?" John asked, knowing how much of their fortune had already been spent on their Union activities.

"You know we will care for the girls. When the war ends, you can return," Eliza pressed.

In the end, the tormented man had trudged off to war, leaving behind his despondent family.

Days later, on the afternoon of the planned escape, the stunning news arrived that Elizabeth's brother had deserted the army. Hidden in a safe house, he sent word to Elizabeth, asking her to come.

"I'm going too," Eliza insisted.

"You should stay with the children," her daughter urged.

"He's my son," Eliza said firmly. "The children are fine with the servants."

Just after dark, the two women, disguised in coarse clothes, wearing sunbonnets and carrying baskets, slipped out through the back of the house and made their way by foot to a working-class section of Richmond. Unknown to Elizabeth, that very night the planned escape from Libby was already under way.

⁓

Rose and Hamilton, the first to crawl out of the stifling, cramped grave, pulled themselves through the opening into the brisk, fresh air. The cold night watched with a thousand eyes as they nervously peered into the darkness, dusted off their clothes, and walked onto Dock Street along the canal parallel to the James River. After two blocks they turned left and began to make their way to Church Hill and the Van Lew mansion.

Behind them the others slowly emerged from the tunnel and began inching their way through the dark toward their designated safe houses. By twos and threes they walked away from the great hole, hidden by the fence, breathing the clean air and hunched against the cold. After the thirty men had all left and the promised hour passed, Hobart quietly made his way around the cavernous cell above the kitchen, quietly spreading the word to a few men at a time, instructing them to move slowly and deliberately. As a diversion, a small group of prisoners began singing and dancing in a corner of one of the cells. One by one, the gaunt men, hungry for freedom, slipped into the shadows behind the fireplace and down the rope.

At first the exodus went smoothly. But as word began to seep through the great cells above the kitchen, an elation took hold. More men came down into the pitch-dark dining room where General Hobart was leading an orderly exit. Mindful of the guards behind the thick stone walls in the next room, the men kept silent as they shifted about. While Hobart struggled to subdue the anxious men, the descent into the east cellar continued, one by one. For awhile the would-be fugitives stood quietly in line, waiting their turn.

But soon, as more men streamed in, they began pushing and shoving to get to the front of the line. Two or three men jumped into the hole without using the rope. When it became clear he could no longer control the men, Hobart took his leave, disappearing into the gaping fireplace. At one point the men thought they heard a sentry call out and they hurried from the kitchen in a panic, scrambling up the wooden stairs to their cells. Two men remained hidden behind the fireplace, too frightened to move. Presently an ominous light moved slowly down the long hallway and into the doorway of the kitchen, where it stopped.

"Who's here?" They heard the gruff voice of the hated Erasmus Ross. They froze, their breath stuck in their throats as they waited. Ross stood a long while in the doorway but he never entered the room. At last the flickering light faded down the hallway. Uncertain whether they should risk plunging into the unknown darkness below, the men carefully replaced the bricks in the fireplace and crept back to their cells to wait another day.

Slipping from shadow to shadow through the streets of Richmond, Elizabeth and her mother reached the humble house where John had taken refuge. The small cottage stood dark, its curtains drawn tightly. Elizabeth knocked gently and immediately the door opened. As they stole through the opening, a light appeared in the back of the house and a woman whispered, "Come."

When they entered the dimly lit kitchen, John leapt from a bench into the arms of his mother and sister and the three tearfully clung to each other. He looked gaunt and tired. Choking back sobs, Elizabeth took the hands of the woman sheltering her brother.

"Martha, we cannot thank you enough. And Frank, you are so kind," she said, turning to the man seated at the end of the table.

"No, we can never thank you enough," Eliza echoed.

The thin woman, her hair pulled back in a bun, nodded and smiled anxiously. "Did anyone follow you?" she asked.

"No one," Elizabeth answered. "We left after dark. We made sure."

Visibly relieved, the woman invited them to sit on the benches running along both sides of the table. A black stove on one side of the room gave off a stream of warmth as a large kettle steamed on top. At one end of the soot-covered wall behind the range, a narrow doorway stood etched in the dark glow. A small child—two or three years old, Elizabeth guessed—stood leaning against the doorway, peering at the unexpected guests, a finger thrust in her mouth. Just beyond, a square window over a wash basin watched blindly, its curtains drawn tight and its glass pane cold against the February air. In a corner a crude wooden cabinet stood, its door slightly open.

"Please," Elizabeth heard the woman say, "take some tea." Martha poured from the kettle as the scent of chamomile rose from the mugs. With a large knife she cut slices from a round loaf of bread.

"I need to leave as soon as possible, Bet, mother," John said nervously to the two visitors, turning to each in turn.

"We brought you money and some clothes, John," Eliza responded.

"In the morning, I'll arrange for William Rowley to lead you out," Elizabeth added. "There's no one better or braver."

John lowered his head, despondent. "I've let you down. And the girls . . ."

"No, no. You are doing exactly what we begged you to do," Elizabeth interrupted.

"You have no choice, my son."

"It's late," Martha said. "You should not be walking through the city with so many dangerous characters about. You both must spend the night."

"But . . ." Elizabeth began to object, aware of the woman's poverty and the cramped space.

"Please, Miss Van Lew. It's not the first time," Martha said, referring to other prisoners she and Frank had sheltered. "We *are* able to help," she added proudly.

"You are very kind. Yes, we'll gladly stay."

That night, John slept in the child's room and Eliza and her daughter were given the couple's bed. The family retired to their small sitting room and unrolled mats on the floor, where they slept.

Elizabeth spent a fretful night worrying about John, about the danger of his flight, about the business, about the risks to William Rowley, about the girls who would not see their father for a long time. But something else took hold in her mind, a terrible premonition, a nameless dread that grew as the night passed. What? She could not identify the feeling, but it filled her with trepidation as she lay awake blindly staring into the darkness.

⁓

While Elizabeth struggled with the demons hovering over her sleepless-ness, Captain Rose and Major Hamilton picked their way through the dark streets of Richmond to Church Hill, hugging the shadows of the oak, pine, and hickory trees. Suddenly it rose before them—the white mansion, gray in the darkness, with its Doric portico fronting Grace Street. Looking to their rear and all sides, the two men stepped across the street and made their way around the grounds of the three-storied structure with its gabled roof. At the back of the mansion, the porch with its massive columns looked out across terraced gardens, the finest in Richmond, with privet hedges, box bushes, wisteria, dogwood and mag-nolia trees waiting, dormant, to burst into spring. Beyond the gardens the James River wound through the darkness, indifferent to the turmoil on its banks.

As directed, Rose and Hamilton made their way around the building to the servants' quarters on Twenty-fourth Street and knocked on the door. The black man who answered appeared startled to see them. They hastily explained that they had just escaped from Libby Prison and that Miss Van Lew had prepared a room for them.

With Elizabeth and her mother gone from the house, an apprehen-sion swept over Peter Roane. Who were these men? Could they be Con-federate detectives set on entrapping his mistress? Torn about what to do, Peter asked the men to leave. Alarmed, the fugitives pleaded to be let in.

"Please, ask Miss Van Lew," Rose implored the man.

But Peter feared betraying her absence, knowing where she had gone. His mind raced. How could he risk admitting the wrong people? There had been numerous attempts to entrap the Van Lews. With Eliza also gone, there was no way to know who the men were. Desperate, Peter shut and bolted the door without responding, leaving Rose and Hamilton dumbstruck at the unexpected rebuff. Within minutes the two terrified men disappeared into the grip of the cold darkness.

＊⁓＊

When at last dawn made its way across the gray sky, Elizabeth had already risen and dressed. Exhausted and anxious from her sleepless night, she left Eliza in bed and quietly made her way down the rough wooden stairway to the kitchen. Martha was already at the stove, stirring the embers and adding kindling and logs. The winter cold had seeped through the kitchen walls during the night and Elizabeth pulled her shawl tightly around her shoulders.

"I hope you slept well," Martha said, as she prepared to cook porridge.

"Only worry kept me awake, Martha. The bed was most comfortable."

"Frank left early to get William Rowley."

After a few minutes, Eliza came down, followed shortly by John.

"We'll wait for Peter to come," Elizabeth told them. "He's bringing supplies for Martha and John this morning. He knows what to do when we don't return." With the curtains still drawn, they sat waiting at the kitchen table in the dim light, talking softly, and eating a simple breakfast with Martha and her daughter.

When Peter arrived in the farm wagon and carried two sacks into the house, he seemed agitated.

"I didn't know what to do." He shook his head repeatedly.

"What is it, Peter?" Elizabeth asked immediately, her foreboding boiling to the surface. "Has something happened?"

"Two men come to the door . . . late last night . . ." he said haltingly.

Elizabeth shot a glance at Eliza. "Who . . .?"

"I don't know. They say they escape from Libby, but . . ."

"Dear God," exclaimed Eliza.

A pallor descended over Elizabeth and the words stuck in her throat.

Peter groaned. "Did I do wrong, Miz Lizzie? I thought maybe they be Confederates. A trap."

"It's not your fault, Peter . . ." Elizabeth started to respond.

"It's my fault," John interrupted, striking his chest, "my fault . . ."

"No, no!" Elizabeth said emphatically. "It's no one's fault. It's a terrible coincidence."

"Soldiers is all over da streets this morning," Peter said.

Just then Frank entered the house and hurried into the room. "There are roadblocks and soldiers everywhere. I turned back."

"Do you know why?" John asked anxiously.

"Everyone is talking. There was a big prison break from Libby last night. No one discovered the escape till roll call this morning," Frank answered breathlessly. "Over a hundred men escaped."

Again Peter groaned aloud. Surely then, Elizabeth concluded with painful regret, Rose and another prisoner had been turned away from her home. As the gravity of the situation swept over her, Elizabeth looked at her brother in despair. She immediately understood the impact on him, a deserter.

"This changes everything, John," she said gently touching his hand. "Getting through the line now may not be possible."

John's brow knit in dread and his words froze.

"But what can we do now?" an anxious Eliza asked.

Her daughter sat silently, her thoughts a jumble. Fretfully, she twisted the fringe of her shawl with her fingers, as everyone watched. At last Elizabeth spoke, a slight tremble in her voice. "We'll have to appeal to John Winder."

"I don't know …" her brother said nervously. "I've deserted my regiment."

"He's helped us before. He'll help again," Elizabeth said firmly, as much to convince herself as the others. "Desperate situations sometimes require desperate remedies."

Everyone agreed that John should stay with Martha and Frank. Elizabeth and her mother immediately returned home with Peter in the farm wagon.

Elizabeth made her way to General Winder's office after hurriedly changing her clothes. As Peter wound their carriage through the streets, they passed Confederate soldiers everywhere searching for the fugitives. Her heart still ached at the thought of Colonel Rose being turned away from her home and, now, the subject of such a massive hunt. Her mind twisted about in self-blame. Peter was right—those other attempts to entrap her had frightened them all. I should have told Peter to expect the fugitives, she thought. But I'm always home—there was no reason to tell him ahead of time. How was it possible, of all nights? Rushing out like that, the shocking news of John's desertion . . . I wasn't thinking. But I should have thought. Still . . .

Arriving at General Winder's office, Elizabeth found Philip Cash-meyer in the outer office. Now head detective under the general, the patrician-looking Cashmeyer greeted her stiffly. She noted uncomfortably how his eyes scrutinized her.

"So much activity on the streets, Mr. Cashmeyer," she said, as though put out by the inconvenience of it all. "It's hard for a lady to venture out. What ever has happened?"

"You've not heard of the prison break, then?" He scrutinized her face some more.

"I had heard something. But with so many rumors, it's hard to know what is true."

"I'm afraid it's true, Miss Van Lew. The streets of Richmond are crawling with 109 fugitives. But we shall find them—every one!"

"Amazing!" Elizabeth responded in mock surprise.

"Some have already been brought to justice." He hesitated, watching her carefully. "Perhaps you know Robert Ford . . ." His face immobile, he waited for her reply.

"Who?" She asked, making a great effort not to betray herself.

"Robert Ford, the captured Negro Union soldier." Elizabeth stood frozen in place. "He no doubt helped the prisoners escape. Dick Turner whipped him nearly to death—five hundred lashes."

A terror gripped Elizabeth, not only at the thought of Robert's torture, but for herself and Abbey Green. Had he revealed their names? Why was Cashmeyer telling her this? Her face had turned to stone as she strained to hide her feelings.

Composing herself inside, she addressed the detective, "I have every confidence the guilty parties will be brought to justice, Mr. Cashmeyer. Is General Winder available?"

"Of course," he bowed slightly.

General Winder received her kindly. "What a pleasure, Miss Van Lew."

"I hope, general, you'll still think that when you hear my request," she smiled.

"More requests for prison visits, then?"

"No, no. I'm afraid this is personal and more pressing," Elizabeth answered, as Winder cocked his head a bit and grasped his chin. "It's about John."

"Your brother?"

"As you know, he's not been in the best of health for a long time," she lied.

"No, I didn't know," Winder interrupted. "I'm sorry to hear this. I've always liked John—fine man."

"He was conscripted into the service recently." Winder stopped and looked curiously at her. "He's really not physically fit to serve and has left," she continued as delicately as she could.

"Left?"

"Left the service, general. I'm hoping you can help?"

After a stunned silence, Winder echoed, "Left the service?" He began pacing the floor and running his fingers through his disheveled mass of gray hair. "You mean he simply left his regiment?"

"He was not well enough to continue." Her heart raced as she tried to appear calm. Desertion meant imprisonment at the very least.

After what seemed a long time to Elizabeth, General Winder spoke. "Have John come in to see me tomorrow morning. I'll see what I can do." He wrote something on a piece of paper as he spoke.

"How can I thank you?" Elizabeth asked.

"Take this to John. It'll provide safe passage through the city. I'll expect him in the morning." Then, bowing ever so slightly, "Please give your mother my best."

"And Mrs. Winder," Elizabeth smiled as she moved to leave. "You are so kind."

When she opened the door of Winder's office to leave, she saw Detective Cashmeyer move away from the opening as though he had been listening. He nodded slightly, his face inscrutable. A terrible unease came over her again as she smiled at the man and quickly made her exit.

<hr />

Immediately on arriving home she sent a message to Abbey Green, asking what she knew of the Ford matter. Abbey came calling later that evening.

"Turner whipped Robert nearly to death," Abbey angrily told Elizabeth. "But he bore it without ever betraying anyone." The two women sat silently marveling at the courage of this extraordinary man. Anger, sadness, relief, gratitude—a swirl of emotions overtook the women as they thought about the brave black man who endured what few could have.

"I'll be leaving Richmond soon," Abbey said unexpectedly.

She startled Elizabeth. "Leaving? But why?"

"I've been so involved, Elizabeth, as you know. But I'm worried for my family. This was too close . . ."

"We'll miss you terribly, Abbey, but I understand." Elizabeth felt a tug at her heart. They had all grown so close, almost without realizing it, risking so much together. "You'll have to be very careful getting out."

Abbey smiled. "I'll have help."

The next morning John learned that the general was unable to get him a medical deferment but that he was to report to Winder's company, the Eighteenth Virginia Regiment. "That way I can protect you," Winder had said simply. When John reported to the unit, he learned they were stationed in Richmond. To everyone's amazement, he was able to return to running his business.

In the aftermath of the great escape, Richmond Unionists again fell under suspicion. The press attacked those "traitors among us" who had helped the prisoners escape and warned of the murder and mayhem fugitives meant to visit on their city. As a result, many found their homes under surveillance and their movements followed. The Van Lews did not escape notice. Authorities threw up a guard at the Van Lew mansion to the great dismay of Elizabeth and her family.

After leaving the Van Lew home in desperation, Rose and Hamilton uneasily stole through the dark city streets following the North Star. At one point the two men suddenly came upon two Confederate guards chatting as they shivered in the cold. Hamilton immediately fell back in panic and headed east across a tree-covered yard. Rose, being too close to the men to flee, pulled his threadbare overcoat tightly around his shoulders to cover his blue uniform and boldly walked on. They paid him no mind. Alone now, Rose searched the darkness for his friend who had vanished into the night shadows. Emotionally and physically drained, alone, he headed north again, following his star.

Slipping through the gloom, Rose at last came to the Richmond and York River Railroad tracks heading east. Following the tracks, he moved toward the inner peninsula, which he had heard in prison Union forces controlled. But aware that land in these parts changed hands back and forth, he could not be sure. As the first rays of dawn appeared in the night sky he strained to see. Ahead lay the Chickahominy River, its bridge guarded by Confederate pickets. Quickly turning south, he pushed through the thick underbrush and trees. Along the river bank ahead, break of day revealed a Confederate cavalry camp sluggishly rousing itself from slumber. Rose slunk back, deep into the woods. Exhausted, fearful about moving in daylight, he found a large sycamore log on the ground among the trees, hollow from long decay. Quickly he buried himself in the log, covering his body with fallen branches and decomposing leaves. As the stinging February cold reached into the log, Rose struggled to sleep. Hunger, cold, and the sounds of camp in the distance—horses, shouts, and an occasional shot—conspired to torment his wakeful dozing.

When at last darkness fell, he rose from the dead sycamore, shook off his cramps, and began to steal quietly downstream through the sheltering trees. When the Confederate camp had moved out of sight, Rose left the protection of the woods and searched for a place to ford the Chickahominy River. Plunging in at what appeared to be a shallow spot, he waded into the bitterly cold waters thrashing about against the current and the uneven river bed that left him at points up to his waist in deep, wet pits. He made shore shivering in his soaked clothing. All morning he trudged through the woods heading east, fighting off fever, chills, and hunger. Again he stumbled onto a Confederate camp and retreated quickly into the dense woods. Finding a pit in the broken ground, he again buried himself under the forest refuse. Exhausted he fell into a deep sleep till the hoot of a nearby owl woke him. Surrounded by darkness, it was his third night outside Libby Prison. His teeth chattering, he tried to rise from the pit but his wet clothes had nearly frozen on his stiff body.

Shunning the roads and open fields, forcing himself onward, Rose hurried through the swampy marshes in his path. In the dim moonlight, struggling to see, he doubled his guard, alert for the slightest movement.

Having finished the pieces of bread he took from Libby on the first night out, his hungry stomach rumbled and his limbs ached. Every step a torment, he moved uneasily over frozen, uneven ground, through creeks and bogs. When he could stand the cold no longer, he pushed deep into an isolated cedar grove. Taking a handful of hidden matches from under his cap, he risked a small fire to keep himself alive.

Dodging Confederate pickets the whole way, Rose spent the next day walking and resting. Late on the third afternoon, while moving of necessity across an open area, he suddenly spotted a Confederate soldier on horse who appeared to see him. As the man shouted an alert to his comrades in the distance, Rose broke into a fevered run across a laurel thicket in the open field. As the sound of horses and shouting grew near, he dove into a dry gully that seemed to run the length of the field. Concealed by the rambling brush creeping over the land and crawling on his stomach, he painfully dragged himself to the other end of the ditch, cutting his hands on the jagged stones and thorny briars. When he emerged at the end of the gully in a stand of trees, he could see the puzzled Confederates still searching the open field.

That night Rose kept moving till midnight when he collapsed under a great white pine. Completely spent, he slept soundly till morning. At dawn, barely able to move, he pulled his limbs along a path that led up a gentle slope. All at once he spotted three men emerging over the horizon. Before his legs could flee he spotted the blue uniforms and fell to the ground in joy as the men moved toward him. But as they approached, an uneasy premonition suddenly swept over his joy as the men spotted him and called him forward. In a terrible instant Rose spotted the gray shirt under one of the open blue shirts and realized they were Confederates in Union disguise.

As the men got so close he could feel their breath, Rose became like a man possessed in his rage. Some force within lunged forward and knocked one of the men to the ground. Grabbing the man's pistol, Rose swiftly turned on the other two who had already raised their weapons in the air. Swinging their musket handles violently, they bashed him about the head and body. In an instant the pistol in his bruised hand discharged into the air and the battered body of the fugitive from Libby crashed to the frozen ground.

Chapter 7

A MOST EXQUISITE EVENING COVERED THE BEGINNING OF THEIR DRIVE south to Richmond. As the advance Union force of five hundred men confidently set out from Stevensburg in late February, countless stars in a clear sky followed their movements through the night shadows. On the banks of the Rapidan River the cavalry fell on a small force of rebel pickets. After a brief skirmish they easily captured the group and forded on horseback the rushing waters shivering in the silver moonlight.

At the head of the march a tall, slender young officer, twenty-one years old, rode a splendid black stallion. His handsome face sported a goatee and his golden blond hair, almost reddish in cast, added to his patrician look. As he rode, a crutch fastened to his saddle bounced with the animal's gallop. Only seven months before, death had narrowly failed to swallow the young man at Gettysburg. But it had taken one of his limbs so that now, surprisingly vigorous, he moved about on a wooden leg.

Everyone in Washington of any importance, including President Lincoln, knew the charming young cavalry officer, as they knew his father. People outside Washington knew him too, for the Northern press frequently extolled the heroic deeds of Colonel Ulric Dahlgren, son of the commander of the Union fleet in the waters off Charleston, Admiral John Dahlgren. But none of his feats to date would match the mission now passionately undertaken with the dashing, ambitious Major General Judson Kilpatrick.

Leading the main force of 3,500 men behind Dahlgren's advance party, Kilpatrick proposed to storm Richmond, free Union prisoners, and capture Jefferson Davis and his cabinet. The successful outcome of this attack stood in Kilpatrick's mind as the ultimate glory that would further his goal of one day becoming president of the United States. Failure would be avoided at all cost.

The audacious plan involved a total of four thousand cavalry riding south from Stevensburg through the killing fields of Chancellorsville into Confederate-held territory. The advance party led by Dahlgren would veer southwest to Goochland Courthouse, cross the James River, and prepare to breech Richmond from the south with the aim of freeing Union prisoners. For his part, Kilpatrick would ride south and advance to the northern outskirts of the city, drawing its defenders to fight his larger force so that Dahlgren could steal into Richmond. All the while two large diversionary forces would move down their west flank. The audacious, long-haired Brigadier General George Armstrong Custer would lead his men down to Charlottesville, as conspicuously and with as much noise as possible, their aim to be seen and to draw Lee's men away from Richmond. Two other regiments under General Sedgwick would also create a diversion as they headed west toward Madison Court House.

After capturing the Confederate pickets and easily crossing the Rapidan River, Dahlgren sent word back to Kilpatrick, an hour behind him, that all was well. Satisfied that their movements had not alerted Confederate forces, Dahlgren led his men under the moonlit sky on a fast ride to Spotsylvania Courthouse, their next marker. But unknown to him, two interlopers, Confederate scouts Dan Tanner and Hugh Scott, known as iron scouts for their seeming invincibility, had spotted the skirmish on the river bank. In disguise, wearing Union uniforms, they melted into the rear of Dahlgren's line.

As Dahlgren's cavalry galloped through the countryside past Spotsylvania, they could see the great Confederate encampment in the vicinity of Fredericksburg, its campfires lighting the horizon. Just before dawn broke, clouds appeared, inching across the sky, banishing the stars and moon. As the men rode on, the sky grew more menacing and the clouds turned almost black. Dahlgren anxiously eyed the ominous heavens, hoping the storm would linger there until his mission ended.

As reports reached General Robert E. Lee in Richmond of the forces bearing down on Charlottesville and Madison Court House, he hastened to depart to Orange Court House, his headquarters west of the capital. Unaware of Union troops riding south to strike the city, Lee boarded a Virginia Central Railroad train heading northwest out of Richmond.

By now Dahlgren's path veered southwest as he continued the relentless drive, his troops enjoying only brief rest stops. They met few signs of resistance, but everywhere the remnants of war stood—burned buildings, abandoned farms, discarded blockades, scorched earth where crops once grew. Ahead lay Frederick's Hall Station, a stop along the Virginia Central Railroad. As Dahlgren approached, the men could hear the distant whistle of a train passing through, heading west. When they arrived, the sound of the receding train grew faint as it retreated. Unknown to them, it carried the man who commanded the Confederate forces, a man whose capture, had they arrived minutes earlier, would likely have dealt a decisive blow to the rebel cause. After tearing up the train tracks, the cavalry continued its ride south.

All along the way, slaves began to attach themselves to the Union line in hopes of finding freedom. Alone, in twos, in families, in groups they came. Some fled their masters; others had been left behind as their owners escaped previous Union onslaughts and the leveling of their plantations. All believed the men in blue would protect them.

❧

Behind Dahlgren, Judson Kilpatrick's men pushed south, crossing the Virginia Central train tracks at Beaver Dam Station. They managed to capture the station's telegraph operator before a message could be sent to Richmond. After setting fire to the cluster of buildings comprising the tiny town, they rested briefly, waiting for darkness to resume their march south. Overhead the threatening clouds parted, sending a drenching rain on the weary men and horses. Before long the temperature dropped and the rain mixed with snow.

To the west of Kilpatrick, Dahlgren moved slowly toward the James River through dense underbrush that choked the ground around thick stands of trees. In the darkness icy sleetlike rain and freezing wind battered the men and horses. At midnight they stopped to rest for awhile and eat. But the rain kept them from building fires to cook and keep warm, and the mud and cold kept them from sleep. Around the edges of their encampment, black folks huddled under their blankets against the rain and cold and ate the scraps of food they had quickly packed when spotting the Union line. Occasionally sniper fire rang out in the pitch dark against the drowsy men from nearby farmers and home guards who stalked them.

By the second evening of their march, Richmond already knew of the advancing force. Unknown to Kilpatrick, the two iron scouts had left Dahlgren's party and raced off to warn General Wade Hampton of the impending attack. With troops numbering less than one-tenth the invading forces, Hampton rode his men hard to catch the invaders. At the same time he sent couriers to alert nearby Confederate militia and authorities in Richmond. Lee, worried about the forces advancing from the west, knew nothing of the danger to Richmond.

Before reaching the James River, Dahlgren sent a party out to destroy buildings, canal locks, granaries, and whatever stock could not be taken. On the morning of March 1, the men stopped to rest on the grounds of Sabot Hill, an expansive plantation, home of the new Confederate Secretary of War, James Seddon. As the men huddled on the wet grounds, Dahlgren made his way to the door of the great mansion on his crutch.

Mrs. Sallie Seddon answered the door when her frightened servants would not, and stared at the man. Dahlgren politely asked if Mr. Seddon was at home and identified himself.

"Ulric Dahlgren?" she asked. "Are you related to Admiral John Dahlgren?"

When he nodded affirmatively, she exclaimed, "Little Ully! I knew you as a small child. Why, your mother and I were classmates in Philadelphia. Before she married your father, he was my beau. Come in. Come in." As they moved to the parlor, she added, "Mr. Seddon will be very sorry to have missed you."

Seated together on the great overstuffed sofas, they spoke of Dahlgren's childhood, his mother, his father, her girlhood, and other pleasantries. The war had suddenly vanished and with it all enmity. They drank from a twenty-year-old bottle of blackberry wine as they chatted. Outside the Union troops lounging on the soggy lawn disappeared behind the great parlor windows. But in the distance, unnoticed, a servant rode out from the barn behind the great white house to alert authorities about the Yankees. At last the charming Ulric took his leave and Sallie Seddon walked him out, watching from the veranda as he motioned to his men to mount. Turning to the woman on the great porch, Dahlgren bowed and rode away.

At the James River they searched for a place to cross. Their guide was a former slave named Martin Robinson, who had helped Elizabeth's Union underground in Richmond during the Libby Prison outbreak, leading several fugitives to safety. New to Dahlgren's party, he proceeded to lead them along the river, having assured Dahlgren he knew the area in great detail. When they reached Jude's Ferry, Robinson stood puzzled at the depth of the raging river. Had the rains swollen the river and sent its waters rushing in a driving torrent or was he at the wrong place?

Impatiently, Dahlgren quizzed the man who appeared baffled. *Everything* depended on fording the James River and approaching the city from the south. Failure to cross would scuttle the whole plan for taking Richmond. When it became clear they could not cross, a frustrated Dahlgren began to suspect that Robinson had deliberately misled them. Furious at this unexpected, disastrous turn of events, he ordered the terrified black man taken and hung from a nearby oak tree. On a great branch overhanging the river, Robinson's body was left to dangle in the cold rain while Dahlgren and his men rode away.

As the slaves moving far to the rear of the line approached the hanging black man, they gasped in wonder at the ominous sight. Had the Confederates done this terrible thing? Or were they not as safe with the bluecoats as they thought?

When no possibility of fording the swiftly moving river presented itself as they rode along its shores, Dahlgren was forced to abandon their plan to storm Richmond from the south. Consulting his officers, he decided to join Kilpatrick's force north of the city. In a coordinated effort, they could still enter Richmond, he thought, and throw open the prison doors. As they moved closer to the city along the north side of the James River, they heard gunfire in the distance. Assuming Kilpatrick had begun his assault, they pressed on.

Within five miles of Richmond, Kilpatrick waited for the signal that Dahlgren had reached the city. But the rain made the firing of flare signals impossible, he assumed, so Kilpatrick hesitated. In fact, Dahlgren had sent a rider to inform Kilpatrick of the change of plans and urge a coordinated attack from the north. He never arrived, having fallen into enemy hands.

Harassed by snipers and rebel artillery and facing the fortifications around Richmond, Kilpatrick wavered. Unsure of what lay ahead, he sent a few men forward to skirmish and determine the strength of rebel defenses. But where were the defenses, the scouting party wondered as they came on one unfortified line of barricades after another? Still,

Kilpatrick moved his men in an agonizingly slow manner, all bustle and no speed. In the nation's capital, the brash warrior and womanizer had boasted of storming Richmond. Now he seemed paralyzed, unable to move, indecisive. By afternoon, having started under a black dawn, he had barely moved two miles.

Every excuse seeped into Kilpatrick's mind in those precious hours on the Brook Pike. Open fields had to be traversed, making them ripe for cannon fire. The ground grew more slippery with mud as rain began falling again and turning to snow. The conditions for cavalry movement were terrible. His men were wet and exhausted. The rebels had too many guns and more moved against him by the hour. The city would surely be heavily fortified. Dahlgren had failed him—where was Dahlgren?

In fact, his indecision gave the enemy ample time to build their defenses. At dawn a few scattered guns challenged his advance. By afternoon the guns had multiplied. A small force of local militia, many of them amateur guards standing in for Confederate forces fighting elsewhere, had stolen the mighty Kilpatrick's nerve. With an easy victory in his grasp, he sent the order to his advance party of skirmishers. Fall back. Cover the retreat of Kilpatrick's massed cavalry turning back to the north.

A determined Ulric Dahlgren forged ahead, knowing nothing of Kilpatrick's indecision. Within a few miles of the city, dusk began to fall on the darkest of days and enemy fire grew more intense. Suddenly, the sounds of battle north of the city, where he presumed Kilpatrick to be, stopped. Puzzled, Dahlgren again dispatched scouts to find Kilpatrick. Again they disappeared.

Although the situation looked bleak, Dahlgren determined to charge the enemy, even if it was no longer possible to storm Richmond. To retreat without a fight meant dishonor to the seasoned fighter. He quickly assessed the situation.

First Dahlgren would have to deal with the Negro masses in his wake. They posed a tactical problem, slowing his movement, diverting the attention of his troops. He could not be responsible for fighting a war and leading slaves to safety at the same time. No. The hundreds of slaves who had taken it on themselves to join their march could no longer move with them. Regretfully, they must be abandoned and make their way to freedom on their own.

Dahlgren sent two officers to the rear of his long column to inform the slaves they must stop following or be shot. When the men addressed the huddled crowds with loud shouts, a great gasp rose through the air. Several people pushed forward and pleaded with the officers.

"Runaway slaves is hung, sah," one man declared.

"They's children here. Do'n leave us, sah," a woman begged.

The officers averted their eyes in shame, but they knew the order would stand. As the crowd surged forward, one of the men ordered the cavalry at the rear of Dahlgren's line, close to the slaves, to aim their guns against the mass of people. The crowd fell back in despair.

The Negro problem settled, Dahlgren prepared to charge the faceless rebels ahead. Before the attack, he moved up and down his line of men, encouraging the men, praising their valor, and wishing them Godspeed.

For over two miles they charged, driving the enemy back. Dahlgren led each attack. With every rush, their adversaries fired and fell backward toward the city. Throughout, the brutal weather continued as cold sleet now fell and a bitter wind sliced their bodies. At last Dahlgren crossed into the city's outer limits, but by then he had lost many of his men. His small force badly reduced, he ordered a withdrawal.

Slowly his cavalry moved through the pitch blackness and icy rain in the direction of Kilpatrick's force. Behind him, roughly half his remaining men followed under Captain Mitchell. Lack of transport forced Dahlgren to leave the wounded behind with one volunteer assistant surgeon.

In Richmond all that day, residents had moved about in fear while the crash of guns covered the city. Troops rushed through the streets heading north. Equipment and artillery rolled past. Messengers on horseback raced to the presidential mansion and the war department. The bell in Capitol Square relentlessly pealed its call to arms as civilian home guards donned their uniforms, grabbed their muskets, and left their homes and places of work. Fearing the worst, many people hung around the capitol in the driving rain, huddled under umbrellas, desperate for news. Others, hearing the fighting to the north, tried to flee the city from the south, but the mud-clogged roads stopped them at every turn.

Everywhere rumors raced through the streets, shops, and homes of Richmond. Hundreds of slaves had massed outside the city, planning to murder and rape its citizens. Twenty thousand Union soldiers were marching against the city. The Secretary of War's family had been taken hostage by the Yankee beasts. The government was preparing to abandon them and flee south. Union prisoners would surely break out of Libby, Castle Thunder, Belle Isle, and other prisons and overrun their streets . . .

At the Van Lew home, Elizabeth, her mother, and brother dared to hope for liberation from the endless nightmare of war. The two frightened little girls whimpered and clung to their father as the cannon crashes and gunfire burst in the distance. When the pealing bells spread their call to arms, John reluctantly donned his uniform and departed to join his regiment. No one spoke as they waited and clutched at hope in the gaslight of the parlor.

By afternoon word flew through Richmond that a second attack against the city had begun from the west. What was left of the home militia—old men, wounded soldiers, students, boys, factory workers, government employees—sped into action. Trained for such a moment, they marched out to meet Dahlgren's force in an orderly manner. And although they fell back several times in the face of the superior force, they exacted a toll on the enemy. By nightfall the Yankees quit the attack and appeared headed north. But uncertainty hovered over the city as its residents spent a panicked night.

By morning, an eerie quiet descended over Richmond. The blare of fighting stopped and in its place a stream of wounded and dead poured into the city on wagons and horses. Families clogged the streets frantically searching for loved ones. Screams of despair or cries of joy pierced the air when an identification was made. By late morning the victors began marching Union prisoners captured in the fighting through the streets toward the very prisons they had sought to empty.

At the Van Lew home, near despair settled in. Was this the awaited attempt to take Richmond by General Butler? Had Butler sent the recommended forty thousand men against Richmond and failed? Had he tried to take the city with too few men? Or was this another Union strike, not by Butler at all? Had the Federals merely pulled back to regroup and attack again? The questions tormented Elizabeth.

◦━◦

Kilpatrick and his men had spent a miserable night retreating along the Mechanicsville Pike heading for the safety of General Butler's line. But struggling against the storm battering down on them, the bitter cold, and the mucky mud, they ground to a stop. Without tents, soaked to the skin, the hungry, exhausted men built a few sputtering fires in a vain attempt to keep warm.

After midnight a small contingent of Confederates under General Wade Hampton, with his scouts, Tanner and Scott, caught up to the forsaken troops. Aiming their two cannon on the dispirited cavalry huddled around their miserable fires, they fired volley after volley. After their cannon fire devastated the closely packed troops, they began their charge. With both sides firing in the darkness now, the shots became random. Terrified, those Union forces not killed or badly wounded fled in panic into the pitch blackness, on horseback and on foot. Throughout the night the pursuit continued. Rebels, joined by local militia, captured some who fled in confusion from their main group.

Before long after the attack, Kilpatrick and some of his men regrouped and headed east, beaten by the pitiless downpour the whole way. By dawn, as the outline of a landscape emerged into view, Kilpatrick prepared his troops to meet Hampton's cavalry at Old Church on the Williamsburg Road. Without the element of surprise that served them well during the night, Wade Hampton's small force chose to abandon the fight and Kilpatrick dragged the remnants of his exhausted men onward toward the safety of the Union line.

After leaving Richmond, Ulric Dahlgren's men rode northeast through the darkness to rejoin Kilpatrick. The pitiless cold and rain beat down on the weary men as they inched their way through the darkness and dense woods. Everywhere icy branches angrily struck their faces and bodies as they hacked their way around fallen limbs and tree trunks. Underneath, puddles of water and mud sucked at their feet, pulling them to the ground. Near Hungary Station, Dahlgren stopped to give his men a desperately needed rest and allow Captain Mitchell's rear guard to catch up. When no sign of Mitchell appeared, he anxiously sent scouts to find them. When at last his scouts returned, they reported no contact with Mitchell's men. His troops badly divided and fearing Confederate forces in pursuit, Dahlgren ordered his men northeast again in search of Kilpatrick, who meanwhile drove his men southeast.

Four days after leaving Stevensburg, three units of Northern cavalry moved in different directions, struggling to connect with each other and reach sanctuary among Butler's Federal forces on the peninsula. Having lost Dahlgren in the darkness, Captain Mitchell led his men through the gray dawn. Trailed the whole way by firing Confederate soldiers, militia, and ragtag rebel sympathizers, Mitchell guided his men in different directions, first one way, then another, as enemy fire intensified. Forced to leave his dead and wounded, he forged ahead, sending scouts to find a way out. By late afternoon they stumbled on Kilpatrick's troops moving away from their Old Church stand toward Tunstall Station, which Mitchell was approaching, having lost one-third of his men.

That morning Dahlgren reached the Pamunkey River with what was left of his troops. Swollen from the rain, fording looked impossible. But urging his men on, now only eighty strong, a couple of men braved the rushing current and swam the river pulling a long rope. Once across, they secured their end of the rope to a tree trunk. The rest of Dahlgren's men slowly, painfully, wrestled the rushing waters as they clung to the rope strung across the river. One by one they emerged on the other side.

Thinking themselves undetected, they moved quickly northeast toward the Mattaponi River. The rain had mercifully stopped. Finding a raft hidden in the brush along the river bank, they began their crossing in small groups. Unexpectedly, a small band of Confederate cavalry opened fire. Dahlgren, on his crutch, rallied his men, who returned fire as the raft came and went, ferrying the men across. Only with the last crossing did Dahlgren leave. They headed southeast, under fire the whole way from scattered snipers. By late afternoon, when the completely exhausted men and horses could move no further, they stopped near King and Queen Court House to rest and eat. Before midnight, Dahlgren woke his men and they mounted their horses. Again the rain began. As they moved anxiously through the night, Dahlgren fretted that his scouts, sent ahead, had not returned.

Suddenly, a volley of bullets rang out from the darkness. Horses and men in the front part of the Union line crashed to the ground. In a panic the ambushed men whirled about, slamming into each other, searching for an escape in the black night. Breaking through a rail fence alongside the road, some dashed away from the bloody scene. In the chaos others gave up in despair and sat on the cold ground, waiting for the light of day to take them.

On the bloody road bodies lay scattered. Among the corpses rested a mud covered dead man with a wooden leg.

—◦—

In Richmond, on the second day of March, as the dead and wounded spilled into the city and anxious families searched among the bodies, the morning newspapers boasted about repulsing the Yankee attack on the city. Elizabeth and her fellow Unionists despaired. Within days, a more ominous report reached Richmonders.

The press indignantly screeched the news that incriminating papers had been found on the body of Ulric Dahlgren, commander of the ill-fated attempt to capture Richmond. The newspapers claimed that the "Dahlgren Papers," as they were called, revealed the sinister nature of the Union's designs in the attack. The captured documents purported to detail Dahlgren's instructions to his men containing three elements: release Union prisoners, kill Jefferson Davis and his Cabinet, burn the city. The accounts plunged the residents of Richmond into a frenzy of rage as they confirmed long-held beliefs that the barbaric Yankees could never be expected to abide by the rules of war.

While Elizabeth Van Lew and her family cast about for some word of what had happened, news of the "Dahlgren Papers" broke. Convinced the documents were fabricated, Elizabeth slipped away at night, avoiding the surveillance still on her home, to counsel with her Unionist friends.

She went to the home of Thomas McNiven and found him there with Frederick Lohmann.

"It's a lie cooked up by the government," McNiven assured her.

"People are demoralized. They need to whip everyone into a rage," Lohmann added. "What better way than to tell people their homes are to be burned and their lives threatened?"

"I've spoken with Palmer, Stearns, and the Holmes family," McNiven told her. "Everybody agrees the papers are forged."

"And I've been in touch with Rowley," Lohmann said. "He's convinced of the same."

"It doesn't make sense that an honorable man such as Dahlgren would be part of such a vicious plot. It's contrary to all rules of war." Elizabeth, experienced in the arts of deception, wanted to believe it was all a government hoax.

"Besides," McNiven interjected, "no one seems to have actually seen these papers. Wouldn't the government put them on display if they really existed?"

The next morning Elizabeth put some food in a basket and set out for the almshouses, worried that the recent shelling and cannon battering around the city must have terribly shaken Emmie and the others.

"I've neglected them badly," she told Eliza has she headed out the door.

She found Emmie in her dingy room seated by a window, lost in thought.

"Emmie?" She said softly.

The elderly woman turned and a broad smile spread across her face when she spotted her visitor. "Lizzie!"

Hugging the frail woman in her rocker, Elizabeth pulled up a stool and took Emmie's hand. "I haven't been here for awhile. I've been remiss. Can you forgive me?"

"Hush, girl. You been so good to me. Better than anyone," Emmie replied, squeezing Elizabeth's hand. "But I did miss hearin' the news, Lizzie. I thought them Yankees were coming, what with all the commotion. Nobody tells us nothin' here."

"I'm afraid the Union's not here yet," Elizabeth said, a touch of despair in her voice. "Did all the noise scare you?"

"Not much kin scare me these days. With the grim reaper breathin' on my neck, ain't no big noises gonna frighten me."

Elizabeth laughed. "Well then, you're braver than I am."

"Tell me, Lizzie, what's happening? Is this cursed war ever gonna end? I'd like to see a few Yankees before I go."

"Now where you going, Emmie?" Elizabeth teased.

"Well, I sure hope it ain't to everlasting fire. I do *not* like fire," she said emphatically.

"What have you ever done to even think that," her friend chuckled.

"I done my share a harm along the way. Chased a few men I oughn't of."

Elizabeth burst into laughter. "You are wicked, Emmie!"

"But tell me, Lizzie. What's really happenin'?"

"Far as I can tell—and nobody knows for sure—the Confederates pushed back a Union attack on the city. Seems like they came pretty close. But all they have to show for it is more men taken prisoner and many more dead and wounded. It's dreadful."

"Somethin' I never understand, Lizzie. Why them boys, all of them, gonna follow Davis and Lincoln—whoever—and throw themselves in front of bullets and cannon. Why you suppose they do it?"

Elizabeth nodded sadly. "It's something I don't understand, Emmie. Men rushing to get themselves killed over something that has nothing to do with them, like slavery."

"Men is shor a strange bunch, ain't they?" Emmie said. "They make out like they's so strong, so all powerful. But when the boss man gives the order, they ain't so strong no more. Then they turn to sheep."

"I used to think it was ignorance," Elizabeth said. "But maybe you're right. Maybe those who seem strong are really weak . . ." She thought about it. "You know, Emmie, there's a lot of desertion from the Confederate army . . ."

"Lord, I'm glad to hear that," Emmie jumped in. "They's some hope then. Takes a lot a guts to desert, seems to me. They sayin', you ain't gonna make me die for nothin'."

"Then what passes for weakness is really strength . . ."

"Lord, Lord," Emmie said again.

The two women sat quietly together for awhile.

"You got time for a game of whist, Lizzie."

"I surely do, Emmie."

❧

Although the Dahlgren affair dominated their concerns, a strange side-show unfolded for Elizabeth and her network in the midst of the turmoil. Word reached them from Erasmus Ross that prison insiders were buzzing about the arrest of General Winder's head detective, Philip Cashmeyer, on March 9 for "holding treasonable intercourse with the enemy." Authorities were holding him in Castle Thunder. The news stunned Elizabeth who always felt a sinister presence when she met Cashmeyer during her visits to Winder's office and elsewhere.

"Could that man truly be a Unionist?" Elizabeth asked Ross in a meeting at the home of his uncle, Franklin Stearns.

"It would seem so," Ross replied. "They arrested him at City Point where he was delivering Union prisoners for exchange under the flag-of-truce. Someone saw Cashmeyer pass a bundle to one of the Union prisoners before he was handed over."

"Did they actually see what was in the package?" Elizabeth asked, intensely curious.

"Yes. Confederate guards took the bundle from the prisoner before he was exchanged. It contained letters written in German, his native tongue, as well as documents and orders from General Winder's office. They took Cashmeyer into custody on the spot."

Elizabeth fell speechless. How was it possible they had not known, she thought?

"He may not be in prison long," Ross continued. "He's asserting his innocence. Claims the package was for his wife in Baltimore. That he was trying to impress his wife with his importance as a Confederate official.

I doubt that, but he's one of Winder's favorites and, you know, we all believe what we want to believe . . ."

———

Despite Union reverses in the Kilpatrick-Dahlgren fiasco, the Confederacy hung by a thread. Food scarcity, manpower shortages, not enough horses, lack of fuel, a crumbling infrastructure, troops stretched perilously thin, dwindling munitions, a badly devalued currency, a dearth of medicine and doctors for the wounded . . . But the news that Yankees planned to burn their city, their homes to the ground and kill their leaders whipped Richmonders into a renewed fury against the North and pushed their own suffering into the background. Calls for the immediate execution of prisoners taken in the Dahlgren raid echoed through the city.

But for Unionists, another tragedy had unfolded, the desecration of the body of Colonel Dahlgren. On the battlefield where he fell, Confederates took his possessions, stripped the corpse, ripped off his wooden leg, cut off a finger from his hand, and threw his body into a muddy pit by the road where he had fallen. After the "Dahlgren Papers" story broke, his body was retrieved from its muddy grave and hurried back to the capital. At the York River Railroad station authorities put the corpse on display in a plain pine box. As a mark of contempt, a gray Confederate uniform now clothed Dahlgren's lifeless body as a steady stream of the curious filed past the open casket to view and revile the hated Yankee. At the side of his coffin, Dahlgren's wooden leg stood, also on display as spectators hurled curses at the corpse.

From the railroad depot, authorities later spirited Ulric Dahlgren's body to a secret burial place, despite pleas by his father, Admiral John Dahlgren, for the return of his beloved son's body. Under orders from Jefferson Davis himself, no one was to know where the Dahlgren grave had been dug.

For Elizabeth and Richmond Unionists, the desecration of Dahlgren's body weighed heavily. The outrage roused a deep sadness and indignation in Elizabeth. What want of decency could motivate such barbaric behavior against an inanimate body? She vowed to find the body in its secret hiding place and move it to friendly care. They, loyal Unionists, would act as Dahlgren's family in the absence of his blood kin.

The surveillance of her home having ended—more for lack of manpower than anything else, she suspected—Elizabeth went to the bakery in the light of day to order bread. While examining the loaves, she spoke in hushed tones to Thomas McNiven about the urgency of finding the burial site of Colonel Dahlgren's body and removing it to caring hands.

"You're proposing a grave robbery?" McNiven said with surprise.

"If you must put it that way," Elizabeth whispered, smiling. "But first we must locate the grave."

"I'll contact Lohmann," McNiven said. "He knows Lipscomb." Martin Meredith Lipscomb was the person responsible for the burial of Federal prisoners who died in Confederate hands in Richmond. A bricklayer with a thirst for elective office, Lipscomb was currently engaged in the unlikely pursuit of the office of mayor.

When Lohmann visited Lipscomb at his Franklin Street home, he appealed to the man on humanitarian grounds. Taking care to give no hint of Unionist interest in the matter, Lohmann made his case for the importance of finding the body so it could be properly buried with religious rites.

"I'm hoping you can help ease the terrible grief of Dalhgren's father who is distraught at the thought he may never see the remains of his son or provide a true Christian burial. Imagine what any father would feel."

"I have to tell you, Frederick," Lipscomb said, "I was not involved in burying the man." He sniffed with disdain. "Davis himself ordered the burial and bypassed my office." His voice revealed the hint of a grudge.

"I'm surprised, Martin—after all your loyal service," Lohmann commiserated. The long friendship of the two men went way back to a time when they had worked together. "Is there *any* way we can find out where the body is buried?"

Lipscomb hesitated, thinking. "Perhaps Gabe . . ."

"Gabe?" Lohmann asked.

"Gabriel," Lipscomb continued. "He's the slave who digs the graves at Oakwood Cemetery. He likely dug it."

"But will he talk?"

"He will for me," Lipscomb said with self-importance.

The next day the two men went to Oakwood Cemetery on the eastern outskirts of Richmond. Lipscomb urged the nervous man at length to show them Dalhgren's burial spot. After much hesitation and Lipscomb's assurances that no one would ever know, Gabriel led them to a corner of the cemetery not far from the entrance. There, under a small sapling, the slave pointed to the ground which had been carefully smoothed over and covered with dirt clumps full of grass to look as though it had lain untouched. No headstone or marker of any kind distinguished the grave. Thanking the anxious man, Lohmann and Lipscomb left.

Elizabeth Van Lew, armed with knowledge of Dahlgren's whereabouts, began arrangements to remove the body—diggers to disinter the corpse, a wagon and driver to carry it away, passes to move through the city, a suitable burial ground, a chance for Unionists to pay their last respects, and money to pay the diggers, purchase a metal coffin and more. A month after the death of Ulric Dahlgren, Elizabeth completed her organization of the grave robbery.

On April 6, Federick Lohmann, his brother John, and Martin Lipscomb drove a farm wagon into Oakwood Cemetery in the dead of night. Remnants of a late-winter snowstorm lay on the ground in patches. Overhead, another storm threatened, for which the schemers gave thanks. A biting wind, lightening bolts, claps of thunder, and ominous black clouds conspired to keep Richmonders indoors. As the squeaking wagon entered the cemetery, the men looked about for anyone who may have followed them.

Seeing no one, they moved to the sapling over Dahlgren's grave where Gabriel and two other black men waited in the shadows of nearby trees.

Quickly the workers dug into the wet earth of the shallow grave till their shovels hit the coarse pine box. Lifting the coffin from the ground, the men pried open the top as they covered their noses against the stench. Unwilling to risk lighting a candle, Lohmann felt around in the dark cavity. Finding only one leg, he confirmed that it was Ulric Dahlgren whose body filled the black void. Lipscomb hastily refastened the lid on the coffin, while Frederick Lohmann paid Gabriel and the other diggers fifteen hundred Confederate dollars. As the creaking farm wagon pulled away with its cargo, the three black men rapidly plowed the dirt back into the empty grave, replaced the grassy clumps and replanted the sapling on the spot.

After dropping off Lipscomb, the Lohmann brothers drove the wagon through the rain to William Rowley's farm on the outskirts of the city. There they placed the coffin in a small building on the farmstead, used by its owner as a workshop. Rowley left the house and sat by the coffin in the outbuilding all night, keeping watch over its precious contents.

The next morning the Lohmanns returned with a metal coffin, a rarity in Richmond in these hard times, that Lipscomb procured for them. With Rowley's help, they carefully transferred the remains to the new casket. Throughout the morning and early afternoon, at great risk to all of them, a steady stream of Unionists stole out to the farm to pay their last respects and pray over the body—Charles Palmer, Franklin Stearns, Sarah Wardwell, Elmira Holmes, Frederick Lohmann, Eliza and Elizabeth Van Lew, and others. Together they mourned the passing of Ulric Dahlgren, brave and noble in their view. Before sealing the coffin for the last time, Elizabeth carefully cut some locks of hair from the dead man's head to send as a memento to his grieving father, Admiral Dahlgren. Next she placed a blue military blanket over the body as a final gesture of respect.

Then the men sealed the coffin and carried it out to the wagon. Covering it with dirt, they tightly arranged a number of peach trees ready for planting over the surface of the wagon, obscuring the coffin beneath. The Lohmann brothers set out on foot ahead of the wagon, flanking the sides of the Brook Turnpike, their destination the farm of a German friend and Unionist, Robert Orrock. Behind them Rowley guided the mule-drawn wagon down the pike. The journey along the heavily guarded thoroughfare was fraught with danger. Discovery meant imprisonment or death and, likely, torture to discover the accomplices. But conviction beat in Rowley's iron heart and he forged ahead to meet the Confederate pickets along the route.

The first and second meeting with guards went smoothly and they waved Rowley on. Approaching the last picket on the turnpike, he sensed trouble. Everyone was being stopped. As he pulled up to the barricade beside a tent, a Confederate lieutenant stood eying his wagon. Rowley stopped and dropped his reins casually, trying hard to appear indifferent. He heard the lieutenant order the guard on duty to search his wagon before disappearing into a tent. Just as the guard drew near him, another loaded farm wagon pulled up to pass. Seeing Rowley casually relaxed behind his mules, he moved toward the other wagon and proceeded to search its contents.

When he finished, the guard returned to Rowley and asked, "Whose trees are these?" But before he could respond, the guard looked closely at his face and asked, "You look familiar. Do I know you?"

"We've met," Rowley answered. "I visited your house sometime back. You had a group of people over. My wife and I . . ."

"Ahh, yes. I do remember you." With that the two men engaged in friendly talk. Then the guard asked again, "But whose trees are those?"

"The peach trees belong to a German in the country. I'm delivering them for planting."

Just then another wagon pulled up and the guard left to search it. When he returned, the guard and Rowley again exchanged pleasantries about the peach trees, transplanting them and the weather.

At this point, the lieutenant stuck his head out of the tent and called out testily, "How long does it take to search a wagon? Get it done so the farmer can move on." And he disappeared back into the tent.

The guard leaned in and said quietly to Rowley, "It would be a shame to tear up those trees. You've packed them so nicely. I won't hold you any longer. Your honest face is good enough for me." With a wave of his hand, he motioned Rowley on.

A short distance ahead the Lohmann brothers waited anxiously, having observed the scene at the picket. When the wagon pulled alongside them, they climbed onto it, seating themselves on each side of Rowley who nodded and smiled. They drove on until reaching Yellow Tavern, where the Lohmanns directed Rowley to get off the turnpike. About ten miles down the road they arrived in Glenn Allen at the farm of Robert Orrock, a Unionist whose code name was "Quick." In a remote spot on the farm, the men hastily dug a burial place in the cold ground. After removing the peach trees, they lifted the coffin from the wagon and lowered Ulric Dahlgren into his third grave, knowing it would not be his last. After refilling the black hole, they carefully planted a peach tree over the body.

❧

While Dahlgren's multiple burials at last brought him to rest, his captured men found none. The "Dahlgren Papers" fueled continued calls for the immediate hanging of all Union prisoners captured during the ill-conceived raid on Richmond. In speeches and in the press, the government was urged to show no mercy and proceed with the executions. One of the most vocal advocates for hanging all the captives was Sallie Seddon, who angrily denounced the men and Dahlgren.

An exhausted Jefferson Davis grappled with the Dahlgren affair's aftermath, the increasingly noisy press surrounding the infamous "papers," and public outrage at the presumed Northern plot. To the east and north of Richmond, Grant's troops massed, ready to strike. He spent long, joyless days working in his office at the capital as Varina worried about his health, his difficulty sleeping, and his failure to eat. Each day she walked to his office around noon with tempting food that she coaxed him to eat.

On the last day of April, Varina, pregnant with her sixth child, strode to the capital through a gentle breeze with her basket of food, feeling cheered by the warm weather, the bright sunshine, and the profusion of blossoms everywhere. Along the way she chatted with various passersby.

At home, her children played, running through the house, teasing each other and enjoying the warm sun on the lawn as their nurse and servants watched. But shortly after his mother left, five-year-old Joe wandered away from his Irish nurse, Catherine, and scrambled onto the banister of the second story balcony, tottering and peering down. Within seconds, he lost his footing and crashed to the brick pavement below.

Mary Bowser was cutting flowers in the garden for the dinner table when she heard the child's pitiful scream and the ominous thud a few feet away. Dropping everything, she rushed to little Joe, only to find him unconscious. Mary anxiously patted his cheek and forehead. Still he didn't move. She screamed for help.

His brother Jeff, playing on the lawn at the time of the accident, dashed over and began calling, "Little Joe, wake up, wake up!" When the child didn't answer, Jeff began praying out loud, "God, please wake little Joe. Please wake Little Joe. Please God!"

One of the slaves ran from the house, followed by Catherine, and picked up little Joe. "Go get them," he said to Mary ". . . at the office." As she quickly turned to leave, she heard Catherine's spine-chilling wails rise into the empty air. Mary ran the three blocks to the Davis office, cobblestones flying past under her feet, trees and people rushing by. She darted up the steps and rushed into the president's office.

"Please come quickly, Mr. Davis, Miz Davis," she pleaded, breathlessly looking from one to the other. "An accident . . . little Joe . . ."

Varina instantly flew out the door followed by her startled husband. Mary ran back to the house behind the pair. By the time they arrived, a police officer and three neighbors were trying to revive the child who had been moved indoors and lay immobile on a sofa. Margaret stood sobbing and clinging to Jeff behind the sofa. Varina threw herself on the floor by little Joe and began rubbing the child's face and calling him back, calling, calling, continuing her ministrations long after the body had gone cold.

The boy's father stood paralyzed over the two, watching the soul drain from the joy of his life. A bright light bathed every corner of the room and breezes gently blew the filmy curtains from the great windows. A terrible silence descended over the place, broken only by Varina's violent sobbing.

In the midst of the anguish a courier arrived with an urgent message for the president. Davis stood staring at the paper, uncomprehending, unable to focus. Stricken, he looked to Varina, to the corpse of his child, to the paper. He could not understand or speak for a long time. At last he handed the paper back to the courier and in a heart-broken, shaking voice, he told the man, "I must have this day with my little child."

That night little Joe lay in the drawing room surrounded by cascades of flowers, little Joe who a few nights earlier had jostled his way through visitors at a reception in that same room to climb on his father's knee, say his bedtime prayers, and kiss him goodnight. After the wake, Jefferson Davis shut himself in his room and paced the floor all night long.

At the funeral the next day, throngs of people came to share the grief of the first family. Hundreds of schoolchildren marched behind the funeral carriage carrying flowers and boughs to throw on the casket. At the gravesite, Varina, despondent and ashen, stood silently staring into the deep pit ready to swallow another of her children, while her husband stood straight as an arrow, clear against the blue sky, his face immobile in its searing pain.

The Dahlgren affair would not go away, despite the personal calamity of Jefferson Davis. Public cries for the hanging of all prisoners captured during the Dahlgren raid continued relentlessly. He and his Cabinet argued for hours about the matter. Davis counseled no, while Secretary of War Seddon pressed for the executions. After failing to agree, they wrote to General Robert E. Lee, asking him to make the decision. In the end, his response settled the matter: *I do not think reason or reflection would justify such a course. I think it better to do right, even if we suffer in so doing, than to incur the reproach of our consciences and posterity.*

So Lee spared the lives of Dahlgren's men. But their lives did not fare well in Libby Prison. Cast into a basement dungeon, they found themselves in cold darkness, save for a single precious candle, surrounded by stone, mold, vermin and rats, straw for bedding, and very little food.

But the hapless men had the sympathy of Colonel Thomas Rose, mastermind behind the great Libby tunnel escape. After the severe beating and recapture, he too had suffered the cruel indignities of the cellar dungeon. Ever resolute, he secretly dug a hole through the first floor to the dungeon cavern. Through the hole he dropped playing cards with a note for the men to signal the absence of the guard by turning the King's face up below the opening. When the King appeared in the dim candle-light, Rose lowered corn bread and scraps of meat down to the hungry men in the stone tomb, using a broken bottle tied to a rope . . .

CHAPTER 8

A DREADFUL TREMOR SWEPT OVER THE SLAVES LEFT BEHIND ON THE north shore of the James River in the wake of Dahlgren's departure as word spread from those in front that the Union army meant to leave them behind. Sobs and wails rose from the crowd abandoned at gunpoint not far from the western outskirts of Richmond. A cold rain fell again and a bitterly cold wind lashed icy spears at the runaways as they struggled to comprehend their situation and think what to do.

Among them a small group had taken shelter under a huge white pine, its thick branches laden with blue-green needles reaching in all directions. Sitting on the wet ground, Kriszy rested her tired back against the smooth, gray bark of the tree's trunk as she nursed her infant son, little Wash. Her husband, Holdy, stood stooped under the branches, talking in hushed tones to Elijah as the two men searched frantically for a plan. Behind her Bula, with no one in the world but her two children, hummed softly and tried to soothe six-year-old Adaline and twelve-year-old Elum, shivering in the cold.

In the distance Kriszy could see the others slowly begin to melt away. Some retraced their steps northwest. Others began to move west hugging the James River. Still others slid into the dense trees in search of hiding places and a means of escape. A few began to follow the Union line at a distance, hoping for a change of heart.

Kriszy watched uneasily as Holdy and Elijah spoke with animated gestures against the howling wind. She could not hear the words, but she saw the desperation in Holdy's face. Dusk began to fall and dark shadows crept over the two agitated men. Had they really thought they had a chance at freedom when they fled their plantation near Goochland Courthouse to follow the Union troops? A knot formed deep in her bowels and twisted this way and that. This much she knew: There was no going back.

The cold rain continued to fall, hard and driving, and the sheltering pine gave way to the downpour. Kriszy stopped nursing and pulled the blanket tightly around Wash, who whimpered in protest. Bula curled her body around Adaline and Elum as best she could. Holdy and Elijah turned back to the two women.

"Come now," Holdy said taking Kriszy's hand and lifting her from the ground.

Elijah helped Bula and the children to their feet and took the lead through the dense stand of trees as the darkness grew. The mucky ground sloshed around their shoes kicking up mud and splashing dirty water at their skirts and pants. When they reached the open fields, Elijah strained his eyes, searching in all directions, then motioned them forward with a wave of his arm.

The rain had turned to sleet when Elijah thought he saw a structure in the distance. The small group crept along, slipping on the sucking ground and struggling to keep from falling. Bula pulled Adaline along as she clung to Elum. Holdy kept his arm over Kriszy and the baby in a protective gesture.

"Wait here," Elijah ordered.

He edged closer to the building outlined against the dark sky. No sound or light came from the great plantation house and he soon realized it had been burned and abandoned. He hurried back to Holdy and the others and motioned them forward again. Inside the faint smell of smoke and charred wood still lingered.

"Yous be careful," Elijah cautioned as they picked and stumbled their way through blackened wood and burnt remnants of furniture. "Here," he said when he found a room still covered by a portion of the roof.

On one side a broken window let in the wind and rain, but at the other end the windows stood intact, surrounded by charred sills. Bula moved to the area by the closed window with the children and motioned Kriszy to come. Their drenched blankets and clothes clung to their bodies. The children shivered as Bula pulled off the blankets.

"We needs a fire for baby 'n the children, Holdy," Kriszy said.

Holdy looked at Elijah who seemed to consider the situation as he looked around the room. A large brick fireplace stood in the middle of one wall. Without a word, he peeled his blanket from his back and moved to the broken window. Reaching to the top of the sill, he tucked the blanket into the damaged shards above the window until he completely covered the opening. When Holdy saw what he was doing, he took his own wet blanket and covered the other window. Silently the two men moved about the rooms picking up and breaking pieces of wooden furniture. Elum and Bula joined them and soon a pile of wood grew.

From a charred upholstered chair Holdy pulled out the cotton filling and handed it to his friend who spread it in the fireplace. A man of few words, Elijah said, "Small," as he placed a few pieces of wood in the hearth and patted the air in front with the open palms of his hands. Everyone understood the danger of detection without the words. Then he pulled a tin box of matches from deep in his pockets and lit the cotton batting under the wood.

A heavenly warmth spread over them as the small group huddled in front of the fireplace. Kriszy pulled the wet clothes off little Wash and hung them over the mantle, holding him near the fire as he whimpered softly. The others took off their outer garments and hung them to dry as well.

As Elijah stood naked to the waist, his back to Kriszy, she saw the long, dark, leathery lines, angry across his skin. She winced, remembering that horrible day when the master ordered all his slaves into the barn. Elijah had been tied around his wrists with leather thongs fastened to a beam above, arms extended so taut over his head that his feet barely touched the ground. When the master gave the signal for the whipping to begin, most turned away. But he signaled the lash to stop and commanded them all to watch. Kriszy remembered glancing at Bula who had to bear the children's terror at the sight. During the beating Elijah bit his lip so badly to keep from screaming that blood covered his chin and neck. The sounds of the flogging and Elijah's muffled groans swept over her again, the terrible scene tormenting her thoughts. After the whipping, as Elijah hung suspended in pain, blood pouring from the deep cuts across his back, his tormentor warned them all in a howling voice about stealing from their master. Elijah's crime: after being refused a doctor, he took medicine from the big house for his sick, fevered wife, who died shortly afterward.

Kriszy turned quickly from the old wounds on Elijah's back to baby Wash, grateful he had not witnessed the torture and degradation of a whipping. And he must never, she vowed to herself, even as she pushed back the certain knowledge they would all be flogged, and far worse, if caught.

Elijah left the room then and stepped around the debris until he found the kitchen. The outside wall had burned to the ground and the roof was gone in this part of the house. The rain had stopped. In the dark he began poking around outside the kitchen, straining to see, till he spotted the plank covering a hole in the ground a few feet from the kitchen. Pulling at the latch of the heavy wooden door, Elijah opened the gaping hole to the root cellar. Staring into the blackness, he thought better of descending and made his way back to the others.

"What you find, Elijah?" Holdy asked.

"I done found the root cellah," Elijah answered as he poked about the wood pile. When he found the right piece, he stuck it into the fire and soon he had a small torch.

Holdy followed him through the rubble to the kitchen and into the night darkness. As Elijah lowered the flame into the opening, wooden steps appeared. Carefully he placed his foot on the first step and made his way into the disappearing darkness in the large underground storage area.

"You see any food?" Holdy called down.

Elijah grunted as he searched about, pulling open barrel tops and crates and poking into corners. Holdy could see the torch light moving over dark shadows below. At last his friend began to ascend the ladder holding the torch in one hand and a sack in the other. Holdy took the bag as Elijah went back down. Shortly he re-emerged carrying a pile of musty flour sacks and pulled himself out. Together they closed the heavy wooden door and made their way back to the warmth of the fireplace.

The women and children watched as Holdy poured the contents of the sack onto the floor. A few sweet potatoes, turnips and dried ears of corn lay before them.

"Thas good, Elijah," Bula said gratefully.

"They's a bit mo down there," Elijah answered as Bula and Kriszy picked around the woodpile for sticks with a sharp point. After they roasted the roots and corn, they ate hungrily. Then they settled on the hard floor to sleep as best they could using the flour sacks for coverings.

Unable to sleep, Kriszy anxiously stared at the eerie flickerings dancing across the room as she held the baby close to her body and worried. Even with the fire, the room was cold and damp. She knew the fire would have to go out before morning or someone might see the smoke from a distance. Wash whimpered in his sleep and Holdy lay silent and still. She tried to see the future, even tomorrow, but she saw nothing. The fire died and it was approaching dawn before Kriszy fell into an exhausted sleep.

Bula woke with a start the next morning when the sounds of battle started in the distance, gunfire and cannon bursts. The others still slept, worn out by the flight and fear. She noticed Elijah was already gone. "Goin' to find help," he had told them the night before.

⚊⚊

Before dawn Elijah left the rubble of the manor and slipped through the muddy countryside making his way toward Richmond. Should he be stopped, he carried a pass in his pocket allowing him to enter and leave the city. Elijah regularly drove the plantation wagon, laden with farm produce, into the hungry capital to sell at market.

But today he walked, hugging the trees along the river road, fighting the cold morning air. The first streaks of light spread across the dark gray sky when he heard cannon and gunfire erupt in the direction of Richmond. The closer he got to the capital the louder the sounds of war became. The road was deserted. He alone seemed to rush toward battle.

As he neared the city Elijah veered off the main road taken by the soldiers who abandoned them and away from the sounds of battle just north of the city, closely following the James River to the southeast. He made his way through the trees lining the river still swollen from the rains, as the mucky ground sucked at his thick work boots and roots reached out from the mud to clutch at his feet. He would enter the city along the river, passing by the Tredegar Iron Works, into the center of town and the marketplace. He knew of slaves escaping north and he meant to find out how.

As he approached the city, Elijah saw the Confederate home guards manning a checkpoint. Taking a deep breath and whispering to the good Lord, he strode boldly to the picket. Over the thunderous din of mortar in the distance, the picket asked to see his papers and Elijah pulled out his pass. The young man peered at the document, then at the tall, hefty black man in front of him and back to the paper. He handed Elijah the pass and with a quick wave of his hand motioned him forward.

Walking quickly on the road along the river, Elijah soon spotted the Iron Works ahead. On his right stood Belle Isle in the middle of the James River where, he'd heard, hundreds of Union prisoners languished and many died in the open without shelter. Passing the Iron Works and the State Armory, he made his way toward the marketplace. Alarm bells clanged in the air calling men to their posts and warning citizens—as though they needed any warning, Elijah thought to himself. People moved anxiously about the streets distracted by worry over what would happen to them if the city fell, searching for any shred of news. No one knew whether a thousand or fifty thousand Yankees were charging north of the city.

When Elijah approached the marketplace he noticed fewer stalls than normal, but more people scrambling to buy whatever they could for the expected siege. Cautiously he moved behind his friend Lemuel's stall from the Brody plantation in Charles City east of Richmond.

"Didn' spect ta see you today, Elijah. How you git through the fighting?" Lemuel asked, since he would have had to drive from the west through the Union line.

"Not selling today," Elijah answered. Then looking around, he pulled Lemuel back from his stall. "I's need help."

"What kind a help?" his friend asked, puzzled.

"I need ta know . . ." He hesitated and looked around again. "How are friens git to the North?"

Lemuel glanced to all sides instinctively. "You gonna flee?"

"Yes, sah," he answered.

"But the war almost over and you be free. Why you want to go run now?"

"We done already flee," Elijah said. We got to find 'r way out."

Lemuel stared at him. "We?"

"Small bunch a us from the plantation. You know who help 'r friens?" Elijah asked urgently.

"Jus what I hear tell," Lemuel said, shaking his head. "Don know fer shor."

Just then a woman called to them. "You boys working or talking?"

"Yes, ma'am," Lemuel answered, hurrying to wait on her.

Elijah slouched back, glancing around at the row of stalls behind which black men and a few women stood, hurrying to wait on nervous shoppers as the cannon blasts and musket fire continued thumping and shaking the air. *Which one?* he thought. *Or maybe someone else not here. Anyway, had to be a black person helping the slaves escape.*

When Lemuel returned he nodded in the direction of a row of stalls across from his.

Elijah looked puzzled. "Which one?"

"Try da man selling sweet potatoes an beans." He motioned his head in the direction of the second stall. "White shirt, white hair, straw hat. I hear tell he knows somethin'. But I ain't shor so be careful."

"Who is he?" Elijah asked. Although he had seen the man many times at market and had even greeted him in the past, he knew nothing about the black man in the thick jacket, his breath freezing in white puffs of mist as he moved about.

"Brisby his name. William Brisby. A free man. Own his own farm over by New Kent."

Elijah thanked his friend and edged across the cobblestones to the wagons behind the stalls. He studied the middle-aged black man of medium build piling sweet potatoes onto a makeshift wooden table. After a few minutes the man caught his eye and the two looked at each other. Brisby returned to his work, but Elijah stood still, watching. Finally the farmer moved back toward his wagon.

"You need something, my man?" he asked.

"Yes, sah, I needs somethin," Elijah answered.

"You hungry?" Brisby inquired.

"No," came the response.

The farmer looked at him with narrowed eyes in his weather-beaten face, his manner questioning and searching. "What then?"

"I needs to go North," Elijah blurted out at last, his voice barely a whisper.

Brisby quickly turned and made a circle with his eyes, examining the crowd, then turning back to the brawny man. "You can unload my wagon," he said in an audible voice for others to hear, ignoring the request. "You a good worker?"

"Yes, sah," Elijah said quickly and climbed on the wagon as Brisby returned to stacking sweet potatoes. In the background the battle north of the city raged on as people anxiously milled about in the cold and rumors flew through the marketplace.

Elijah kept busy, unloading, sweeping, tending Brisby's horse. As he moved about, Brisby quietly asked a number of questions.

"Where you from?"

"Goochland Courthouse."

"You must have a pass. I seen you selling here."

"Yes . . ." Elijah hesitated. "But da others got none."

Brisby started and his face broke into a frown. "How many others?"

"They's seven of us."

Brisby let out a whistling breath and stared at the man, his mind racing. "Seven!"

"Yas, sah. A baby and two young uns."

Brisby kept busy, shifting the piles of potatoes.

"Are they in the city?"

"No, sah, outside. Near Westham. We got lef by da Union Army we was following. I spec that's them," he said nodding in the direction of the battle.

At last Brisby told him what to do in a hushed voice. "You got to get them into the city so we can get them out to safety east of the city. That's where the Union line is. You can't go north around the city." He nodded toward the fighting. "You can't cross the James to the south. That's Confederates. Nope, you got to get them into the city. Then we'll take you east."

Elijah looked alarmed at the prospect of bringing his group into the Confederate capital.

"The home guard is busy fighting north of the city. This is a good time," Brisby tried to reassure him. "You needs to get them around the pickets. At night. Don't try it in the daylight."

Brisby continued waiting on customers between his whispered bits of advice.

"There's a lady can help. She's the best one to take that many. Which way you come in today."

When Elijah explained he had come by the river, Brisby nodded in approval. "That's the best way. Her house is just up from the river after you pass the prisons." And he proceeded to detail how to find the lady's mansion, what entrance to go to, tips about moving through the city at night. Elijah knew the city well and listened carefully, all the while wondering about this white lady Brisby was talking about.

— ·◦· —

By late morning the bombardment north of the city stopped suddenly as Elijah made his way out of Richmond. The air had turned bitter and he hunched against the wind as he moved. By afternoon as he was approaching the burned-out manor, the fighting erupted again. At the building he picked his way through the debris to the room where he left the others. A panic tightened his chest as he saw the empty room, the cold fireplace and the blankets on the windows mocking his wordless questions. Except for the window coverings every trace of them was gone.

"Holdy," he called out desperately as he worked his way through the rubble, room by room. When he reached the kitchen, he hastened to the root cellar. Pulling open the plank door, he called again, "Holdy."

"Elijah!" a voice exclaimed. Holdy appeared at the bottom of the steps, a huge grin on his face. "You back!" The others crowded around Holdy.

"What you doin' down there?" Elijah asked. "Scare me half to death."

"We saw a group of rebs comin cross da fields so we grabbed ever'thin and come down here," Holdy explained as he climbed the ladder. "Been here since mornin."

Elijah frowned, dismayed to hear of Confederate troops close by. One by one they emerged from the root cellar and he led them back to the room. Little Wash whimpered and fussed in Kriszy's arms and Adaline looked frightened. Elijah explained what they were going to do, going into the city and all. He could see the fear in their faces and wanted to comfort them.

"Ain't nothin ahead of us bad as wha we lef behind," Elijah told them firmly, looking them squarely in the eyes. "A fine lady gonna help us." He saw the curiosity and questions creep into their faces.

"Why a fine lady wan ta help us?" Bula asked skeptically.

"I dunno," Elijah answered, shaking his head. "Jes a good person maybe. Now you all rest. We leavin after dark."

Before they left, Elijah and Holdy made a small fire in the fireplace to roast a few sweet potatoes. No one had eaten since the night before. Gathering their things, wrapping themselves in their blankets, the small group of desperate fugitives picked their way out of the rubble and into the dark night. Elijah led the way while Holdy followed at the rear.

A cold drizzle began to fall again. Straining to see in the pitch darkness, they picked their way through the broken, yellowed cornstalks tripping their legs as they moved through the fields. For awhile they kept moving through the muddy countryside with its remnants of dried stalks and scratchy brush. An eerie silence covered the land. Neither moon nor stars could be seen, only blackness and shadows. Elijah moved instinctively over familiar ground and thought of the years driving the farm wagon and walking, again and again, back and forth, back and forth.

"Don't never want ta come this way agin," he thought to himself. "Never, never . . ."

"Come. Stay close to me," he said to the small band clutching hands in a moving chain. Then he veered toward the river, crossing the dark main road leading into Richmond and edging down toward the James. They ducked into the thick stand of trees lining the river, stumbling over rocks and brambles in the dark. They had not gone far when the sound of horses driving down the road overtook them.

"Down!" Elijah ordered, as they fell to the soggy ground. Little Wash began to cry and Kriszy frantically covered his mouth, pressing it mute while Holdy threw his arm over her for protection. The horses rode swiftly by, three, four, maybe five. They could not tell for sure who the riders were.

"Quickly," Elijah urged, pulling them up from the ground, and beginning his move forward again.

Bula hugged a tearful Adaline and tugged at Elum's arm as they stumbled on. Kriszy shushed and pleaded with the infant in her arms as he cried and whimpered on and off. They hurried at a near run through the vegetation, the rushing river to their right, black and angry, charging to the sea. The night grew colder as the towering trees dashed past, snapping their branches against the faces and bodies disturbing their rest, tangling and pulling at their blankets and clothes. The runners' panting grew heavier as they lumbered against the icy air that stole the breath from their lungs.

At last they saw the dim lights of the city ahead. Elijah stopped and pulled them around him in a circle.

"Da pickets is ahead," he whispered. "This be the hard part." He pointed in the shadows to the river's edge. "We gonna crawl along da slope o' da bank. Kriszy, yous keep da lil one quiet. Everyone keep quiet," he warned. "It be more quiet if'n we spread out. Jes do what I do."

With that Elijah plunged toward the river and scrambled down its bank. Slippery rocks, scraggy brush, and tangled roots covered the slope leading down to the river. Slowly the line of fugitives picked their way down to the edge of the menacing James, hanging onto scrub and roots. The swollen river lapped and tugged at their feet as they crawled along its edge, sending icy shivers up their legs.

Soon they could hear the sound of Confederate pickets talking at their post on the road above. Inch by inch they moved. Holdy gripped Kriszy's arm tightly as she held Wash who had fallen silent at last. Moments dragged on endlessly until they emerged from the river bank a good distance from the sentries.

The drizzle began to turn to cold rain. Elijah peered into the blackness and started walking toward a cluster of buildings off the road. The others crept anxiously behind him, their eyes darting left and right until Elijah led them into a narrow alley between two brick buildings. It was after midnight and the streets had fallen silent as exhausted Richmonders took to their beds after two days of listening to crashing cannons and gunfire at their door.

Slowly the small party of slaves crept on, hugging the dark structures, passing the Iron Works and keeping to the water's edge, eluding an occasional drunk stumbling along the road. Elijah stopped them as they approached Libby Prison rising ominously against the canal paralleling the river and he moved ahead stealthily to look for sentries. When he saw that they stood by the barred doors, behind a fence, he motioned his group forward. They made their way furtively past the prison and turned left onto Twenty-second Street. Like shadows they slithered from tree to tree along the road, past sleeping houses and stables and gardens dormant in the winter cold.

As the small band climbed Church Hill and the homes grew more magnificent, their uneasiness intensified. At one point they heard voices approaching and slid quickly behind some tall hedges. Two Confederate soldiers walked by talking loudly and gesturing.

"Hurry," Elijah said when they had passed.

His tattered party continued up the hill. There at last it stood against the gray sky, taking up a whole city block. Elijah ran Brisby's words through his mind and quickly walked up to the imposing, three-story mansion, swinging around toward the back, his weary, breathless followers in tow. No lights appeared in the curtained windows or any sign of activity. Had Brisby told the lady to expect them as promised? Elijah nervously tapped on the door, lightly at first, then louder as no reply came. After a few moments the door swung open and a tall black man peered out into the darkness surrounding them.

"My name is Elijah and . . ."

"Come in, quickly, quickly," the black man urged, motioning the shabby group into a dark room. One by one they slipped through the open door, hesitant about dragging their sodden clothes and muddy shoes into the fine home. "Hurry. Pay da floor no mind," the man in the entrance said, reading their wavering steps. At last the door closed behind them and Elijah, Kriszy, Holdy, Wash, Bula, Adaline, and Elum found themselves in total darkness as the keeper of the door fumbled about. At last a small candle flickered on and spread a tiny light over them. They appeared to be in a kitchen.

"Wait here," the man said. "I git the Missus."

They watched with apprehension as the candle moved away through a doorway, leaving them again in darkness. Elizabeth had dozed on a sofa in the parlor and woke with a start when Peter called to her.

"They's here, Miz Lizzie."

Elizabeth rose quickly and followed Peter to the kitchen. The sight of the slaves stung her heart when she saw how wet and cold they were.

"This here Miz Lizzie. And my name is Peter," the man with the candle said.

"We are so pleased to have you," Elizabeth said kindly. "Let's get you out of those wet clothes." She reached for the whimpering infant and taking him from Kriszy Elizabeth led them to a large drawing room where a fireplace glowed, spreading warmth and light over the weary, frightened group. Thick velvet drapes had been drawn tightly over the windows. A pile of clothes rested on one chair and towels on another.

"We's thank you, Miz Lizzie," Elijah said bowing in Elizabeth's direction. "This here is Holdy, Kriszy, an you got baby Wash." He pointed in turn to each. "An Bula with hers, Elum and Adaline. My name is Elijah." Elizabeth smiled warmly to each in turn.

"You must be hungry. Here are some clothes and towels to dry off. Baby things too. Please get yourselves comfortable and we'll bring you some food. There's a screen to change behind," Elizabeth pointed to a fine woven silk screen with three folding panels at one end of the room, a nicety completely foreign to their meager existence. Handing the baby back to Kriszy, she left the room and shut the door.

After a while Peter, Caroline, and Elizabeth brought chicken soup, bread, and dried apples, a feast for the famished wanderers. The hot soup spread its warmth to every bone in their bodies, washing away, for awhile at least, the dread that had taken residence there. For Adaline and Elum, Elizabeth brought colorful pieces of hard candy that brought smiles to their faces.

When they finished Elizabeth led them up the great staircase past the third floor and the servants' quarters to the attic stairs. Once there, Peter pushed back the large box concealing the opening. Thick coverings had been nailed over the small windows next to the chimney flue. Mats and blankets lined the floor and a large chamber pot sat behind another screen.

"I'm sorry to put you here," Elizabeth apologized. "But you'll be safest here in case . . ."

"This fine, Miz Lizzie," Elijah assured her.

"We real grateful," Kriszy added, clutching her baby.

"It may be a day or two before Mr. Brisby can start you over to the Union line. Now you get some sleep," Elizabeth told them. Leaving them with a hurricane lamp, she and Peter pushed the box back over the opening.

—❦—

By morning Kriszy woke to find the baby listless and feverish. When Elizabeth and Caroline came with food they found Kriszy and Holdy frantic with worry for little Wash.

"He burning up," Kriszy said, her face twisted with apprehension.

"You and the baby come with me, Kriszy," Elizabeth said.

She brought them down a flight of stairs to one of the servants' rooms.

"Caroline, get my mother."

When Eliza entered the room her daughter was already applying cool, wet cloths to the infant's forehead. The baby's breathing had turned laborious. "Fever, mother. Send Peter for the doctor." When Eliza looked at her with concern, she reached out her arm to her mother. "It'll be alright. We'll tell the doctor Kriszy is our newest servant." With that Eliza turned and quickly left the room.

For three frantic days Kriszy tended the feverish baby with the help of Elizabeth and the servants, doing what the doctor had said. The baby wouldn't eat so Kriszy dripped water and milk into its mouth. They applied compresses and rubbed ointments on the baby's chest. His mother never left his side and barely ate herself, though Elizabeth and Eliza coaxed food on her.

In the attic above, Holdy waited anxiously for each bit of news that came about his sick child. For everyone the fretful hours dragged by and the escape to Union lines seemed to vanish into an empty future.

In the parlor below, Elizabeth blamed herself. "This is my fault. I should not have put that baby in the attic," she told Eliza, berating herself.

Eliza would have none of it. "You must stop this," she responded firmly. "That baby is sick because they spent days out in the cold and rain. You *had* to put them in the secret room. What if someone followed or saw them coming here? Bet, you take too much on yourself. This is all hard enough without you . . ." She caught herself.

"It's just that I keep thinking I could have done something differently," Elizabeth said as though she had heard nothing her mother said.

Eliza shook her head in exasperation. "You must stop," she repeated.

On the fifth day the baby seemed recovered enough to travel, so Elizabeth sent word to Brisby at the market. Word came back that Brisby would take them east the next night. They would have to leave on foot— too dangerous to hide so many in the farm wagon as he usually did, he told Peter.

When the time came to leave, Elizabeth tearfully hugged each person.

"You done save our lives, Miz Lizzie," Elijah said.

"You're not safe yet, Elijah," Elizabeth answered with a smile.

Remembering her initial skepticism about "the fine lady" who was going to help them, Bula told Elizabeth, "You *is* a good person."

"Mr. Brisby has gotten many, many slaves over to the Union side," Elizabeth assured them. "He's the best."

In the kitchen Brisby waited as they put on the warm coats and sweaters Elizabeth had gotten for them. Cautioning everyone to keep quiet and do exactly as he said, he opened the door and peered into the late-night darkness. When Peter, waiting in the garden, gave him the all clear signal, Brisby stepped out. One by one the little band of freedom seekers followed, the cold, fresh air splashing against their faces.

Elizabeth watched intently from the doorway as they became shadow spirits drifting away through the trees and bushes in the winter garden, slipping through the sleeping magnolias and dogwoods, creeping past the great mansions of Church Hill, hurrying past the rushing waters below. After they disappeared into the night she could see them flying, soaring above the rooftops, higher and higher, away from the plantations and prisons of Richmond, away from endless labor, away from squalor and chains, away from degradation.

Sweet liberty waited. And they came.

CHAPTER 9

AN ADVANCE DETACHMENT ARRIVED ON THE ABANDONED CHANCELlorsville battlefield late in the day while overhead a clear blue spring sky spread a blanket of warmth over the fields. The line of men broke into fingers across the pasture as they got ready to make camp. But slowly, one by one, a somber mood took hold, sending shivers of dread under their skin and through their hearts. Strewn on the ground in all directions lay the bones of dead men decaying in the sun. The snow and rains of winter had eaten away at the shallow graves, pushing the empty skulls to the surface to watch a fresh crop of fodder prepare to join them.

Eyes averted, the men dug their tent poles into the ground, only to hit more human bones, indistinguishable as Union or Confederate. The dead lay together as they might have lain as comrades on a wilderness hike. The macabre scene stung the campers' spirits and they looked skyward, through the swinging branches covered with shifting leaves, for a reason to hope. As the sparks and smoke of their campfires rushed to the fading heavens, darkness banished the bones, which disappeared again into the earth.

Behind them, the Army of the Potomac, 110,000 strong, led by General George Meade, rested at a distance as the whippoorwills sang mournfully. Alongside Meade, General Ulysses S. Grant, commander of all Union forces, directed the campaign into the Virginia wilderness north of Richmond. By morning on a beautiful day in early May, the great mass of men crossed the swollen Rapidan River over pontoon bridges with pomp and ceremony, flags and banners flying, drums and bugles blaring, soldiers marching in formation.

Among the men marched Major Allen Lee Rockwell. In the flickering sunshine he saw Elizabeth's clear blue eyes watching him move, a mute smile on her worried face. In his breast pocket he carried her latest letter and the brooch she had given him when they parted. As he walked, Rockwell touched the pocket lovingly. Beneath his feet spring wildflowers in a profusion of brilliant colors—violets, chickweed, lady's slippers, columbine, snapdragons—ran quickly past.

By midmorning the men entered the vast wooded area known as the Wilderness. The deeper they moved through the trees, the more dense the tangled forest and brush became. Moving slowly, hacking their way through the claustrophobic scrub, they struggled to advance. Overhead a thick canopy of branches pushed back the sun as it struggled to follow the men. Gradually a strange darkness settled over them on this sunniest of days. To Rockwell it seemed they had suddenly entered a fearsome primeval jungle full of unfamiliar and hellish plants where only wild things grew.

Around noon shots rang out. A Confederate line, appearing abruptly out of the trees, threw itself against them in the confusing tangle of wild vegetation that clawed and stabbed at their legs and arms as they moved. A tumult of bullets, sabers, orders, and screams pierced the air, turning everything to chaos.

As he fought, Rockwell lost sight of his men in the thicket of vines and smoke. The opposing lines disappeared in a crush of bodies. To his right a bullet hit a Union comrade in the head, so close his blood splattered over Rockwell. In horror he realized there was no help for the man here in the Wilderness, no surgeon, not even an orderly to carry him away. Rockwell fired, but at whom? A haze of smoke seeped through the impenetrable woods and the fighting on both sides became a wild hunt for an enemy heard but not seen.

All day the blind men fought, ducking behind trees, shooting the enemy, shooting themselves, clashing at close quarters, firing into the distance. The Union's advantage in numbers faded in the face of entrenched

Confederate defenses. All afternoon they fought. As the dimness of day descended into blackness, pits in the ground, ravines, and fallen logs offered sanctuary as the men dug in to wait for darkness to pass.

Throughout the night, sounds of the wounded, moaning and crying for help that never came, rose from the bloody ground and sporadic sniping cut the eerie darkness as Rockwell lay sleepless and tormented in his trench. A kind of despair filled the corners of his heart at the senseless slaughter, and he thought to himself that he would die there. In places throughout the forest, dry leaves had caught the sparks of fighting. Smoldering for a long while, they burst into flames here and there, spreading quickly through the dry underbrush, choking the fetid air and burning many wounded men to death as they cried in agony.

It was more than Rockwell could bear and he thought he would go mad as screams pierced the burning blackness. But then he imagined Elizabeth, looked into her ocean eyes, saw her sweet smile, listened to her calm voice, felt the gentle touch of her fingers on his arm, and smelled the scent of jasmine on her skin. Gradually an unexpected tranquillity took hold of him as he willed himself in Richmond by her side.

At last dawn crept over the haunted tangle of darkness, held at bay by the dense scrub and woods. For a second day the battle raged in the center, on the right flank, on the left flank. The world tore at itself in a madness too terrible to contemplate. After two days, the Confederates had driven back the Union forces of General Grant, a man who had vowed he would never retreat. Some of the men managed to carry out a few of the wounded as they pulled back. Rockwell, moving backward haltingly through the dim light, stumbled and fell over an injured soldier. Lifting the man onto his shoulders, he half-carried, half-dragged him out of the ghostly Wilderness, back to the safety of the Union line. Behind him, the Northern dead and wounded, numbering seventeen thousand, lay throughout the bloody Wilderness.

Unlike the generals before him, Grant would not pull back. His plan to deliver a number of strikes against Lee involved simultaneous attacks by Meade north of Richmond, Butler south of the city moving up the James River, and Franz Sigel hammering Confederate forces in the Shenandoah Valley to the west to prevent them from joining Lee. In Georgia, General Sherman would engage Johnston, and Nathaniel Banks would take the port city of Mobile, Alabama. The coordinated attacks would grip Confederate forces in a vise, with the rebel capital the prize.

So he directed the troops south in a crescent movement that swung to the east of Lee's parallel move south. However, Grant's immediate objective, Spotsylvania, had been anticipated by Lee who arrived there shortly before the Union troops. For days the two armies continued crippling each other, fighting, maiming, and killing around Spotsylvania. Even the earth convulsed under the steady hammering of gunfire and the sun hid in shame at the sight. Between the Confederate and Union lines, a mass of breathless and wounded bodies piled over the bloody earth as charge after charge added to the nauseating gore and stench.

Still Grant continued his sweep south and Lee fought him to a standoff every step of the way. The hit-and-move game of the generals sped toward Cold Harbor, a crossroads some ten miles northeast of Richmond near the Chickahominy River. May had already passed into June as Lee dug in at Cold Harbor to meet the Union Hydra that refused to fall.

◦~◦

In Richmond Elizabeth anxiously waited through the weeks of fighting for news—news of the battles, who won, who lost, news of Grant's advance, news of a coming strike against Richmond. As always, the Richmond newspapers painted a rosy picture of Lee's victories and Grant's inadequacies. The terrible sounds and the acrid smoke of battle reached Richmond as Grant pushed south. Everywhere in the city people existed on a ration of dried beans and peas, corn bread, and bacon-fat drippings, with the poor suffering the most. Their men gone to war, women carried on as best they could.

But mostly Elizabeth worried about the lack of word from Allen. Her heavy heart whispered that he must surely be involved in the cruel campaign in the wilds north of Richmond. His letters stopped abruptly in early May. She feared the worst as news of casualty figures on both sides seeped back to the capital.

At night, alone in her room, Elizabeth tossed and turned in fitful sleep and wakefulness. "I'm so worried, Poppa," she said to the phantom in her dreams.

He grudgingly roused himself from sleep and listened. Being woken from a sound sleep was very annoying.

"I'm dreadfully worried about Allen."

You really like that man?

"Of course." She was a bit indignant.

Your track record with men is not the greatest.

She ignored him. "The worst thing is not knowing. Do you know where he is?"

How would I know?

"Aren't the dead supposed to see everything . . . know what's happening?"

Where did you get that idea? We sleep a lot.

"I'm terrified he's dead . . ."

Another dead fiancé? What would that say about being engaged to you?

She sat bolt upright in bed, suddenly wide awake. He went back to sleep.

<hr />

The month of May tore at Elizabeth for another reason as well. The Confederacy called up her brother's regiment and John suddenly got word that they would move out to join Lee's forces. When Grant's troops had massed on the Rapidan River, Lee prepared to throw everything in the path of his expected advance. Her brother's rapid reversal of fortune hit the Van Lew household hard. This time, no appeal could be made to General Winder whose protection had fled with the winter snows. That very month, the general was transferred to North Carolina to the infamous Andersonville Prison where he was to run the whole Confederate prison system east of the Mississippi River.

"I cannot be part of this," John said somberly to his sister and mother as they sat in the parlor after hearing the order. His ashen face stared out the window.

"Then you must leave now," Elizabeth said firmly.

"The time has come, John," Eliza added sadly.

John's head dropped and he sat silently, his eyes downcast, his shoulders drooping, his hands clenched.

"The girls, the business, you both . . ." he sighed at last, his voice barely audible.

"Your life!" Eliza responded, a harsh edge to her voice. "To die for a cause you believe in is one thing. To die for something evil is another. No. The time has come, John."

"She's right," Elizabeth said softly, touching his arm. "There isn't much time. You have to get to William Rowley quickly."

John looked at them both in desperation.

"There's no other way, John," Elizabeth said, her voice almost a whisper.

John rose from his seat. A weak smile crossed his face and with a wordless nod, he left the room and climbed the great staircase to prepare a few things to take to Rowley's farm.

John's desertion from the Confederate army a second time and the terrifying flight they knew was coming for him left Elizabeth and her mother badly shaken. Coupled with Allen's disappearance, the days dragged on into June as worries swelled and a suffocating aura filled every room in the mansion.

On the battlefield Grant's troops had caught up with Lee at Cold Harbor and his men made camp with a troubled expectation of yet another combat to come. Around the campfires, men rested uneasily. Despairing, some jotted farewell notes to loved ones and tucked them in their pockets. Rockwell took Elizabeth's letter from his shirt, reread it and turned it over to write. But every time the pencil moved to the crumpled page, no words formed. An incoherence, an emptiness kept the letters from joining together. Surrounded by madness for weeks, the words of life and normalcy evaporated from his paralyzed fingers into the rising mist. In the end he refolded the sheet and tucked it back in the dark place over his heart.

At one point as the men sat about fighting their personal demons, thinking their thoughts of life and death, a young enlisted man, hardly more than a boy, wrote his name and address in uneven letters on a scrap of paper. Taking a piece of wire, he pinned the paper to the back of his coat. Others saw what he did, and wanting to be identified for loved ones at home should they fall to rebel fire, began writing their own identities on bits of paper and cloth and affixing it to their own coats. Silently the act spread through the great camp and those with hope wrote themselves into the future.

Before dawn the bugles shouted a call to the wakeful men who shook the torpor from their limbs. By the time everyone assembled to attack, brilliant red and purple streaks began to spread over the gray dawn. Across the misty fields and wooded areas, entrenched in ravines, streams, ditches, and tree lines, Confederate troops had every advantage.

Thousands of eyes anxiously watched the blue line advance, struggling to keep from firing too soon. From the onslaught rose a terrible cacophony—a shouting of orders, battle cries, screeches to give courage, and the tramping of feet, as the disturbed earth jumped in protest. The eyes watched as rifles advanced, bayonets glistened in the rising sun, and flags waved. When at last the order to shoot rose from the trembling ground, the men in gray stood in unison from behind their trenches and breastworks and musket fire deafened the still air. Wave after wave of Union men collapsed under the ravaging volleys as great mounds of ephemeral dust rose where the bodies fell.

Allen Rockwell watched in horror as his comrades charged and fell in front of him. As the bullets cut down the line before him, he moved into position with his men, facing certain death, his mind suddenly devoid of thought and his heart empty of feeling. A terrible blackness descended over him although the sun had broken through the gray dawn above, and he stood at the edge of a dark bottomless pit. Through the blackness he sensed a slight fluttering, ghostly wisps of movement rising from the carnage, disturbing the air ever so faintly. Something lightly brushed his face before it rose like a curl of smoke disappearing into the sucking void.

But suddenly Grant ordered the charges stopped. Not ten minutes had passed from the first rush at the enemy. Yet on the vast killing fields many thousands of Union soldiers lay dead and wounded across the four mile length of the opposing sides. The general swore to himself with remorse at the waste of it. His officers refused to consider another such charge—even if Jesus Christ himself ordered it, one said.

Stunned by the command to stop, Rockwell and his men pulled back in disbelief, away from the waiting eyes and muskets. The blackness lifted and evaporated and the dark, open pit at his feet slowly disappeared as Rockwell realized he had been spared. In a stupor, he could not grasp why.

"This is murder," he thought to himself bitterly, "but they call it war," as he stumbled and pitched backwards, inebriated with the enormity of the loss.

For three days the armies faced each other in the summer heat, waiting. Between them the corpses moldered in piles and a stench filled the air. Men on both sides, nauseated and sickened by the unendurable sights and smells, gasped for air through their muffled faces. Only the shifting winds gave momentary relief. Every now and then corpses shifted, betraying a wounded soldier, consigned too early to the graveyard. A few managed to crawl away. Others lingered in agony on the open crypt. At one point Rockwell watched in horror from a trench as a wounded man on the pile of despair struggled to rise and in plain sight slit his own throat. Rockwell quickly averted his eyes and, staring at the ground, saw dust instead.

Fearing any gesture of weakness or defeat, neither Grant nor Lee would give ground and ask for a truce so the bodies could be taken away and the wounded tended. So they sat.

———

On the outskirts of Richmond, as the fighting raged, John Van Lew hid for days in an outbuilding on William Rowley's farm. The sounds of battle he had eluded sporadically broke through the walls of his hiding place. When Rowley thought they had a chance, the two men, carrying a bundle of supplies each, slipped out under a starless sky and headed south around the outskirts of the city. With the troops distracted elsewhere, only the home guard watched the roads in and out of the capital.

Below Richmond, Rowley led John along the Richmond and Petersburg Railroad tracks for a short distance, away from the sounds of war coming from the northeast. Then they looped east across the James River, heading for the Chickahominy River below Cold Harbor and Union lines. Rowley, skilled by now at avoiding the Confederate pickets scattered through the area, sidestepped the roads, moving instead through farmland and orchards. After picking their way through the mosquito-infested Chickahominy swamps, they forded the river at a shallow, rocky point. Crossing the Richmond and West Point Railroad tracks, the two men swung northwest up the peninsula toward Cold Harbor. The sounds of battle had grown ominously still.

Rowley and his charge cautiously approached the first Union picket in sight and declared their intentions. When a guard approached, John asked to be taken to someone in authority. Rowley bid his friend goodbye and headed back on his perilous journey to the center of the cauldron.

A Union picket searched John for weapons, then led him into camp, taking him to Federal army scout Judson Knight. The two men spoke at length as John explained his predicament and his desertion from a Confederate regiment. Knight immediately tried to recruit John as a Union scout, but John declined and indicated his determination to get to family in Philadelphia.

John had more to say. He spoke to Knight about the Union underground in Richmond, about his sister and mother, about Elizabeth's contact with Union prisoners in Confederate jails, about the safe houses for prisoners who escaped, about the network of Unionist guides who made their way regularly through Confederate lines, about the Dahlgren affair, about Elizabeth's communication link with General Butler, about Elizabeth's plant in the Jefferson Davis home.

On hearing about a spy in the Davis mansion, Judson Knight visibly started with excitement. Butler's position had been eclipsed by Grant's command of the eastern theater, he explained to John. Then he probed for details about Elizabeth and her place in the underground effort. He wanted to know about "this Negro, this Mary Bowser"—who was she, did she understand what she was doing, had she gotten any information out. On hearing that she was a former slave freed by the Van Lew family, literate, educated in the North, Knight stared in amazement. At last, convinced of Elizabeth's centrality and Mary's competence, he enthusiastically rose and insisted that John follow him.

Together the men moved into the officer's camp far behind the enlisted men's encampment. At the distant end of camp a large tent stood, nestled among a stand of trees. In front of the tent an open canopy, held in place by large poles, covered a group of wooden chairs on which a few officers sat about. To John it seemed like a large, cloth-covered porch looking out on the grass and trees. The flap of the tent directly behind it was fastened open by a rope, but he could only see a dimness inside.

Judson Knight motioned him to wait and passed under the canopy, disappearing into the darkness of the tent. A few minutes later he emerged and motioned John into the tent. There, seated at a large wooden desk with a lantern, maps spread out before him, sat a bearded man with brown hair, a cigar dangling from his lips. As he rose and turned, John spotted the stars on the right shoulder of the rather ordinary looking man of medium height.

"Ulysses Grant," said the man, extending his right hand as he pulled the cigar from his lips with the other.

"John Van Lew," responded the startled visitor.

"Judson tells me you have information that can help our cause," the general added, his clear blue eyes intent under his high, furrowed forehead. "Please." He motioned to a chair.

His jaw squarely set, his upper lip compressed, Grant listened intently as John repeated what he had told the scout. His brow knit, the general kept his flashing eyes on his guest delivering the unexpected and welcome news. When John had finished, Grant rose.

"Well then, we'll coordinate with General Butler," he said gratefully. "And I'll have Judson work with our intelligence head, George Sharpe, to contact Miss Van Lew. I understand you want to reach Philadelphia."

"I have family there," John answered.

"Then we'll provide safe passage and an escort." Taking John's hand, Grant shook it warmly. "We are most grateful to you and your family."

As John made his way to Philadelphia, William Rowley recrossed the Chickahominy swamp heading back to Richmond where his anxious wife waited. The authorities had called at the farm, looking for her husband and accusing him of failing to report for service in the army. When Rowley arrived home, they were waiting and arrested him.

❧

On the battlefields, the carnage had raged back and forth for a month since crossing the Rapidan, as men passed from sunlight to shadows to the darkness of the grave. During that time, the North lost fifty thousand men, dead and wounded. Still the opposing troops sat at Cold Harbor, facing each other over mounds of corpses.

Finally, on the third night after the killing charges, under a blanket of darkness, Grant led his men out of their trenches south across the Chickahominy River. By pretending to head for Richmond, Grant outwitted Lee, and forced him to move the bulk of his men to the outskirts of the capital. While Lee busily fortified the city, Grant shifted south again, bypassing Richmond and heading for the James River. He objective was to take Petersburg to the capital's south, choking off Richmond's supplies. There, six weeks after the bloody battle in the Wilderness began, unable to breach the defenses of General Beauregard around the city, Grant settled in at City Point on the James River for a long siege of Petersburg.

Now Grant's headquarters, the small town of City Point quickly transformed itself into a bustling Union seaport. Commerce sprang up—barracks for the troops, commissaries, a vast hospital of tents, rows of warehouses, bakeries and stores, docks along the river, and a new railroad spur to move troops and supplies. In contrast, Confederate forces and civilians suffered mightily from a lack of supplies and a strangled transportation system.

The brutal Wilderness Campaign exhausted the troops beyond endurance. At City Point the forces of the North began to rotate short leaves. A great rush started to go home to families, to see loved ones, however briefly, or just to rest in their quarters with blessed nothing to do. Major Allen Lee Rockwell, too, requested a leave although he gave no indication where he would go.

Through it all, secret intelligence from Mary Bowser at the Jefferson Davis house miraculously made its way into the lion's belly in the great Van Lew library where Elizabeth found it, converted it to code, and sent it on its perilous journey to General Butler on the peninsula. Letters were sent by mail under the flag of truce or by courier. Larger packets went to the Van Lew farm south of the city, which served as the first drop-off point. From there the secrets crept from one drop point to another.

Back came messages from her "uncle" with questions and instructions of various kinds. To her great surprise, one letter asked that she deliver an enclosed envelope addressed to Philip Cashmeyer. After a short stay in prison and a rebuke for his "indiscretion," the detective had returned to Winder's office, where the general was shortly informed of his impending transfer. Knowing no other way to contact the man, she anxiously made her way to the former office of General Winder, now departed.

There she met a surprised Cashmeyer.

"Miss Van Lew, you know General Winder is gone," he said.

Looking about to be sure they were alone, Elizabeth pulled out the letter. "I have a message for you."

An anxious look passed over Cashmeyer's face as he opened the envelope. After reading the contents, he turned deadly pale and quickly stuffed the letter deep into his pocket. Taking her elbow, he edged her toward the door.

"Please," he whispered, "you must be prudent. Do not come again. I'll come to you."

Two days later, after darkness had fallen, Cashmeyer appeared at the Van Lew mansion.

"The letter you brought me," he said to Elizabeth, "was from General Butler. I've worked with him for some time."

"You been working with General Butler?" she repeated, surprised.

"He has asked me to join the Richmond Union underground."

Elizabeth's face brightened.

"He feels I'd be more effective working with you instead of doing what I do alone," Cashmeyer continued. "He's right and I'd very much like to join the network."

"That's wonderful news," Elizabeth exclaimed.

"However," he quickly added. "I'll be following General Winder to his new assignment. I only remained behind to tie up loose ends."

A look of disappointment spread over Elizabeth's face. "You're leaving?"

"I can do the most good there, on the inside. Besides, I'm attached to the old man. He's a decent sort. We knew each other in Baltimore. He never supported secession, but when it seemed that Maryland would secede, he could not bear the thought of fighting against his sons, friends, and neighbors. The decision was agonizing for him."

"I'm not surprised to hear that," Elizabeth said, reflecting on her experiences with Winder. "He's been good to our family."

"I'm sorry not to have connected with you before. I wanted to." Cashmeyer smiled and shook his head. "But you are a slippery one. I suspected. I tried to find out. But I never knew for sure if you were really involved."

Elizabeth laughed at his admission. "All those times I met you . . . I felt you suspected, that you knew and were building a case against me. You frightened me," she gently rebuked him.

"On the contrary! I wanted to join you. It was I who was afraid to approach you openly for fear I was wrong and *you* would turn me in." He broke into a laugh. "You are too good at your deceptions." He looked at her. "And now you have another secret to keep."

So Elizabeth and Richmond's Union underground lost Philip Cashmeyer as soon as they found him.

———

In mid-June, more than a month after her brother left home, Elizabeth received word that she was needed at their farm.

"A gentleman at da farm to see you, Miz Lizzie," Peter said.

"At the farm? Who is it, Peter?" she asked uneasily.

He shrugged. "He don't say. But he says it be important."

Puzzled and a bit anxious, she set out on the mule-drawn farm wagon with Peter. As they rode haltingly through Richmond, army carts rumbled through the streets, clogging roads and making a great racket. Weary troops stumbled along and ambulances carried the endless wounded to hospitals and private homes. Beggars stood on street corners and women searched for food in nearly empty shops. The once-spotless roadways were littered and dirty and everywhere a gloom hung under the brilliant summer sun.

Elizabeth's apprehension grew as she approached the family farmhouse about a quarter mile south of the city limits along the Osborne Turnpike. Was it a trap? No one ever called at the farm . . . Peter pulled the wagon to the front of the house. No sign of movement anywhere. Nervously Elizabeth dismounted the wagon and moved to the front door. As she reached for the handle, it swung open.

"Allen!" she gasped in disbelief, clutching her chest.

Rockwell pulled her into the dim room and, glancing quickly down the open road, shut the door. Without a word, he drew her to him and embraced her tightly, pushing back the tears.

"Allen," Elizabeth repeated, her voice shaking. "But how?"

Still Rockwell could not speak. Overcome with emotion, he clung to her, as the unspeakable horrors of the past weeks slowly drained away and he tried to comprehend that she really was there in his arms.

Elizabeth looked deeply into his eyes. She sensed something different, something dreadful lingering there in the dark channels of his mind. "What is it, dear Allen?" she asked softly touching his cheek. "What has happened?" Her blue eyes searched his in the silence. Then, taking his hand and pulling him gently into the parlor, she whispered, "Come, sit with me."

"I have a very short leave," he said at last. "I can't stay long. But I had to see you."

"But how did you get here? There are Confederate troops everywhere."

"I remembered you telling me about your farm on the James River— your descriptions, where you said it was located. I thought it best not to try to get into Richmond." A slight smile moved across his face. For the first time she noticed that he wore civilian clothes. "We're camped at City Point on the James, so I followed the river upstream the whole way. We hold some of the area on the east side of the river between here and City Point now. I got help from a farmer and then some Negroes working in the fields."

Elizabeth held both his hands tightly. "I can't believe it. I've been so worried about you. When your letters stopped, I . . ." She paused, hesitant to ask. "The Wilderness. Were you there?"

His head and shoulders dropped and the calamity of the fighting swept over him again. "Yes, and Spotsylvania . . . Cold Harbor was the worst." The grayness of killing had crawled under his skin and through his body, settling in the phantoms behind his eyes. "War is madness, Elizabeth, madness on both sides."

Sensing his deep anguish, Elizabeth gently kissed his cheek and stroked his hair. "But you are here now. And you're safe." The questions tumbled out. "How long can you stay? Have you eaten? Are you well?"

Her intensity brought another smile to his face. "I'm well now that I see you." Then his face darkened again. "Dear Elizabeth, I cannot stay. It's a very short leave, but I had to see you. I came much of the way on foot and it took me longer than expected. I'll have to make my way back today." Then, seeing her stricken face, "We have a bit of time."

Tearfully they hugged again, embracing each other tightly, kissing passionately, touching, whispering words of love. After a few moments, Elizabeth stopped, pulled back a bit, looked into his eyes. Her fingers gently stroked his forehead, then slid from his cheek to his shoulder. She rose and walked to the parlor entrance. Closing the sliding wooden doors, she shut out the world. Slowly she began to unbutton her dress as Allen showered her with kisses and stroked her back, her neck, her breasts. Looking into her blue eyes, he felt himself buoyed by an ocean wave, weightless, suspended. Elizabeth felt Allen's heart beating in her chest.

Time stopped for them as the lovers eagerly buried themselves in each other. In their boundless fervor, they clung intensely as one.

At last, their overpowering emotions spent, they gathered themselves, dressed, and embraced again.

"I love you, dearest Elizabeth."

"And I love you . . ."

A somber look crept across his face. "Tell me, Elizabeth, have you been well? Are you still reckless with your own safety?" He gently chided her. "I think of you always, and I worry. Your letters have meant so much to me."

"I do what I must, Allen, just as you do." Then she added casually, almost as an afterthought, "I have been contacted by Colonel George Sharpe."

"Sharpe?" Rockwell interrupted, immediately sensing the importance of the name. He knew Sharpe to be Chief of Intelligence for the Army of the Potomac.

"He contacted me on behalf of General Grant," Elizabeth continued.

An apprehension began to creep over Rockwell. This was not chicken soup for prisoners. But before he could speak, Elizabeth tried to reassure him. "I take every precaution, Allen. It is *you* on the battlefield. I just send scraps of information."

Rockwell shook his head. "Scraps of information?" he repeated incredulously.

Elizabeth smiled. "Yes, scraps of information."

A grin moved over his lips. "Scraps . . ."

Suddenly they broke into laughter and a flood of hilarity swept over them. They laughed away the pain of separation, of fear, of death. The pent-up stress that had imprisoned them for so long poured into the room. Having forgotten how to laugh, they rediscovered it with a vengeance.

When the laughter had spent itself, they sat, holding hands, sharing their joy at being together and their fears of separation, talking of different things. But Rockwell did not, could not, talk of the fighting.

At long last Allen sighed, "I must be leaving, dear Elizabeth, though I cannot bear to."

Elizabeth nodded weakly and gently touched his cheek. "We'll be together soon. The end of war is near," she bravely added, though the years had taught her otherwise.

Then she quickly packed what food she had at the farmhouse, food the workers ate, corn bread and vegetables. She called Peter from the place where he had gone to join the other field hands and quickly explained what needed to be done. He immediately got the wagon ready, loading a deep layer of straw in its bed, and brought it to the back of the house.

"Peter will hide you in the farm wagon under some straw," she told Rockwell. "He'll get you through the Confederate lines at this end."

When he started to protest, Elizabeth put her fingers to his lips. "It's what we do, often—for others. There is such a desperate need for food in Richmond that the farm wagons move quite freely. But you must be careful," she said urgently. "The area changes hands frequently."

"And you?" he whispered.

"I'll wait for Peter to get back."

"It seems we are always saying goodbye . . ." he said hesitantly.

Tears welled in her eyes and she choked back a sob. They clung to each other desperately. They kissed, their passion born of love and fear and an unknown future. Finally, without words, he moved away slowly, still holding her hand until he had to let go. She watched as his shadow disappeared onto the wagon behind a shimmering film of tears, her hand touching the gold ring strung around her neck. Her eyes never left the road as the wagon jerked over the rocky dirt surface, vanishing beyond a stand of trees around a bend.

Back in the house Elizabeth threw herself on the sofa where they had lain together not long before and sobbed uncontrollably in joy and sorrow.

CHAPTER 10

As MAJOR ALLEN LEE ROCKWELL CROUCHED WITH HIS HOLLOW-eyed comrades in the trenches around Petersburg, he scrawled a letter to Elizabeth:

> *Words cannot describe the horrors of battle dwelling in the tattered spirits of those of us who crossed the Rapidan and clawed our way through the Wilderness, Spotsylvania, and Cold Harbor. Only the images can be spoken of. The wild chaos of battle charges. The terror of facing the bayonet. The regimental flags flying to sanction the bedlam. Battle cries substituting for courage. Officers yelling commands inaudible over the pandemonium. The crashing of hundreds of cannon blasts. The piercing noise of thousands of muskets firing. Shrieks of pain from wounded men. Unanswered cries for help. The choking smell of gunpowder. The tortured faces of the enemy—his, mine, friends in another day. Exploding bodies. Blood, everywhere blood. Charging over dead bodies. The ground trembling under our feet. Chasms torn open in the earth. Trees charred, mangled, toppled. The stench of death. Clouds of gunpowder smoke swooping over the madness. An angry God throwing piercing rays of fire from the sky.*
>
> *I could not speak of these things when we met, dear Elizabeth. Now I must speak of them if we are to spend a life together. I am changed, Elizabeth, lost, really, and I struggle to find my way back from this abyss of brutality.*

You alone, dear Elizabeth, stand apart from this terrible void. I pray you can love me still.

> *Yours forever,*
> *Allen*
> *29 July, 1864*

⌒

For weeks, a group of coal miners from a Pennsylvania regiment burrowed under the ground. Little by little a tunnel made its way through the earth. The miners dug at an angle toward Elliot's Salient until they reached a depth of thirty feet. The brainchild of General Ambrose Burnside, the dig's purpose was to bomb an opening through Confederate defenses, thereby allowing Union troops to storm the city and take Petersburg. The six-foot-tall, handsome figure with his muttonchop whiskers took personal charge of the digging, poking about, inspecting, instructing the men. As the long hole in the ground advanced, the men placed wooden girders to shore up the passageway. An anomaly in the midst of the siege of Petersburg, the excavation became the talk of the trenches and the brunt of jokes among the men.

While the workers dug, Burnside prepared an inexperienced division for frontline duty, two all-Negro brigades. Blacks, viewed as unsuited for combat, were generally kept away from battle. Burnside believed they were suited, so he set about rigorously training the fresh and enthusiastic men to lead the assault, despite grumblings among some of the men that they would never follow Negroes into battle.

At last the five-hundred-foot tunnel reached its destination. Burnside ordered four tons of gunpowder packed into the breach.

The afternoon before the planned blast, a courier arrived with an order from General Meade at headquarters and approved by Grant: The planned assault must be led by white troops, not the Negro brigades. Fearing public censure from Abolitionists for putting Negroes in the most dangerous positions if anything went wrong, Meade was adamant. Greatly dismayed that his well-rehearsed troops would not lead the charge, Burnside drew lots to pick which division would undertake the frontline duty. His black troops now would bring up the rear.

In the predawn morning of July 30, the troops left their trenches to move forward. Pitch darkness covered the landscape. Unable to see, Rockwell, along with the others, groped his way over the unfamiliar rocky ground, inching slowly forward. When the signal was given and the fuse lit, they waited anxiously. Nothing happened. The engineer in charge hurried into the breach, lantern in hand, to repair a splice as the men fretfully lay in the dark.

Not until the first light of dawn broke across the hot summer sky, did the explosion go off. As a gigantic rumbling and cracking of the earth began, a massive explosion tossed the men about. A mountain of earth erupted above the blast, spewing rocks and earth in every direction. Flames carried a great mushroom cloud into the sky, fire below and smoke above. Lightning and thunder rose from the earth. Rocks, dirt, wooden joists, and body parts rained up to the sky.

From his position Rockwell stared in disbelief at the inferno. The end of the world has begun, he thought in the moment of the earth's first spasm.

Stunned Confederate troops who were not killed in the explosion fell back in a great wave on all sides. Terrified, soot covered, dazed, they staggered away, saving themselves and dragging their wounded comrades. Shouts and screams followed the thunderous eruption as the sun began its quiet ascent in a calm eastern sky.

After the thick black smoke drifted away, Union soldiers gaped in disbelief in the gray morning light. Rockwell could see an enormous crater in the scarred earth. It looked to be some 250 feet in length, about seventy feet wide, maybe ten feet deep at the beginning but becoming deeper still as it progressed. His head throbbing and his heart pounding, his stinging eyes frantically searched for signs of life in and around the disgorged earth but could see no movement.

After the initial shock Rockwell and the others waited anxiously, expecting immediate orders. But nothing happened. Not for five minutes, not for fifteen minutes, not for a half hour. The nervous minutes passed through an endless pause. What madness is this, Rockwell agonized as they waited. To what end have we torn up the earth and killed so many? Surely the enemy is regrouping as we wait.

Not until a full hour had passed did anything take place, and the Union offensive begin. Their commander, General James Ledlie, chosen at the last minute by lot, finally gave the order for his division to line up for the attack. He sent the order through his second-in-command while he retreated to his bunker, where he settled himself in a comfortable chair and hastened to open a bottle of rum—for the purpose of wishing his men Godspeed.

The first division to charge included Rockwell's regiment. As the great mass of men fell into line for the attack they stood before the massive pit. Ahead of them lay the prize, Petersburg. Some twenty miles south of the capital, with its four rail lines and supply depots, it was indispensable to Richmond's survival. Take Petersburg and the Confederate capital falls. The daily shelling of the city by Union troops had failed to bring Petersburg to its knees, but here was Burnside's masterstroke.

Finally the order came to move out. To Rockwell's great dismay the men were commanded to proceed toward Petersburg through the crater. He could not comprehend the order. Not *around* the gorge, but *into* the gorge? He stared in disbelief and alarm as men began to descend into the chasm. So I am to die without seeing Elizabeth again after all, he thought with despair.

As they moved forward over the broken earth a ghastly sight met them. Corpses lay strewn across the bottom of the pit. So many bodies covered the floor it was almost impossible to move without stepping on them. Onward they advanced, grim faces moving slowly across the chasm in a trancelike, shocked state. Averting their eyes as best they could from the gruesome sight at their feet, the men stared forward across the gutted, littered landscape.

We are like stupid sheep moving to a slaughter, Rockwell thought in a flash.

They walked so closely together that Rockwell could hear the heavy breathing of men beside and behind him. All around soldiers carried their muskets, bayonets drawn, all miserable, surrounded by macabre sights, awaiting yet another catastrophe. His brain chewed relentlessly on the sights and sounds of war. The Bible speaks of Judgment Day as an apocalypse with unimaginable suffering. But why do we talk of the apocalypse as something in the future, thought Rockwell bitterly, when life is full of them. His mind rushed over the past and he particularly regretted that his last letter to Elizabeth was one of such despair. Was it not enough that desolation had colonized *his* life? Why had he put this burden on her, he agonized?

A growing unease gripped the thousands of men moving through the gorge as its sides rose higher and higher and they descended deeper and deeper into the immense pit. Looking here and there, searching for some unknown, they huddled together as their march slowed and the claustrophobic walls pressed closer and closer. By the time they reached the Confederate line even the façade of order had disappeared. Dazed and bewildered they milled about helplessly. How were they to scale the steep sides of the crater?

Suddenly, from the top of the precipice, Confederate muskets began spraying the open pit with rifle fire. In the bedlam the trapped soldiers thrashed about searching for cover where none existed. Frantically they returned fire at the hidden enemy above, often cutting their closely packed comrades with their bayonets as they wildly swung their rifles in the chaos of firing. Union bullets sliced the air while rebel bullets hit their mark. Many were trampled as the men lunged backward trying to escape in the direction they had come. All around him Rockwell saw his comrades stagger and fall. Shrieks and moans echoed across the chasm, mixing with the thunder of musket fire.

Meanwhile, eager to prove themselves, men from the Negro brigades in the rear pushed forward against those lurching backwards to safety. From the sky, a blazing sun watched as hundreds of black men rushed forward, pushing open passageways among their tightly packed white comrades moving away from the fighting. In the melee and confusion many Negroes reached the front unaware of the slaughter awaiting them.

Rockwell spotted the blood from his shoulder soaking his sleeve, spreading in ripples across the cloth, before he felt a stinging ache that rapidly worsened. His head pounded, a searing pain shot down his arm and across his chest, the canyon walls spun around and around, his knees buckled under him. He grabbed at the arm of the man next to him as he plunged to the ground, his comrade's bayonet nicking his leg, his head crashing against a sharp rock.

＊

The sun rose high overhead before some survivors began waving a piece of white clothing tied to a bayonet. When Confederate officers saw the flag of surrender through the smoke, they ordered the firing stopped. As the haze of gunfire lifted, rebel troops stared in disbelief at the carnage below, a mass grave for Union soldiers living and dead in a burial chamber of Union design.

Slowly the survivors struggled out of the pit at gunpoint. Many in the rear lines had managed to fall back through the chasm and save themselves, but over a thousand men lay dead on the gutted earth. Thousands more suffered from injuries. Those wounded who could not move were gathered up and hauled out of the massive hole in the ground.

Dazed, his mind reeling, Rockwell became vaguely aware that two men were dragging him out of the pit. As he labored to focus on the ground moving beneath him, shouts began to mount at the top of the chasm walls. The words erupted in a fiendish nightmare.

"Take the white men. Kill the niggers! Kill the niggers." The words rose in a chant. "Kill the niggers! Kill the niggers!"

At the top, before he lost consciousness, Rockwell saw through the dirty, stinging sweat pouring over his eyes that Confederate troops were bayoneting and clubbing to death his black comrades. He tried to cry out, to scream "Stop," but no words came. The horrible shouts and the hideous scene turned gray and slowly faded until silence and blackness enveloped him.

When Rockwell at last opened his eyes, a great expanse of brilliant blue spread before him. A vague memory of eyes exactly like this color blue flashed into his mind, but he could not place them in a face. He became aware that his whole body shook and bounced. His shoulder ached terribly and a sharp throbbing rattled his brain. When he turned his head he saw that he lay in a clattering, lurching wagon packed with men dressed in uniforms, many of them covered with blood, some of them moaning. One of them, a tattered young man, not much more than a boy really, sat beside him, saying something he could not understand and pressing a bloody rag into his stinging shoulder.

Slowly the words took form. "Major, can you hear me? You've lost a lot of blood."

Rockwell tried to speak, but the words came only with the greatest effort. "What . . ."

"We've been captured, sir. They are taking us to Richmond."

Richmond. Another memory stirred in some deep recess of his being where connecting threads had broken and struggled to come together again. Richmond. The word echoed in his mind. Richmond. A question, not a word.

⸻

As the processional of captured Union troops, many walking, some in wagons, slogged north toward the Confederate capital, General Grant stood before the great chasm surveying the calamity. His fury lay buried deep inside.

"This is the saddest affair I have ever witnessed in the war," he thought to himself as he pondered the human cost, lost opportunity, and gross incompetence. He knew as sure as he knew anything that the press and his countrymen in the North would blame him and would call him "butcher" as they always did when things when badly in this war. By evening he had dismissed the commander in charge of the fiasco, General Ledlie, and he put General Burnside on permanent leave.

The siege of Petersburg continued. Not an inch of ground had been gained.

At Union headquarters that same day, a short distance from the great dig, the machine of war ground on, impervious to life and death, suffering and grief. The City Point postal workers sorted the mail as they always did and sent it on its way, including a letter addressed to one Elizabeth Van Lew of Grace Street, Richmond, Virginia.

⸻

Major Rockwell lay on the bare wooden floor in Libby Prison, in pain and struggling to remember. Stone walls surrounded the great chamber on all sides, rough hewn beams covered the ceiling, and small barred windows without glass panes lined one wall. In the dim light emaciated men milled about in the tightly packed room, stepping over those on the floor. Foul smells and moldy air made it hard to breathe. His shoulder, his head, his back ached. An intense thirst raged in his dry mouth. Through the fog of pain, Rockwell became vaguely aware that two men sat at his side, one the young man who helped him in the wagon, the other he did not recognize. The older man was carefully propping a rolled, threadbare jacket under his throbbing head.

"How are you feeling, Major?" the man asked kindly.

Rockwell strained to say the word. "Water . . ."

The young man quickly raised a tin cup to the wounded man's cracked lips. "You've been in and out of consciousness, sir. You couldn't drink anything," he said almost apologetically as the thirsting man sipped the tepid water.

"What is this place?" the wounded man asked feebly.

"We are in Libby Prison, sir. They brought us here after the battle."

Rockwell's mind tossed and turned trying to comprehend. Libby Prison? Battle?

The older man bent over and looked closely at him. He saw more than the bullet wound to the shoulder and the gash on his head.

"This is Colonel Thomas Rose, sir," the young man volunteered.

"At your service, Major," Rose said. Then, looking into the wounded man's eyes, he asked, "And your name?"

Rockwell thrashed about desperately in his consciousness. His name? The frantic flaying continued, but his rambling thoughts had no place to dismount. His face blanched. His eyes grew wild. A realization more terrible than the pain seeped through his body and began to suffocate him, catching his breath, pulling it from his chest. *He did not know his name.* He did not know anything about a battle. He did not know why he was in prison. Who were all these people?

"Major Rockwell, sir," the young man said anxiously. "Are you alright, sir?"

Rockwell. The word sounded foreign. Rockwell.

Colonel Rose touched him arm gently. "You've had a bad blow to your head, Major. You're having trouble remembering. It should pass," he said reassuringly, his voice calm and soothing. "Don't alarm yourself. You need to rest and try to eat a bit." He nodded to the young man who offered bits of corn bread that the ailing man could not eat.

He turned and said something to the men nearby. In a few moments someone passed Rose a blanket, though people did not seem to have blankets. He spread it over Rockwell who had started shivering wildly despite the summer heat.

When at last Rockwell fell asleep, Rose asked the young man what he knew about him.

"I am in Major Rockwell's regiment, sir. I don't know him well, but he's a kind man, always looking after the men." Then he smiled. "He is always writing letters. The day before the explosion, we were in the trenches and he was writing even there. I suspect he's writing to his wife, or maybe a lady friend, since he writes so often."

"His family should be notified," Rose said.

"It's strange," the young man continued. "I saw an envelope one day and it was addressed to someone in Richmond. But he's from New York."

Rose started. "Richmond? Perhaps we should look in his pockets. There may be a family address."

He began reaching into Rockwell's pockets, moving slowly so as not to disturb the exhausted man. In the blood-soaked chest pocket of Rockwell's jacket he felt something small and round. Carefully pulling it out, he saw a fine lady's brooch. Scraping away the dried blood, Rose opened the brooch and stared at the woman's attractive face, a mass of curls tumbling over her forehead. The unfamiliar image stared back at him and gave no sign that on that fateful night of the great escape, he had been denied refuge at her home.

Closing the brooch and replacing it in Rockwell's pocket, Rose continued to search. He pulled out a piece of paper folded into a small rectangle, weathered and torn from multiple readings and endless fingerings. The ink on the paper had smudged and run and he could not decipher much of it. But he saw it for what it was. A love letter brimming with the most intense feelings. Embarrassed to be reading something so private, his eyes swept down the page to the signature. *Yours, Elizabeth*.

Replacing the letter he turned to the young man, "That's it. No address, I'm afraid. Is there no one else in your regiment here who might know of his family?" he asked.

The young man nodded sadly.

When Erasmus Ross appeared a little later to take roll, Colonel Rose waited until he finished canvassing the able-bodied standing at attention and the unwell spread along the cell walls. Then he approached the hated Confederate.

"Sir, that wounded man is badly hurt." He pointed to Rockwell sprawled on the floor.

"I've counted him," Ross answered sharply.

"Yes, but he needs to be down in the infirmary."

"The infirmary is crowded," the clerk interrupted.

"But perhaps he could lie on the floor there. At least a doctor would see him," Rose persisted.

"Not much good that would do. There are no medicines," Ross said impatiently.

"Maybe the doctor could do something. Clean the wound or at least . . ."

But before he finished, Erasmus Ross turned away and strode out of the room without another word, slamming the door behind him. Colonel Rose swore and cursed the man under his breath.

Within minutes, to Rose's great surprise, two guards appeared carrying a stretcher. Motioning the men aside they went directly to Rockwell. The wounded man appeared dazed and bewildered.

As the guards loaded him onto the stretcher, Rose leaned in and whispered, "It'll be better now. A doctor will look after you. Get well."

At the door of the first floor infirmary, Erasmus Ross signaled the guards to put the stretcher down. He began searching the man for weapons or contraband before admitting him to the hospital, as protocol dictated. His hand felt something hard in the chest pocket and he pulled out the brooch. Casually, almost without thinking, Ross flipped open the piece of jewelry.

To his great shock, there, from the brooch, Elizabeth Van Lew stared out at him, the familiar curls bouncing on her forehead, her refined features framed by gold. But how? Had this man stolen the brooch? Had Elizabeth given it to him? He continued rummaging in the man's pockets and pulled out the letter. He immediately recognized Elizabeth's handwriting and her signature. Sensing the danger to Elizabeth of anyone finding these things on a Union soldier, he quickly slipped both objects into his own pocket and motioned the guards to carry the dazed officer into the infirmary.

That evening Erasmus Ross cautiously made his way to the Van Lew mansion, questions spinning in his mind. Oliver, the butler, answered the door and showed Ross to the parlor where Elizabeth, her mother, and her nieces sat.

"Erasmus," Elizabeth said rising. "What a surprise."

Ross greeted everyone and nervously sat down. Annie and little Eliza began chattering with him but soon a strained silence filled the room. Sensing his unwillingness to talk with the girls present, Elizabeth suggested that Eliza get the children ready for bed. After strong protests from the girls, Eliza shepherded them out of the room.

"What is it, Erasmus?" Elizabeth asked.

"I'm not sure what this means," Ross said hesitantly. He dug into his pocket and pulled out the brooch and folded letter.

Elizabeth sank into a chair when she saw what he had. Her voice failed and she turned pale. She could not bring herself to take the objects. Her head swirled madly as she imagined the worst while trying to push it back, back. Ross stared anxiously as she sat speechless.

At last she asked feebly, her voice barely audible, "Where did you find these?"

"I found them on a prisoner, Elizabeth. A very tall man, middle-aged. Union officer. A major . . ."

Elizabeth gasped. She struggled to take it in. Allen, a prisoner again? "But he is at City Point . . ." She reached out her hand to take the objects and clutched them to her breast.

"Then you know him?"

Elizabeth nodded weakly.

"There's more I'm afraid." She was still grappling with the fact that Allen had been taken prisoner when she heard Erasmus say, "He's wounded . . . badly. I'm so sorry, Elizabeth."

Elizabeth felt dizzy and faint. "I must go to him." She began to rise, but Ross quickly stopped her and gently coaxed her back into the chair.

"He's at Libby."

Libby. The one prison where she had never been allowed access. Her heart sank.

"I must go to him, Erasmus," she repeated. "We are to be married."

Ross stood stunned. Married? He ran his fingers through his hair, his brow knit. He would do anything for this woman. "We'll find a way, Elizabeth," he tried to reassure her.

But his mind raced and churned trying to sort it out. So many people to get by. The doctor who came and went on his own timetable. The guards. Prison officials. The orderlies—though they were Union prisoners themselves. Slowly a plan began form in his mind. It would have to be at night when prison officials had retired. It would have to be after the doctor left—he only came once a day, if at all, and seldom at night. The guards he could deal with. The orderlies should be no problem. Church Hill was not far from Libby . . .

Elizabeth broke into his thoughts, pleading. "Tonight, Erasmus."

Ross's thoughts began spinning again. Tonight? The doctor had been there that day around noon . . .

"You and Peter. Come before midnight and wait at the back behind the trees and watch the door. When all is clear I'll signal him to bring you. I'll raise my hand over my head. It will have to be a very short visit. We can't risk . . ."

"Yes, yes, Erasmus. I can't thank you enough."

Before he left, Ross told her about the man who had called his attention to Rockwell. He asked if she knew him, Colonel Thomas Rose. Elizabeth's hand flew to her mouth as she stared in mute astonishment.

Colonel Rose! Then he had not made it to Union lines after all. Her mind flew back to that horrible night when Peter turned Rose away from her door, something she still blamed herself for. And now he had set in motion the means for her to know of Allen's imprisonment.

"I do know him, Erasmus . . ."

Around midnight Ross sent the orderlies upstairs. He told the guard outside the infirmary and those at that end of the prison to take a break. "I'll watch over things here. I can't sleep anyway."

He opened the prison door and stood in the moonlight. Slowly he raised his hand above his head. When he saw a shadow move across the street he closed the door and waited.

Before long he heard a soft tap on the door. Elizabeth slipped in when he opened it. He motioned her to follow him and they silently passed down a narrow corridor to the infirmary. When they entered Elizabeth's eyes frantically searched the large room with its cots lining both walls. The smells of illness hung in the air and low moans rose from some of the patients. Ross moved quickly down the row of beds, then stopped before a cot at the far end.

Elizabeth gasped when she saw Allen and a sob rose in her throat. She barely recognized him. The crusted gash on his head had not been fully cleaned but his bloody shirt was gone and a fresh one now covered his torso. His face was swollen on one side and blackish. She could see the thick bandages on his shoulder bulging under his shirt.

"I did the best I could for him," Erasmus whispered. "I'll watch by the door."

Tears streaming down her face, Elizabeth took Allen's hand. The sleeping man stirred slightly.

"Allen . . . Allen," she said softly, leaning down and kissing his battered face—his lips, his cheeks, his forehead. He felt hot to her touch and he seemed not to hear her. She shook him slightly and his eyelids opened for a moment. Their eyes met but he seemed not to recognize her and he had a terrible, vacant look. Then he closed his eyes again. Kneeling by his bed, she dropped her head on his chest as the tears flowed and she clung tightly to his hand. Erasmus was standing nervously over her again.

"We must go, Elizabeth. I'm sorry," he said apologetically.

"I must get him out of here, Erasmus," she said desperately, turning to her young friend. "He needs to be cared for."

Erasmus frowned and ran his fingers through his hair. "Nothing is possible right now. Let me see what I can do. But now you must leave. It's not safe." Taking her arm he gently lifted her from the cot. She bent and kissed Allen again and followed Ross to the door, turning one more time to look at Allen. He had not moved.

"Have Peter take you home," Ross whispered to the red-eyed woman as she left the prison. "Then have him return with the wagon, park around the corner across the street, and wait for my signal." He motioned to a point beyond where she had waited earlier.

<hr />

Erasmus Ross waited for an opportunity as the guards returned from break. With only a lone guard on duty outside the infirmary door, Ross saw his chance.

"Looks quiet tonight," he said casually to the guard.

The guard nodded and yawned. Ross strolled about the room, checking each cot in turn.

When he got to Rockwell's bed, the wounded man was still in a deep sleep. Ross thought he looked unconscious, so still was he. He waited a few minutes, then looking in all directions he pulled the blanket over Rockwell's face.

Walking back to the guard he spoke as indifferently as he could. "We've lost another one. Get a stretcher and help me get him out of here."

The guard thought nothing of it. Death had taken residence in the place. He rose, yawned again, and moved down the hall, returning shortly with a stretcher. Ross led him down the row of patients.

"That one?" the guard said. "Didn't spect he'd last long."

They placed the covered body on the stretcher and carried the corpse downstairs to the morgue.

"I'll see to the paperwork," Ross said. "I'm leaving soon."

The guard turned and walked back up to the infirmary. Immediately Ross unlocked the outside door nearest the morgue where no guard stood. The dim light from within outlined his shadow in the doorway. He raised his arm and walked back in, leaving the door a crack open. Within moments Peter slipped through the doorway. Without a word the two men quickly lifted Rockwell from the stretcher and carried him to the door.

"I got him, Mista Ross. Be easier." And he carefully slung the wounded man over his shoulder. Ross quickly locked the door and they slipped into the darkness where the farm wagon waited. Peter carefully placed Rockwell in the cart and both men covered him with straw. Almost two in the morning, the city had gone quiet and dark. Moving quickly through the shadowy streets, peering in all directions and nervously listening for sounds, they anxiously inched up Church Hill. At last they reached the mansion and pulled up to the back door. Peter lifted the heavy load as Ross held open the door.

Elizabeth waited apprehensively inside with Eliza. "Bring him up," she said, hurrying up the staircase in front of them. Frightened to see that he was not awake despite all the movement, she tried to compose herself. They placed Rockwell on Elizabeth's bed and tried to make him as comfortable as possible. Still he slept the sleep of the living dead.

When Erasmus Ross began to leave, Elizabeth could not find words to thank him. Instead she reached up and kissed him on the cheek.

Elizabeth stayed by Rockwell's side through the night as Eliza moved in and out of the room with basins of water and clean cloths. She brought soup that they tried to drip down his throat. His hot body trembled slightly now and then, but otherwise few signs of life appeared. Elizabeth swabbed his feverish brow and washed the gash on his head as best she could. The swelling on his face had gone down a bit, but it was still black and blue. She changed the bandage on his shoulder and shuddered to see the angry wound, red, swollen, burning. Using hot compresses she tried to ease the swelling.

While Elizabeth worried about Allen, Eliza fretted about Elizabeth. She saw the pain and despair in her daughter's face. By morning she offered to call a doctor.

"We can say he's a wounded Confederate soldier," she reassured Elizabeth.

When the doctor finally arrived around noon, Elizabeth was frantic with fear over Allen condition. Nothing had changed. The doctor frowned as he examined the patient. The wound had become badly infected and that was the source of the fever, he told them. It didn't help Elizabeth's state of mind that the doctor said more soldiers were dying from infection than from anything else. In the end he suggested little more than what they were already doing: try to bring the fever down with cold cloths on his head, neck, and chest, force liquids down his throat, keep the hot compresses on the shoulder wound. Before he left, he handed Elizabeth a bottle of thick, black syrup for the patient with the caution that she should not expect much.

Elizabeth sat by the bedside despondent for the rest of the day as she frantically tried to bring down the fever and calm the wound. She dripped water, broth, and the foul-smelling black syrup down his throat. When the servants offered several times to take over so she could sleep she refused. Annie and little Eliza crept into the room on and off throughout the day, asking questions about the strange man in her bed and trying to cheer their grieving aunt.

As Elizabeth cared for her fiancé, she spoke to him, kissed him, stroked his hair and cheeks. And cried. A number of times she saw him shiver or move slightly and a momentary hope leapt into her heart. Each time she thought he would wake, but he did not. When darkness crept through the windows of her bedroom, she urged Eliza to go to sleep, assuring her there was nothing more she could do.

In the flickering candlelight the second night, Elizabeth kept watch, her chair pulled up tightly against the bed, her hand holding Allen's. Outside a full moon crept across the sky, bathing the room in an eerie light and casting long shadows over the gloom. In the silence she could hear his breath rising and falling, rising and falling. Sometime after midnight she put her head down on his chest as it rose and fell with every inhalation, her tears dripping over the coverlet. She could feel his heart beating. A terrible fatigue and desolation suddenly came over her and she drifted to sleep, her eyes wet against his body and her hand holding his.

How long she lay there in her exhausted sleep she did not know. But at some point she became vaguely aware of a featherlike touch on her head and she seemed to be floating in a dream, somewhere between consciousness and unconsciousness. Fingers. Fingers wove through her mass of curls, brushing her scalp. They moved lightly like phantoms winding around her head, not real and real. She woke with a start and lifted her head.

In the candlelight she saw Allen looking at her, his eyes wide and searching. His hand rested on her head and his fingers stroked her hair.

"Allen," she whispered looking into his eyes. A sob caught in her throat when no answer came.

The fingers continued to weave gently through her hair and his eyes stared intently at her as though struggling to comprehend some mystery.

"Allen," she said again fearfully. "It's Elizabeth."

The fingers froze for a moment and his eyes narrowed in a flicker of recognition. But then it passed and his eyes kept searching.

A crushing thought enveloped Elizabeth. *He does not know me.* Almost without thinking she reached for the brooch on the bedside table and tenderly taking his hand from her hair, she placed it in his palm. His eyes darted to the object in his hand. A frantic look spread over his face. Gently she opened the brooch in his hand. He watched with an intensity she had never seen. Then his eyes moved from the brooch to her face, back to the brooch and to her face again as he strained to connect the two. At last his eyes locked onto hers. His knit brow began to loosen. A weak smile passed over his lips. His eyes lit up and he struggled to form the words.

"Elizabeth . . . My love . . ."

Overjoyed she threw her head down on his chest again, burying her face in him and sobbing his name, "Allen. Allen, you've come back to me." She lay there for a few moments hugging him tightly.

As she snuggled peacefully against his body in a moment of unimaginable joy, a sudden terror tore through her. She froze, unable to move. A horrible silence and stillness had descended on the room. Without stirring she strained to listen. His breathing no longer filled the silence. His heart no longer pounded in his chest.

Her anguished scream echoed through the mansion after him. "Come back . . ."

⁓

The sun blazed overhead. All around the mingled scent of roses and new mown grass filled the still air. Birds flew overhead and a blue jay chattered in one of the magnolia trees. A curious squirrel darted across the grass, pausing briefly to look at the small group gathered on his turf. The Reverend Philip Price prayed and prayed over the simple pine coffin, his words incomprehensible and endless. Even the death of Jefferson Davis would not bring forth a metal coffin these days, the undertaker had said.

To Elizabeth's right stood her mother, sick with worry for her daughter. On her left, Eliza Carrington grieved for her dear friend. Behind her a few friends lamented her ordeal. Inside, a hollowness filled her being as Elizabeth stood by the gravesite. The cauldron of feelings had given way to emptiness and she watched the cheerless scene before her as if in a dream. Had life become a parade of death and graves then? This endless, shameful war had given her Allen—and taken him away.

At last the praying stopped. The workers lowered the coffin into the ground. One by one those around her came to press her hand, kiss her cheek, and offer condolences again. Then, out of respect for her feelings, they all hung back, leaving her alone with Allen and her grief.

As Elizabeth stood staring at the box in its earthen tomb, a new misery poured into the corners of her emptiness, filling her with an unspeakable loneliness. Fighting back the stinging tears filling her eyes, she kissed the white rose in her hand and dropped it onto the pine coffin. At that moment a soft breeze rose from the perfectly still air, brushed her face, caught a wisp of her hair, and drifted upward in tiny waves.

Elizabeth turned from the family plot and, walking with a determined step, she joined her mother and Eliza at the gate of Shockhoe Cemetery. Together the three women silently made their way back to the Grace Street mansion.

Inside, on the table by the front door, sat a letter addressed to Elizabeth Van Lew from City Point, Virginia.

Chapter 11

News of the formal investigation against Elizabeth came from a friend.

Cyrena King, a member of Richmond's elite and longtime family friend, called at the mansion on a sunny fall day in September. When she appeared at the door unexpectedly, an instant premonition crept over Elizabeth. She didn't know why. After all, Cyrena had called many times before, although not as much since the start of the war.

For awhile they chatted about ordinary things over tea in the great parlor—family, the warm fall weather, the shortages of food, the inconvenience of moving about in the crowded streets . . . All the while a shiver wound its way through Elizabeth, touching nerves here and there, twisting around the recesses of her mind.

At last, setting down her teacup, Cyrena said, "I hesitate to distress you, Elizabeth." She shifted uncomfortably in her seat as she spoke and Elizabeth's shiver grew larger and more aggressive. Glancing at Eliza, she added, "And you, Eliza."

The two women waited.

"I had a visitor some days ago. Most unpleasant." Cyrena continued, "Thomas Doswell. You know him, of course."

"Yes," Eliza responded, her curiosity growing stronger. "He knows our family. He has visited here a number of times over the years. What is it, Cyrena?"

"He's been appointed to John Winder's post as Provost Marshal." They knew this. "He came to my house wanting me to testify against

Elizabeth." The shiver exploded in Elizabeth's chest. "I'm sorry to bring this bad news, but you need to know."

"Testify? Testify about what?" Eliza asked while her daughter sat dumbstruck.

"He's trying to build a case against Elizabeth."

"For what?" Eliza interrupted.

"Disloyalty." Cyrena looked at Elizabeth, pausing.

Elizabeth did not move or betray the emotions swirling within. "Tell me exactly what happened, Cyrena," she said, trying hard to stay calm.

"Doswell came to my house. He told me they've begun a formal investigation of you on the charge of disloyalty to the Confederacy. He asked me to do my duty and give testimony against you. I told him the charge was absurd and I could not help him. He tried to get me to change my mind and when I would not, he left," she recounted, as an ashen Eliza listened in obvious distress.

"I thank you for your loyalty, Cyrena," Elizabeth said, looking closely at her friend.

"I know you're not happy about secession and the war, Elizabeth, but disloyalty . . . And to have a family friend initiate this charge." She hesitated again. "There's more. I received a summons the next day to appear before Doswell. A Detective New came to my house to deliver the summons."

Cyrena opened her purse and pulled out an envelope. "This is it."

She handed the envelope to Elizabeth as her stricken mother watched. The paper read: *Miss King. Captain T. W. Doswell requests that you come to Commissioner Sand's Office on Tenth St. between Broad and Capitol to give testimony against Miss Elizabeth Van Lew on the charge of disloyalty to the Confederacy.* A hammer began to pound in Elizabeth's head. She refolded the paper, put it back in the envelope and handed it to Cyrena.

"When Detective New gave me the summons he assured me you would never know of my testimony and that you would not be present. I had to go with the detective as ordered. They asked me so many questions." Then she quickly added, "I told them nothing, of course. There is nothing to tell. I tried to make them understand. But Doswell insinuated I lied and kept asking me to 'remember' and do my duty."

"You're a good friend, Cyrena," Eliza said.

"I am furious that this is happening without you knowing, Elizabeth, or without a chance to defend yourself."

"I'm indebted to you, Cyrena," Elizabeth responded, suddenly feeling very drained.

"They summoned Reverend Philip Price too. He was brought in the same day and I met him when I left Doswell. I've spoken with him since. I don't know exactly what he said, but he assures me he defended you. Doswell interrogated Price for a long time and kept insisting he 'refresh his memory.'"

"Reverend Price is a close friend of the family. Who else has Doswell tried to intimidate?" Eliza asked.

"I don't know," Cyrena responded, "but I suspect there are more."

After she left, Eliza and Elizabeth sat silently for a long time.

"You need to leave, Bet. Follow John to Philadelphia." Eliza said finally, her voice shaking.

Elizabeth recoiled in disbelief at the suggestion. "Leave?"

"This time they'll make it stick, Bet. You can't risk it anymore—prison, hanging . . . I can't let you do this." Eliza fought back the sobs rushing to her throat.

Elizabeth rose quickly and went to her mother's side. Taking her hand, she spoke soothingly. "I can't let them drive me from my home. I can't agree with them that I'm guilty. I *am* loyal to my country. *They* are the disloyal ones." She stroked her mother's hair as she repeated the familiar mantra. To herself she thought with a searing heart, "The Confederacy has taken my Allen. There is not much more they can do to me."

"I couldn't bear it if anything happened to you," Eliza whispered.

"I know," Elizabeth replied. "This reign of terror will end soon. It must. We need to be strong."

As she spoke the sounds of laughter and running feet came from the hallway. Annie and little Eliza burst into the room. "Is the lady gone, Aunt Lizzie?"

"Yes, Cyrena has left." Elizabeth extended her arms to the girls.

"Then can you play with us now?" Giggling, the girls threw themselves on their aunt and grandmother.

"Of course, Annie." Elizabeth smiled. "Let's play. Let's all play . . ."

———

Across town, unknown to the Van Lews, Captain Doswell's investigation snared an important witness, someone more than willing to give testimony against Elizabeth. The interrogator had gotten nowhere with Cyrena King and Philip Price, but he struck fertile ground with Mary Van Lew.

On being summoned to the interrogation, Mary Van Lew appeared gladly. Captain Doswell asked the questions while Commissioner Alexander Sands listened. An assistant took down her statement as she spoke. In a sworn deposition, Elizabeth's estranged sister-in-law, mother of Annie and little Eliza, told Doswell and Sands everything they wanted to know.

"How well do you know Elizabeth Van Lew?" Doswell asked Mary, knowing well the answer.

"She is my sister-in-law. I know her as well as anyone," Mary responded. "I lived with her and Eliza for years at the Grace Street mansion."

"Then you know her sentiments about the Confederacy well?"

"Of course. She despises the Confederacy and wishes it to fail."

Doswell's head lifted, his eyes narrowed and his brow knit. "In what way does she wish it to 'fail,' as you say?"

"Elizabeth has always been against secession and in favor of the Union. She wants a Federal victory against the South." Then, to emphasize the point, Mary added, "She wants the Confederacy to lose the war."

"Has Elizabeth Van Lew acted on her anti-Confederacy views?" Doswell queried.

"Many times! She has given aid and comfort to the enemy. Why, she brought a Union prisoner into our home and cared for him before he died. I would have none of it and left the house. She also brought food and all kinds of goods to prisoners. I can barely begin to tell you all the things she did for the enemy in prison. And she refused to sew clothes for Confederate soldiers as other Southern ladies did."

"As you no doubt did," the Captain smiled, scrutinizing Mary.

"I had small children to care for and could not. She *would* not."

"Who are the people she consorts with?"

"Most of her friends are pro-Union. When I lived there, they were always coming to the house and speaking against the Confederacy. It upset me greatly," Mary said, stopping and lifting her handkerchief to her lips.

Doswell persisted. "Please, go on."

"She's an abolitionist!" Mary answered indignantly. "She's against slavery and our whole way of life. Elizabeth even sent one of her Negro women north to be educated. Can you imagine?" She looked at Doswell and continued speaking with a harsher edge to her voice. "John Van Lew, her brother, has gone north to support the Union." She hesitated. "I'm sure you know him to be a deserter from the Confederate Army."

"Yes, but our concern here is Elizabeth Van Lew," Doswell said. "Do you have firsthand knowledge that she helped him desert?"

"I can only guess that she did," Mary answered. Then pausing and shifting in her seat, she asked Doswell and Sands, "What will become of my children should Elizabeth be imprisoned or exiled? I do not want them sent away."

"The courts will determine that, Mrs. Van Lew. I'm sure they will look favorably on your wishes because of your cooperation." Then, looking straight at her, Doswell said, "I must ask something unpleasant. I do apologize. But we must be sure that no one thinks you are giving testimony for personal gain."

Mary looked at him indignantly. "Whatever do you mean?"

"Are you willing to renounce all claims to the Van Lew estate, and put that in writing?"

"I can assure you my family has no need of Van Lew money!" Mary responded, annoyed. "The suggestion is absurd. I do this out of loyalty to the Confederacy."

"Of course, of course, Mrs. Van Lew. I was obligated to . . ."

"I'll sign a statement renouncing any claim to the estate. Will that suffice?" Mary added tersely.

"Most definitely," Doswell quickly replied. "You have been most helpful."

After she signed the deposition, Doswell and Commissioner Sands, who had listened silently throughout the interrogation, bowed as Mary Van Lew left the room.

While authorities sought to build a case against Elizabeth for disloyalty, the crouching lion in her library seldom rested. The beast regularly gobbled up and spit out vital Confederate secrets. Elizabeth's sources, especially Mary Bowser at the Jefferson Davis home, fed the lion a steady stream of intelligence: military plans; Confederate troop strength; troop locations; the mining of roads leading into Richmond; conditions in the city; shortages of materials; what was happening to Union prisoners, most of whom remained despite earlier plans to move them south. But the lion's burdens were nothing compared to Elizabeth's.

Though emotionally battered by the death of Allen and frightened by the secret investigation against her, Elizabeth continued her espionage, collecting intelligence, evaluating it, writing reports, and ensuring it reached General Grant. She took the information that appeared mysteriously from the lion, processed it, and encrypted her reports using invisible ink. The tedious process of encoding a message was endlessly laborious. A single message of 300 words involved roughly 1,500 letters. With each letter of the alphabet necessitating a two-digit number, a message this length meant 3,000 painstaking strokes of Elizabeth's pen. After the encoding process, she overwrote the code with a family letter to her "uncle" and fed it back to her lion.

Then the messages furtively disappeared from the beast's belly and the Van Lews' black servants carried it to couriers, Frederick Lohman, James Duke and his sons, and others, and on to Judson Knight and Grant himself. They used various strategies—shoes with hollow soles, farm wagons ostensibly transporting produce, hollow eggshells among baskets of eggs, false-bottom bowls, clothes with secrets sewn inside . . .

Often when Elizabeth worked in the library, a phantom seemed to hover about, watching, listening, judging. Sometimes when she felt the presence, she shook it off or she consigned it to a corner, out of view and out of thought, where it dutifully stayed. The specter mostly crept around when her mind wandered and her work slumped, which happened a lot these days. The weight of Allen's death still crushed her heart and the investigation dampened her spirits even as she carried on.

"Why do you hang around so much?" she silently asked, annoyed at the intrusion. "Dead so long and still you dog me."

I do not hang around. You keep bringing me back. I'd rather be left alone to sleep. You're the one dogging me, he wanted to say indignantly, but he had learned to keep quiet.

"Everything was so simple when you were alive," she said without words to the apparition as she paused in writing her ciphers.

He disagreed—strongly.

"But I do miss you," she continued with a sigh.

He perked up.

"Our talks. Even our arguments. I don't say more than necessary to mother. She worries so," she continued.

A wisp of air brushed her cheek.

"This war ... this horrible war. It's made me so unhappy ... Allen ..." Her breath caught in a sob and she dropped her pen and sat quietly for a long time.

He waited. He had lots of time.

"But it's been strangely good too. All these brave people who've come into my life. People I would never have known." She fingered the gold ring on the chain around her neck. "I know you would have liked them, Poppa. Allen and all the others." Then she added quickly, "White *and* black—even if you couldn't agree with us."

He bristled a bit at the assumption that he wouldn't agree and that she had to emphasize *white and black.*

"I wonder, would I have stayed in this house if you sided with the Confederacy? I just can't picture you opposing Richmond society, however progressive you were. Or repudiating slavery ..."

The phantom took to agitating. Here it comes—*slavery* again! That cursed will. What was I thinking?

"But then, who knows?"

Elizabeth rose and walked to the window. The leaves had begun falling in dead heaps on the ground as a chill wind tossed them about in swirls. "Nothing is ever really simple, is it, Poppa? I work with Unionists who are slave owners—Botts, Stearns ... And I pretend our servants are still our slaves. I have not repudiated Richmond society—though some have repudiated me ... I can make no claim to purity."

He paused in his twisting about, surprised at her admission. *Yes, far from perfect,* he thought.

"We all see it the way we see it, Poppa."

True.

"But I do think you would admire them as I do—especially our Negro comrades. It's more dangerous for them, you know," she said earnestly. "Peter, 'Uncle' Nelson—you know them, and Mary Bowser, Robert Ford, William Brisby, Sylvanus Brown ... So many of them, risking their lives.

Taking escaped prisoners, slaves, Confederate deserters, civilians across rebel lines. Doing dangerous reconnaissance, spying, carrying messages to the Union. So many things they do."

He listened dutifully.

"Negroes caught helping the Union risk so much more—savage beatings, imprisonment, hanging, 'Dead or Alive' postings . . ."

You were always my favorite—good hearted, incredibly bright, precocious— even if a compulsive liar. He wondered how much he was responsible for what she had become? Or was it in spite of him?

She turned from the window and paused. The reproachful lion caught her eye. "And here I am, feeling sorry for myself, wasting time."

A waste of time? Talking to me. He huffed about, stirring the air around her.

Elizabeth waved her arm dismissively. "I have work to do, Poppa." With that she walked back to her desk, sat down and picked up her pen.

The phantom retreated to a corner and pouted. But he wondered. *What* would *I have done?*

⁓

Through it all the specter of Castle Thunder loomed in Elizabeth's thoughts, setting up residence there. Not knowing wore her down and took a toll on Eliza. It did not help that authorities arrested other Unionist comrades during this period and imprisoned them in the infamous Castle. She and her coconspirators watched the arrests with alarm.

But they also took heart when authorities, unable to make their charges stick, or because of wealth and connections, released some of their friends. They especially rejoiced when William Rowley, arrested for failing to report for military service, finally escaped their clutches when he demonstrated that he belonged to the German Baptist Brethren Church. The Dunkards, as they were derisively known, held to nonviolent pacifism, and claimed an inability to serve for religious reasons.

Life in Richmond and the mansion grew more bizarre and surreal each day. Famine stalked the city with supply lines choked, yet Confederate authorities called for fast days to conserve food. Slaves were forced to support the war effort to preserve slavery. Richmond's elite carried on their social lives as usual, even as their way of life crumbled. Women of the upper classes used lace and damask curtains and mosquito nets to make gowns for their balls and receptions. The population of Richmond soared as resources diminished. Fuel supplies disappeared as winter's bitterness approached. A crippled Confederacy fought on, beyond hope. Richmond newspapers spoke of impending victory as defeat loomed nearer.

In their splendid mansion, the Van Lews lived surrounded by the trappings of wealth even as their Unionist efforts and the closing of their business depleted their fortune. Elizabeth played games with the children one day and risked her life for the Union and the abolition of slavery the next. Beneath what normalcy of everyday life remained, the secret proceedings against Elizabeth churned like a seething underground cauldron, threatening a volcanic eruption at any moment.

As usual, Elizabeth continued her work among the poor, struggling to find food for them where there was none. Disheartened but determined, she made her way to Emmie's almshouse. As she approached, the building seemed more decrepit and squalid than usual. Its face wore the look of death so common in the living poor. As she stepped into the dingy hallway, the wooden floor boards groaned under her. Hardly a worker could be seen anywhere, she noted with some alarm. She peered into the rooms as she passed and her heart ached for the abandoned within and for her own inability to do more.

She found Emmie where she always found her, seated in the rocker, staring off, transported to a different place—a better place, Elizabeth hoped.

"Emmie, dear," she called the woman back.

"Lizzie! Sweet girl, you done come."

The elderly woman looked paler than usual, weaker, thinner.

"Are you well, Emmie?"

"Well as kin be expected. This body keeps hangin' on. Don't know how." She gave out a laugh.

"And you, Lizzie?" She looked hard at her visitor. "You got the look o' sadness on you, girl."

Elizabeth managed a weak smile, but a sob made its way relentlessly to her throat. She could not speak.

Emmie touched her hand quietly and waited.

"I . . . I . . ." The sob broke through. "A loss, Emmie. Someone very dear to me . . . very dear." Elizabeth stifled the sob, annoyed at herself for bringing more gloom into the life of this cherished, suffering woman. "But we all have to deal with loss."

"There's only one loss that matters when we is suffering. Our own." She scrutinized Elizabeth's face. "A man, I'm guessin'."

Am I so transparent? Elizabeth thought. "A kind gentle man, Emmie. This wretched war. Everything comes back to this wretched war."

"I'm sorry for you, Lizzie. Women always carry wars on their shoulders. Wars they ain't startin'."

"They don't start them, but they cheer them on, I'm afraid," Elizabeth said, bitterly remembering all the women eager for war in the days of secession fever. Women celebrating in the streets after Bull Run. Women rounding up supporters for the Confederate cause. Women encouraging their sons to join the cause.

"Sometimes we don't have a whit more sense than men, I guess," Emmie said, shaking her head. "We oughta' take our pitchforks to the politicians. Tell 'em we ain't gonna stand for it no more! And we ain't gonna give our sons to war no more!" Her voice rose as she spoke. "What we thinkin'? Bringing sons into this world. All that pain and sufferin'. Then standin' by when they git sent to war and chewed up and killed. Mostly for nothin'. Women could stop it!"

Elizabeth stared at this dear friend, her passion erupting from some hidden well deep in her being.

"I had sons once . . ." Emmie said, a sorrow creeping into her glassy eyes.

Elizabeth took her hand and held it tightly as Emmie seemed to recede into some faraway cavern of the mind. The two sat quietly, covered by a thick blanket of grief.

At last Elizabeth said, "Emmie dear, you want to play a game of whist?"

Emmie's eyes flickered and she looked at her visitor, slowly connecting again. A slight smile broke across her face. "That sounds good, Lizzie, real good."

⁓

At the presidential mansion the frantic search for solutions to a war going badly went on. In mid-September Jefferson Davis convened a council at his home of his generals—Robert E. Lee, Jubal Early, James Longstreet, Braxton Bragg, John Bell Hood, John Breckinridge, Richard Ewell . . . They arrived in all their military splendor, crisp uniforms, brass buttons, stars on their shoulders, polished boots.

At the meeting, black servants and slaves stood at attention, filling coffee cups and glasses of water, offering brandy, serving food, bringing and taking away dishes, emptying ashtrays. Among them was Mary Bowser.

Stern-faced and somber, Jefferson Davis welcomed the group of generals. He began by declaring his will to fight as strong as ever, despite the challenges facing the Confederacy. Then he put the question to his generals.

"What more is required to win this war?"

Lee spoke first and passionately. "I cannot continue to hold my lines with present troop strength. We must have more men. The Union is certain to extend their lines."

General Early immediately joined Lee in his call for more men. "I have been ordered to hold the Shenandoah Valley and rid it of Federal troops, so that we can threaten Washington and force Grant to abandon the Petersburg siege. But we will fail without reinforcements. There simply are not enough men."

"We cannot continue to shift the troops we have from one spot to another," Lee continued. "In August we diverted men from Longstreet's First Corps to help Jubal in the valley campaign. That left our Richmond defenses vulnerable when the Federals attacked at Deep Bottom." He shook his head. "No, we cannot manage successfully with the manpower we have now."

"I'll repeat again what I've been saying," Bragg added. "The situation is dire and has been for some time. I reported last year that only forty percent of the men on my rolls were present for duty. Things have not improved."

"Two-thirds of my men are absent without leave now," Hood said. "We are reduced to fighting a war with a handful of men."

Jefferson Davis listened grimly. "I would put it differently," he said at last. "The Union is Goliath, but we are David. It is not resources that will win this war, but the rightness of our cause."

The generals shifted in their seats, glancing at each other in disbelief.

"I fear, Mr. President," General Lee responded bleakly, "that right does not make might. We need more than virtue to win."

"General Lee is correct," Ewell said. "A good part of our Confederate line is a mere skeleton, ready to collapse at the slightest attack. At Chesterfield the line is so fragile it cannot withstand even a small force thrown against it."

"Gentlemen," Davis interjected. "We have reason to hope that the election will bring us victory if manpower will not. I'm confident Lincoln will not be reelected in November. The North is as weary of war as we are. They will repudiate Lincoln's war through the ballot and that will force the Federals to put an end to their aggression."

"Perhaps," Lee responded. "But meanwhile we fight. And the reality is we fight with too few troops." He paused searching for an answer to the question before them. "Does any possibility exist for increasing troop strength?" When no one volunteered an answer, he continued, "There is hardly anyone left to conscript unless we want to draft young boys and old men. I certainly do not. Do we divert our troops from their lines to track down deserters? I think not. Our congress will not allow slaves to fight in the military. Who is left?" He paused.

Jubal Early spoke next. "General Lee is right. The only question before us now is how to deploy the troops we have most effectively. Should I pull my forces from the valley and help drive Grant from Petersburg?"

"The valley is too critical to abandon, General Early," Lee responded. "With the sea blockade and our railroads strangled, we desperately need the valley. It's our last breadbasket. I would argue against such a move." He looked at Early. "Unless . . . unless an attack on Petersburg cannot be stopped. Then you need to come down. If you come in that circumstance and are too late, you should take a position between Petersburg and Richmond to defend the capital. If Richmond falls, we are lost."

As the men at the meeting spoke in turn, pored over maps, and made tactical decisions, the slaves and servants stood and moved about as needed. One of them, looking indifferent, listened intently.

Late that night, after all the generals had left and everyone in the Davis mansion had retired, Mary Bowser secretly jotted lengthy notes on pieces of paper. When she finished, she folded the papers into tiny squares and stuffed them deep into her apron pocket. The next morning after Thomas McNiven delivered bread, the tiny squares made their way to the hungry lion in the Church Hill mansion, then immediately to General Grant.

❧

Several days after the meeting at the Jefferson Davis home, Union General Philip Sheridan unleashed a series of attacks against Jubal Early's forces in the Shenandoah Valley. First taking Winchester, southwest of Harper's Ferry, then Fisher's Hill, Sheridan devastated Early's command.

The offensive forced Lee to divert troops to the valley, while Grant pummeled Lee around the James River and grabbed Fort Harrison, near Richmond. By mid-October, Cedar Creek also fell to Sheridan, leaving Union forces in control of the Shenandoah.

The loss of the valley meant much more to the Confederacy than another military defeat. With Richmond's food supply more dire than ever, living conditions and morale in the city, already low, ground down rapidly. Galloping inflation, hunger, suspension of business, scarcity of every kind, rampant crime, an epidemic of Confederate desertions, and sheer exhaustion eroded confidence in the war effort and the will to fight on. This news, too, made its way from the hungry lion to City Point, where the information emboldened Grant and his officers.

Even worse, the loss of the Valley had come on the heels of the fall of Atlanta. Most alarming to the citizens of Richmond were reports that Major General William Tecumseh Sherman had ordered the city of Atlanta evacuated by everyone except the Union Army. Would residents of the Virginia capital soon find themselves also driven from their homes to god knows where, they worried?

General Hood, in protesting the Atlanta evacuation order, had told Sherman that the proposal transcended in its cruelty all actions "in the dark history of war." The mayor of Atlanta also objected in vain that the sick, old, and helpless of the population would suffer in appalling and heart-rending ways from such a move. The tall, lean, intense Sherman, his kindly and pleasant face a mass of wrinkles, listened and agreed with Mayor Calhoun. Yet he pointed out that his order was "not designed to meet the humanities of the case but to prepare for the future struggles." He added what all but the delusional would readily admit, "War is cruelty, and you cannot refine it."

Intelligence from Elizabeth's Unionist network had not only furthered the Valley campaign, it also led to the fall of the last Confederate seaport on the Atlantic Ocean. Samuel Ruth, Superintendent of the Richmond,

Fredericksburg, and Potomac Railroad, obtained information about the number of troops Lee had in and around Wilmington, North Carolina, on the Cape Fear River, just north of Fort Fisher. The revelations set in motion a series of Union attacks that eventually led to the fall of the fort.

~

As her espionage accelerated, Elizabeth seethed with indignation at the covert investigation spreading its tentacles through her family, neighborhood, friendships, and enemies. She chafed under the anonymous threats that appeared on her doorstep and the taunts of "Lincoln lover" and "traitor" that sometimes assaulted her as she moved about the capital. Elizabeth did not see herself as an evil spy sullied by the dirty work of surveillance, but as a resister of oppression and a patriot risking her life for the moral causes of abolition and the preservation of the Union. But still Doswell spun his personal reign of terror on her and there was no General Winder to hear an appeal.

Anxious weeks dragged as the investigation ground on. Behind the scenes at Confederate headquarters, authorities grappled with the charges against Elizabeth. Two men in particular, Provost Marshal Isaac Carrington and Inspector General Charles Blackford, held her fate in their hands as they searched Commissioner Sands's report.

"What do you make of this evidence?" Carrington asked the Inspector General.

"The deposition of Mary Van Lew is certainly damning," Blackford responded.

"Is it sufficient? Should more evidence be sought?" Carrington responded. Then, carefully, he added, "The Van Lews are people of wealth and position."

"Yes, and Elizabeth has supporters among some of our best citizens."

"That's true," Carrington replied, thinking uneasily of the Van Lew friendship with his own extended family on Church Hill, especially Eliza

Carrington. What would it mean to have a close friend of his own family found guilty of treason, he thought uncomfortably to himself?

"Yet it seems clear that Miss Van Lew is very unfriendly in her sentiments toward the Confederacy," Blackford said in a vexed manner. His thoughts moved quickly to his mother, Mary Blackford, who had vehemently and openly opposed secession before the war. She still harbored strong Unionist sentiments, although now she only shared them with her son and the rest of her family.

"But has she actually done anything to harm the cause?" Carrington probed.

"Like most members of the female sex, she talks too freely—and in the presence of her female friends who have informed on her," the Inspector General responded, rubbing his forehead. "But I cannot find evidence of anything concrete that she has done against the Confederacy." He nodded his head as his eyes searched the pile of papers in front of him. "And it is obvious that Miss Van Lew's sister-in-law holds a grudge against her. She has lost her children to the Van Lew family."

"The question, then, is whether we should punish her for her opinion," Carrington ventured cautiously.

"That seems unduly harsh for a woman . . . and a person of her position . . ." Blackford stopped each thought in midstream.

"I agree," Carrington jumped in immediately, hoping this would end the deliberations. When Blackford nodded and pushed the papers away, Carrington's uneasiness lifted and he felt greatly relieved at the dilemma resolving itself so easily. He pushed from his mind his own ruling just two months before that it was not expedient to let men "go at large" who had spoken of the Confederacy in a disloyal way. Or that many had already been imprisoned for merely expressing disloyal opinions.

The recorded verdict in the Elizabeth Van Lew case concluded there was no evidence of disloyal activity. Stamped on the document sat the words "no action to be taken." Some time passed before the disposition of the case reached Elizabeth. Eliza Carrington, who had hounded Provost Marshal Isaac Carrington on behalf of her dear friend, rushed to the mansion and found Elizabeth in the parlor.

"Good news," she exclaimed, nearly breathless.

"You've heard something, Eliza?" Elizabeth asked anxiously.

"More than that. It's official. You will *not* be arrested."

"But . . ."

At that moment her mother came into the room.

Elizabeth's effusive friend took her hand. "They could find no hard evidence against you, Bet."

Elizabeth hugged her friend, as tears appeared in her mother's eyes.

"It's over, Bet. Isaac assures me . . ."

After Eliza left, Elizabeth walked onto the veranda, reassured and comforted by the ruling. A strange quiet had settled over the peaceful landscape, the noises of the street suddenly still. In the garden splashes of yellow, orange and magenta chrysanthemums accented the sea of green. Overhead a brilliant, cloudless blue sky covered the fading colors of late fall. Beyond the sloping garden, the James River snaked its way to the great Chesapeake Bay, indifferently watching the comings and goings on both sides of its shore.

A silent whisper rose from the veranda and floated on a breeze, over the twisting river, upward and away, brushing the cheek of a lost love and dissolving in a hush. Taking a deep breath to push back the tears, Elizabeth turned, went into the house, and walked upstairs to her library and the crouching lion.

Chapter 12

News of the election of 1864 raced through Richmond, igniting tremors everywhere and driving away the few remaining shards of optimism. Given the severe manpower, munitions, and supply shortages suffered by the South, all expectation and hope rested on the defeat of the North's war president. But Union voters reelected Abraham Lincoln. That left divine intervention as the last good hope of victory for the Confederacy.

The war slogged on.

However, rebel supporters were not alone in their despondency. Elizabeth and Richmond Unionists looked at the calendar. Four years. For four years the North had somehow managed to snatch defeat from the jaws of victory—again and again. Against all odds the South tenaciously hung on, victorious in defeat. Almost two years after the Emancipation Proclamation and as the United States Congress stood ready to abolish slavery with the Thirteenth Amendment to the Constitution, slavery still gripped the South. Six months after the siege and bombardment of Petersburg began, Petersburg had not fallen. Despite numerous Union attempts to storm the Confederate capital, despite enemy troops surrounding it on all sides, despite numerous calls for its evacuation, shabby, hungry, and crime-ridden Richmond still stood.

Defeat was everywhere. But where was victory?

Just over a week before the Holy Day of Christmas, people woke to the news that General Hood lost Nashville to the Union after two days of bitter fighting. Days later, more bad news. Word came that General Sherman captured Savannah from the Confederacy and was charging toward the Carolinas. Morale in the capital sank to lows not seen before.

At the Davis mansion, Varina took comfort in her six-month-old baby girl, although the face of little Joe followed her everywhere. The years of stress and loss had aged her prematurely as flecks of gray appeared in her black hair, her skin turned sallow, and her big, dark eyes had narrowed as though to shut out the world. Baby Varina, called "Winnie" or "Piecake" in the Davis family's fondness for nicknames, offered a measure of solace to the gaunt and weary president as well.

As conditions in Richmond worsened and many of the city's elites fled south, Varina had sent her eldest child, Margaret—"Maggie" they called her—away to safety with her dear friend Mary Boykin Chestnut. But disaster followed them closely as Sherman's advance drove them from city to city. So Maggie returned to Richmond as the elegant Mrs. Chestnut was reduced to selling butter and eggs and her few remaining gowns. Varina, too, began to sell her silk evening dresses and finally her carriage and horses. Some prominent citizens bought the horses and carriage back in kindness and returned them to Varina, neglecting to consider that she could barely feed them.

A dreary Christmas came and went in homes across Richmond, where women struggled to put any food on the table, let alone a holiday feast. Their men lay in distant trenches, Union prisons, hospitals, or unmarked graves. Even in the homes of the capital's elites, famine stalked at the doors. The Davis family rations, too, shriveled to corn meal, flour, and rice, occasionally a bit of meat. There was little food to be found at any price, while the Confederate dollar plunged in value.

The Van Lew home was no exception. Eliza struggled to feed her family and servants and the girls sometimes went to bed complaining of hunger. Their financial reversals grew more severe by the day. Having lost the income from their once thriving and lucrative hardware business, and having expended their considerable fortune for four years on Unionist causes—bribing officials, buying food and goods for Union prisoners, supporting safe houses, assisting fleeing slaves, paying workers and couriers—the Van Lew household suffered as almost everyone did. Still the war dragged on.

On the battlefield at the arrival of the New Year, snow, cold, and mud conspired with hunger, depression, and the incessant din of war. General Lee reported to Jefferson Davis that he had only two days of meager rations for his ill-clothed, tattered army.

Somehow, through it all, life went on. Here and there happy moments materialized.

In mid-January a celebratory mood covered the entrance to beautiful St. Paul's Episcopal Church on Capitol Square where many of Richmond's elite worshipped. Guests milled about waiting for the happy arrival of a wedding party. When the clomping of horses' hooves and the wheels of the bridal carriage signaled the approach of the beautiful bride, an excitement spread through the glittering crowd.

A cheer rose from the gathering as the carriage door opened and Hetty Cary began to step down. Suddenly one of the horses bolted and Hetty's white, filmy tulle veil caught on the door as she grabbed the handle, ripping in two. A gasp rose from the guests as they witnessed the ominous portent, not knowing that another omen had hovered over the bride barely an hour earlier. While putting on her gown, a hand mirror crashed to the floor and broke as Hetty admired her reflected image. But here under a glorious, cloudless blue sky, only hope caressed the bride bathed by bright sunshine.

In the church, the young, handsome groom waited for the long delayed marriage. Major General John Pegram, wounded in the Wilderness fighting, had recovered and been granted a short leave. The Reverend Dr. Minnigerode presided over the cheerful occasion in the stately church. After the marriage and celebration, the happy bride followed her husband to establish a home near the front lines. News of the grand wedding appeared in the Richmond press, as did all marriages among the city's elites.

At the Grace Street mansion, too, life went on. But January ushered in more dangers to the Unionist cause in Richmond. Elizabeth sat in the parlor scanning the *Whig* while Eliza read to the girls. At one point, Elizabeth groaned and dropped the paper into her lap.

"Unbelievable," she said in disgust.

Eliza glanced up from the children's book.

"Listen to what the *Whig* is saying about the war." She picked up the paper again and read, "*Far from being depressed, there is every reason to feel hopeful.*"

"Hopeful about what?" Eliza asked.

"There's nothing hopeful that I can see in the article. But they persist in trying to tell a completely dispirited people to hope for the impossible," Elizabeth responded. Her eyes continued moving over the page. "Oh, no!" she blurted suddenly.

"What?" Eliza looked alarmed.

Her daughter stood and began pacing with the newspaper as she read, her voice quivering. "Frederick Lohmann and James Duke have been arrested."

Eliza, grown frail and thin from the years of stress, dropped her book.

"What's wrong, Granmama?" Annie asked.

"There's more," Elizabeth added somberly. "They've also arrested three of James's sons." She read the names from the article, "Moses Duke, Thomas Duke, and William Duke." She stopped pacing suddenly. The room became eerily silent as the girls searched the faces of their grandmother and aunt. Elizabeth said nothing but continued staring at the paper.

Finally Eliza asked anxiously, dreading the answer, "Please, Bet. Tell me what is happening."

"They've arrested Samuel Ruth," Elizabeth responded, her voice trembling.

Eliza gasped. Ruth arrested! Ruth, head of the Richmond, Fredericksburg, and Potomac Railroad! Ruth, another of her daughter's most important collaborators!

"They dragged Samuel from his office and threw him into Castle Thunder. They're *all* in Castle Thunder," Elizabeth went on gravely, her eyes racing across the page.

The girls began tugging at their grandmother's sleeve impatiently. "Finish our story, granmama, please," little Eliza pleaded, picking up the book.

A wordless shadow snaked around the room and settled over the two women. Eliza sat silent and immobile, as though the child had not spoken.

"Come, girls," Elizabeth said softly. "I'll finish reading your book."

For days, the newspapers raged about the arrests, passing judgment, rendering verdicts, condemning or arguing for one or the other prisoner. The *Richmond Sentinel* proclaimed that Ruth was "*long and favorably known in this city as a most efficient railroad officer, and a respectable, prudent and cautious man.*" The *Whig* also dismissed the allegations against Ruth as "*trumped up.*" He could not be guilty. Lohmann, an ordinary working man, on the other hand, was presumed guilty in the press.

Once again, connections carried the day. Ruth was released shortly for insufficient evidence. Duke and his sons also escaped the noose through their connections and were freed. Lohmann, however, languished in solitary confinement at Castle Thunder. Elizabeth's heart broke for her kindly friend suffering in a stone dungeon and for her own inability to help him.

─ ❧ ─

In early February, the press again blazed with inflammatory information about a strange meeting that had taken place aboard a Federal steamer in Hampton Roads Sound at the mouth of the James River. But this time Elizabeth had heard the news already from Mary Bowser at the president's mansion. A feeler had made its way to Jefferson Davis suggesting a peace conference between North and South. Determined to fight on,

Davis nonetheless saw such a meeting as a tool to inflame passions about the North's intransigence and to motivate the troops to fight on.

Davis appointed his vice president, Alexander Stephens, Assistant Secretary of War John Campbell, and Senator Robert Hunter to meet with the Federals. At a preliminary meeting, General Grant received Stephens and Hunter who discussed the possibly of a peace conference. Impressed by the fact that Davis had sent moderates and knowing of the dire conditions in the Confederate capital and in the military from his "lady in Richmond," Grant wrote to President Lincoln. He relayed to Lincoln his sense that the South lay in ruins and must at last understand that defeat was imminent. He believed, he said, the men were sincere. It would be well at least to talk with them. Lincoln telegraphed his response immediately. He would undertake the journey at once and meet the Confederate delegates. The next morning, Lincoln arrived with Secretary of State William Seward and boarded a Federal steamer at Hampton Roads.

At the meeting, after the usual pleasantries, the five men sat around a wooden table in a cabin aboard ship in the middle of the sound. The Confederate delegates expected a discussion with the normal give and take of negotiations—concessions on all sides. But such an expectation could only be predicated on both sides operating from a position of strength, a position assumed by the South despite its obvious fiction given the state of things.

Vice President Stephens made the first proposal. "We are here to propose an armistice, Mr. Lincoln . . ."

"An armistice, Mr. Stephens?" Lincoln leaned forward and listened, his furrowed face and dark eyes intent.

"Yes, an armistice, so that we can present a united front against the French and drive them out of Mexico," Stephens responded earnestly. "This would enable our two countries to reaffirm the Monroe Doctrine."

Lincoln's face went white and his brows knit. "You mean enable *our country* to reaffirm the Monroe Doctrine."

Flustered, Stephens stammered a reply. "No, sir . . . I . . . I meant exactly what I said. *Our two countries.*"

"We seek a harmonious reconciliation of our two countries," Hunter interjected with emphasis.

"Gentlemen," Lincoln said with a steady, deep voice, "we have fought and died for four bloody years and plundered the national treasury to reunite our country. You cannot believe that at this late juncture we would be prepared to abandon our goal."

"We talk not of our past struggles," said Stephens, gaining his composure. "We want what is best for both North and South. Surely you agree that both sides must have what is best for them."

"I agree that what is best for the country is reunification and the abolition of slavery," Lincoln responded, his words calm and measured.

"But our country cannot accept your country's . . ."

"Mr. Stephens," Lincoln cut in, "you know that I do not recognize the South as anything but a region of the Union. The indispensable conditions for these negotiations are the reunification of North and South under a single Federal authority and the abolition of slavery." He stopped and his sad, penetrating eyes looked squarely at the three men as Seward watched quietly.

Stephens, Hunter, and Campbell looked dumbstruck and no one spoke.

At last Campbell found his voice. "But you are asking us to make an unconditional surrender!"

"After the acceptance of these two conditions, everything is on the table for discussion. You will find me most accommodating to your desires," Lincoln continued, unmoved.

Vice President Stephens stood up stiffly. "We bid you good day, sir." Hunter and Campbell rose immediately, nodded and bowed slightly at the president and the three men left the cabin.

For a long time Lincoln and Seward sat quietly at the table, as the bones of dead men crowded into the room and the air swirled around them. Lincoln stared at the apparitions that gathered around his shoulders. Stooped, his head down, he rose awkwardly from the table and left the room of death.

After the Hampton Roads conference, Jefferson Davis used the North's "intransigence" to fire up crowds as he rose from one platform after another to denounce Lincoln's failure to negotiate. The Southern press echoed Davis' condemnation of Federal obstinacy and for awhile passions flared. But people did not so easily forget their misery or their dead.

❦

In February, news arrived in Richmond of the death of General John Henry Winder, in charge of all Confederate prisons east of the Mississippi—the papers said of fatigue and stress. The Van Lews mourned for the man who had so often been their protector, although others did not feel so kindly. Conditions in Southern prisons were universally horrendous with contaminated water, little food, and even less medical attention and sanitation. Many hundreds of Union prisoners died every week of starvation and disease.

Eliza had communicated occasionally with Mrs. Winder after the general left Richmond. His wife sadly relayed his ongoing misery and strain at being unable to provide better for the captives in his prisons and his constant struggles to find them food at a time when Confederate troops fared little better. Two months before he died, Winder had implored Richmond authorities to release all Union prisoners and allow them to go home since the South could not feed or provide for them. They had flatly refused.

That same month Federal scout Judson Knight slipped through Confederate lines and made his way to the Van Lew mansion. He came to report that a new agent, an Englishman known only as Pole, would serve as his agent in Richmond while posing as a Confederate sympathizer. The introduction of an unknown person into the network at this time of danger for Unionists unsettled Elizabeth greatly. She could not shake a premonition of something terribly amiss. She questioned Knight closely. How long had he known the man? Not long. Then why take him on at this critical time? He comes recommended. By whom? A friend.

"Our group will not be happy about this unknown person introduced into our midst. I am not comfortable with this," she told Knight firmly. "I ask that you reconsider."

Trying to hide his irritation, Knight dismissed her uncertainty with a wave of his hand. "There is nothing to worry about, dear lady, *nothing*," he said. "You can rely on Pole."

"If you are wrong, our people will pay the price," Elizabeth responded gravely, her foreboding stronger than ever.

And pay they did. When Pole arrived in Richmond, he immediately reported to the Provost Marshal's office, fingering the Unionists assigned to work directly with him, William White and Lemuel Babcock. Authorities immediately arrested both men. During the interrogation, detectives ordered the men to tell everything they knew about the other "traitors" in their midst. But Babcock and White stood firm.

At one point, a frustrated interrogator held a gun to White's head. "Tell me what you know or I'll blow your brains out."

Unflinching, White looked the detective in the eye and responded defiantly, "Then blow away."

Both men quickly found themselves in Castle Thunder in solitary confinement.

When she heard of Pole's betrayal, Elizabeth dashed a furious note to Judson Knight. *"Your entirely cavalier introduction of a new man, despite my concerns and objections, has cost our brave numbers dearly. No new agents! Eliza Jones."*

Troubled by the scope of the arrests, Elizabeth took the unprecedented step of calling a meeting of her remaining Richmond network. With

Lohmann, Babcock, White, and others in prison, she needed to determine the resolve of the others. Those who could come met at Rowley's farm on the outskirts of the city, away from the prowling eyes of Richmond neighbors and detectives. Though they knew each other well and worked together, this was the first time they had gathered in one room. Heartened by their presence, Elizabeth reviewed with them where they stood.

"We cannot know if any one of us is next. So the question now," she said earnestly, "is whether anyone wishes to leave the group—or depart Richmond. Some of our comrades have left already—Abbey Green, Burnham Wardwell, William Fay . . . Many of you have families to think of. It would be completely understandable if some feel they cannot continue because of the increased danger. Truly, we would all understand. Everyone has given so much already."

A silence fell over the room as Elizabeth scanned the somber faces, black and white. A kind of raw pain lurked in their eyes, under their knit brows. The gray shadows of unwanted and discarded memories had settled under their skin and the weight of hiding and sneaking about had seeped into their shoulders. No one moved in the heavy silence.

After a few minutes, Thomas McNiven spoke with a sweep of his arm around the room. "Well, there you have your answer, Elizabeth."

"Yes," added Samuel Ruth, newly released from prison, a bitter edge to his voice. "We have not come this far to abandon the cause."

Erasmus Ross nodded in agreement.

"I've sent my sons North since we got out of prison. I've nothing to lose now," James Duke said quietly.

Rowley spoke next. "I have been to prison. I'll go again if need be."

"Yes. I would go to prison to help free my people," said black farmer William Brisby.

"I'm still in," Franklin Stearns said simply.

"There is no way I will stop now," Charles Palmer added.

Another black farmer, Sylvanus Brown, also agreed to continue the fight, although a reward had been posted on his head, dead or alive.

Elizabeth fought back tears as she listened to them. "My friends, I have not suffered what most of you have. Yet you go on."

McNiven smiled. "Don't despair, Elizabeth. You may yet see the inside of a Castle Thunder dungeon!" With that the group broke into peals of laughter as a broad grin spread across Elizabeth's face.

"Well, then," she said when the laughter died down, "we must redouble our efforts. There is some good news. Our source in the War Department says that Sherman is sweeping through North Carolina. Apparently he's heading for City Point to join Grant. The end is surely near and Grant will need information now more than ever. Samuel has gotten a report we need to act on."

"I've learned that Davis is planning to send four hundred thousand pounds of tobacco to Hamilton's Crossing. It'll be taken from there to the Potomac River where it'll be traded for bacon and other food. We must stop this from happening or it will again prolong the fight," Ruth told the group. "We'll have to get word to Grant. I can get the information to Charles Carter. He's not coming into the city now because of surveillance, but he's sending a Negro in with produce twice a week. He'll get word to Sharpe who'll give it to Grant."

"Our source in the War Department has also told us that Lee plans to attack Fort Stedman. He's waiting to move his artillery until the ground is dry enough. That should take a while," Elizabeth continued. "They are desperate to break Grant's siege at some point along the line. I'm coding the message for Grant now. We all need to continue doing what we've been doing. But with greater care than ever," she added, looking earnestly at each in turn.

"And the railroad?" Duke asked, turning to Samuel.

"The trains run into problems every now and then, as always," Ruth smiled. "You know—too slow, interrupted service, mechanical breakdowns, miscommunications . . ."

"And the newspaper calls you a '*most efficient railroad officer*,'" McNiven said, breaking into laughter again.

"And do we know, Elizabeth, how the Northern newspaper ads are going?" Palmer asked, referring to the plan hatched by Ruth and their group to have the Northern press place ads calling on Confederate engineers, mechanics, and other critical tradesmen to desert to the Union and be paid a premium. The ads had been spirited across the lines and widely circulated in the Confederacy.

"Extremely well, we're told." Elizabeth responded. "Large numbers have deserted already. Samuel can confirm that the action is threatening the railroads and other vital services."

Ruth nodded in agreement.

"It's also critical that we keep feeding Grant information about the deteriorating conditions and troop movements in the Richmond area," Elizabeth told them. "We've heard that Lee has ordered large numbers of Confederate troops down the Danville Road . . ."

"That must mean they're retreating west to Lynchburg," Sylvanus Brown interjected. "West is the only possible escape. They can't go south from Petersburg, or east, or north . . ."

"You're right, Sylvanus," Elizabeth responded. "Where else could they be going?"

"If they make it through, Lee can regroup and fight on," Brisby said, alarmed.

"Break Grant's siege with some units and get other units out of Grant's reach . . ." Ross said, putting it all together.

"And authorities are at last planning for the evacuation of Richmond. We've learned that all the tobacco, cotton, and other warehouses have been turned over to the Provost Marshal to prevent looting when the evacuation begins," Elizabeth added. "We know Lee has wanted this evacuation for some time, but Davis has refused."

"What does our source in the Davis mansion say?" Duke asked Elizabeth.

"That Davis still believes he can continue the fight and he's prepared to move the government to a safe place if necessary. Davis will not acknowledge defeat."

They continued exchanging information as darkness fell, then reviewed their plans. By the time they were ready to leave, everyone had turned somber again. The specter of arrest at any moment, the thought of their comrades in harsh prison conditions, anxiety for an end to come quickly, and the phantom of the unknown were surely taking their toll, Elizabeth thought. They bid each other Godspeed, hugged warmly, and slipped out quietly one by one through Rowley's back door, into the black night.

In the distance a train wailed mournfully as it approached Richmond. In one of the freight cars, Hetty Cary Pegram sat on the coarse, rattling floor, her arm draped over a pine coffin. Her husband of three weeks, killed leading a cavalry charge at Hatcher's Run, lay lifeless in the casket. Hetty's tears washed over the crude wooden box as her heart fixed on the handsome face of John Pegram, her lover, her friend, her soulmate. A line swirled madly through her mind, the words churning with the wheels on the train tracks: like a flower broken in the stalk, like a flower broken in the stalk, like a flower broken in the stalk . . .

Chapter 13

A steady drizzle fell on the capital three days before the end of March, matching the gloomy mood of Richmonders as a collective depression infected the city. Auction houses and pawn shops overflowed with the memories and scraps of former lives, abandoned in preference for food. Grocery stores, nearly empty, sold what little they had for exorbitant prices. A barrel of flour fetched a thousand dollars. An epidemic of counterfeiting the near worthless Confederate dollar spread so rapidly, hardly anyone troubled to distinguish the real from the fake. Along the alleyways and side streets, women of the night plied their craft and hustlers tried to survive on the slender pickings of Richmond's destitute citizens.

To keep warm, many had retreated to a single room in their homes, usually a bedroom, with whatever sticks of furniture, pots and pans, and personal items still remained. If they were lucky, coal and scraps of wood to feed their insatiable fireplaces or stoves stood ready. A small supply of rice or potatoes, dried peas, maybe some dried apples, kept them alive, if not satisfied. And with them always, faith, wavering at times, in General Robert E. Lee and his ragged, hungry army.

Rumors of imminent Union attacks, threatened evacuations, and the collapse of the Confederate government continually ran through the city. Tittle-tattle about this or that general or official or their families fed the hungry where there was little food. And, for many, a sore, like a canker, inflamed all this pain—the thought of traitors in their midst who had contributed to this appalling state of affairs.

Their horses commandeered for the war effort, weary people moved about on foot. The dilapidated rail lines south to Petersburg and southwest to Danville still ran, barely, and never on time. The others did not. In the harbor on the James River, the tattered remnants of the Confederate fleet under Admiral Semmes, steamers and ironclads, waited, like the rest of the military around Richmond, oblivious of what was transpiring around Petersburg.

A little over a week earlier the Confederate Congress had disbanded, fleeing the city. Jefferson Davis's emergency decrees were not acted on—who would do these things and with what? And for almost a month the removal from the city of government property not in use proceeded—archives and documents, provisions, artillery and machines, the remnants of medical supplies. A standing order for the destruction of tobacco and cotton should Richmond fall hung over the city's merchants.

But the press continued to put the best face on Confederate defeats, referring to battles as "no battle" and to the many wounded and captured as "scarcely anyone hurt." And at the grand Richmond Metropolitan Hall, a new production opened to rave reviews in the newspapers.

Some engaged in communal denial. In mansions around the city festive social gatherings, flippantly called "starvation parties," were held where young women and men, mostly soldiers, danced to the music of a fiddler or piano player. Ornate crystal bowls lined long, linen-covered tables down one wall. Filled with water, the bowls reflected the admonition against refreshments at social gatherings. But around the room, young dancers swirled to music, flouting those who decreed the tunes sinful and contrary to church teachings.

In the White House of the Confederacy, fearful for their safety and on the verge of leaving for the front lines, Jefferson Davis told Varina to take the children and leave Richmond immediately. She pleaded to remain, scornful of fleeing. He would have none of it.

"If I live you can come to me when the struggle is over, but I do not expect to survive the destruction of constitutional liberty," he told her.

Then he handed her a gun and showed her how to use it.

"If the enemy is approaching, you must leave," he cautioned. "But if you cannot flee, use the gun to force your assailants to kill you."

After dismissing the hired servants who would not be traveling with her, Varina packed clothes for herself and the children. Her husband gave her a pile of Confederate bills and all the pieces of gold he had, keeping only one five dollar piece for himself. From the worthless paper, his image mocked her. He refused, however, to let her take the barrel of flour or any food, telling her it must be left for the people who desperately needed it.

At the carriage, their four children cried and clung desperately to their father in the cold drizzle, begging him to let them stay. Little Jeff, especially frantic at the thought of leaving his father, asserted that he could fight alongside the men. Grief-stricken, Davis almost relented in the face of all the pleading, but in the end he hustled them into the carriage and showered kisses on them all, believing he would never see them again.

Darkness began to creep over the carriage as they made their way to the train station. Maggie still sobbed at leaving her father and little Jeff kept asking why they had to leave. Outside the curtained windows covered with rivulets of water, the dreary, deserted streets passed by in the rain. The eerie stillness tormented Varina as she strained to hear some sign of life in the city over the rattling carriage wheels.

At the station the forlorn family climbed aboard the train. Accompanied by Jefferson Davis's secretary, Burton Harrison, pressed into escort service by his boss, and three servants, Varina, her children, her young sister Margaret, and the daughters of the Secretary of the Treasury, Helen and Eliza Trenholm, settled into the rickety, unkempt rail car. None of its former plushness remained. During the long years of war, the paint had slowly peeled from most of its exterior walls and the rich varnishes inside the car chipped away, leaving only dingy wood. Rips and stains littered the once lovely, upholstered seats and soiled, crusted floors ran the length of the car. Varina thought there must be fleas and there were. Above the discolored windows grimy lamps gave off a smoky light. Behind them in a boxcar rode the carriage horses of the First Lady of the Confederacy.

At ten in the evening the train finally lurched out of the station to Varina's great relief. But barely twelve miles from their starting point, the train faltered as it strained to climb a grade, then died.

All night the Davis family and the others sat and waited. Rain continued to fall and skate its way across the railcar roof, searching for cracks and breaks. Taking advantage of the many crevices, water made its way inside, soaking everyone and forcing the children to lay on soggy bedding. When the young ones got hungry, Varina scrambled to buy milk and crackers that cost her the ungodly sum of one hundred Confederate dollars. Dispirited and exhausted, they would not arrive in Danville, Virginia, for three days.

At the Van Lew mansion that same day a familiar face had rejoined the household. Mary Bowser returned from the Davis household, where the president now sat alone, writing reports, memos, directives, and appeals.

"The end is truly near, Miss Lizzie," she assured Elizabeth. "The family is gone and he is alone with his slaves."

"Then we must be ready to welcome General Grant and the troops," Elizabeth said.

She left the room and returned shortly with a huge twenty-five-foot flag proudly sporting its stars and stripes. Long hidden, the flag shimmered as Elizabeth spread it across the parlor floor. She slowly ran her fingers over the red, white, and blue satiny material, examining it for damage. In the colors a ripple moved slightly and touched her fingertips, sliding into her veins and through her heart. "You will not be here to see it, Allen," her mind whispered to her aching heart.

Satisfied that the flag was intact, she left the room again to find Peter.

"I need you to check the flagpole on top of the house," she told him. "Five long years it has sat unused. See if it's still sturdy enough to hold the flag."

After he scrambled onto the roof, Peter returned. "It still be solid, Miz Lizzie," he assured her.

So they anxiously waited for the moment of deliverance with their precious flag ready.

⌒⌒

At City Point, where the Appomattox River flowed into the James, a visitor from Washington had taken up residence on a captured blockade runner, *Malvern*, accompanied by his wife and son, Tad. Those who saw him thought the tall, lanky man with a scruffy black beard, dressed in an ill-fitting, long black coat, black pants, and black stovepipe hat looked exactly like an undertaker presiding over the rituals of death. Those who knew him remarked to each other how fatigued he looked, how much he had aged under the burden of war and its ghosts. His hollow eyes and drawn cheeks, his ever thinner frame, and his heavily lined face gave him the look of the walking wounded.

All around the bustling waterfront where the *Malvern* docked, the business of war came and went. Tugboats, barges, and ships of every kind moved men and materials to and from the warehouses, barracks, and military headquarters.

Each day Abraham Lincoln left the ship to confer with his generals, visit the troops, and see the most recent crop of captive Confederate soldiers. He marveled at the decrepit shape of these prisoners. Many had no uniforms, some no shoes. They hung about under guard wrapped in strange coverings, horse blankets, pieces of canvas transformed from tents or carpets. They stared at the tall man in black as he walked past, few of them aware that the president of the United States walked among them.

On Tuesday morning, March 28, he made his way to Ulysses Grant's headquarters for an important consultation. As he sat, the general peered at a great map spread across his desk. Joining them in the room were William Sherman, fresh from his sweep through Georgia and the Carolinas, mud on his boots and his jacket shabby and rumpled from wear in the field; George Meade, thin, tall, stooped with the cares of holding life and death in his hands; and Philip Sheridan, short, fidgety, and anxious to be on with the deed.

"Thanks to our lady in Richmond, we sent Lee's generals packing when he tried to break our line at Fort Stedman," Grant told the president. "The noose is tightening." A cigar in an ashtray on the map was streaming wisps of smoke as he ran his pen along the forty-mile Union line east and south of Petersburg.

Lincoln watched his hand intently.

"This afternoon Phil takes his men toward Dinwiddie Courthouse." Grant stabbed his pen at a point on the map twelve miles southwest of Petersburg. "That should flush Lee from his positions on that side of Petersburg."

Grant put his cigar back in his mouth and took a deep puff, gray smoke circling his head. "I intend to make an end of this nasty business here." His hand plunked down on the map below Petersburg. "One more desperate and bloody battle!"

Lincoln's head jerked up from the map in alarm. "My God! Can't you spare more spilling of blood?"

"I mean to take Five Forks to finish Lee. It will take blood," Grant responded simply, referring to the critical crossroads southwest of Petersburg.

Lincoln peered at the map again. "And what will this blood give us?"

"It will destroy Richmond's last rail link and cut Lee's forces in two. He and Johnston must not join forces in the Carolinas. All the pressure will force Lee to take troops away from Petersburg. Then we strike our final blow. Petersburg falls . . . then Richmond."

The next morning, Lincoln appeared on the grounds of Grant's headquarters to wish him success. They stood about in the early morning chill, talking the talk of optimists. But they had done that before. As Grant was leaving, he walked to his cabin, where his wife, Julia, stood in the doorway, and kissed her goodbye. Together the two men strode to the rail station and Lincoln fought back tears in sadness as the train with his generals pulled away from City Point, horses loaded onto the baggage cars, a mournful whistle cutting the cool air under a gray sky, to rendezvous with Sheridan's cavalry.

By evening a cold drizzle spread over the area as Little Phil's men drove across the clay fields and down the Vaughan Road. Along the way, rebel sniper fire increasingly dogged them. By dusk they found themselves in full battle with the enemy. Against the quickly darkening sky, blazing streaks of cannon fire lashed the horizon looping over the sizzling flashes of thousands of musket shots. In a happier day, at a huge Sunday picnic perhaps, the fireworks would have inspired and excited revelry and celebration. But now they rose to the sky over bloody and mangled bodies.

During the fight the drizzle turned to a driving rain and by the time the clash ended, the mucky ground had turned to a giant quagmire, sucking at the horses and pulling their legs into the ground, swallowing wagon wheels and spitting up grimy ooze. Pushing on at turtle speed, dragging his troops along, trundling six hundred wagons across fields of water and through thick pine stands, Phil Sheridan moved toward Dinwiddie Courthouse. Supply carts led by frustrated, barking teamsters sank into the mud. Horses felt the ground shift under them and the steady downpour soaked the men through. Stalled by the worsening conditions, Sheridan impatiently stalked about, rain running down his uniform, creeping into his boots, and pouring off his brimmed hat when he tilted his head. He vowed to strike on despite the weather.

By Thursday they arrived at the tiny spot on the map, no more than a handful of deserted ramshackle buildings, including a rickety tavern held up by poles and barely able to push back against the heavy rain. Without tents, without their mess wagons stalled behind in the sucking earth, they stopped there. Four miles ahead lay Five Forks, the Confederate stronghold in Little Phil's sights.

Behind Sheridan, Grant and his officers left their rail car. Riding their horses, they labored against the hostile heavens above and churning earth beneath. Along the way they passed abandoned farmhouses with apricot, peach, and cherry trees in blossom, battered by the rain. They made camp at last in a flooded cornfield and waited, thinking Sheridan would surely be too mired in mud to continue the offensive. But Sheridan was adamant. After appeals back and forth, he prevailed in his insistence that his men move forward.

By Saturday morning, the rain had stopped and Sheridan's men began a slow slog through the mucky ooze toward their objective. The sun still hid behind gray clouds and a damp smoky fog rolled over the land.

Meanwhile, just two miles northeast of Five Forks at an encampment along Hatcher's Run, Confederate Major General George Pickett, in charge of the critical crossroads, had accepted an invitation from a colleague, Tom Rosser. The daring young Rosser, a cavalry officer, tall, big-shouldered, hard-drinking, proposed an early afternoon shad bake along the river. The previous day, Lee had ordered Pickett and his nephew, Fitzhugh Lee, to "hold Five Forks at all hazards." But believing that the mud-sodden grounds would prevent any movement of Union troops, the two men had hurried to the diversion offered by the hard-partying officer who never failed to have good whiskey on hand.

On the outskirts of Five Forks, Sheridan, accompanied by Major General George Armstrong Custer and his cavalry, waited impatiently for more troops to fall in. Not far away Pickett, Fitz Lee, and Rosser spent a pleasant couple of hours eating succulent fish fresh off the hot coals, drinking whiskey, and joking on the banks of Hatcher's Run as a warm sun at last emerged from behind the clouds.

At four o'clock, Sheridan ordered the attack against Pickett's men, lined behind log fortifications. Determined to boost the spirits of his men with a bit of flair, he positioned his musicians, dressed in spiffy uniforms and carrying their instruments, at the head of his line on the best horses he could find. With music filling the air, Sheridan's men began to sing, loudly, lustily.

Leading the charge on his magnificent horse, Sheridan shouted to the men in front, "Boys, let's show these fellows a real April Fool's Day!"

When he got word of a battle well under way at Five Forks, an alarmed Pickett rushed back from his shad bake, riding hard over the clay hills and through thick pine groves. But Fitz Lee, who first ordered one of his men to determine exactly what was going on, failed to leave in time. For the rest of the day and into the night the fighting raged. Little Phil rallied his men the whole time, carrying a flag, hurling encouragement, riding in front as bullets cut the air in all directions.

A Methodist Church at Gravelly Run became the makeshift hospital for the injured. In the small, whitewashed wooden building, Union and Confederate wounded lay tightly packed, side by side, their screams of pain and blood mingling as one. Outside the church, a steady stream of Confederate prisoners under guard, some five thousand in all before it was done, trudged in relief away from the slaughter. Other rebel survivors slipped from their posts in disarray until there was only Union jubilation left.

Back in Richmond, the editors of the *Sentinel* wrote in their Saturday, April 1, edition that they were "*very hopeful of the campaign which is opening*" because, they argued, the Confederacy enjoys "*a large advantage.*"

- ❦ -

On Sunday morning, Elizabeth rose early after an anxious night full of questions. No one really knew what was happening. Part of the previous day had passed in eerie quiet except for an excitement in the afternoon caused by one of General Longstreet's divisions unexpectedly coming into the city from the east near White Oak Swamp and marching south in the direction of Petersburg. By evening the distant sounds of cannon fire pushed across Richmond coming from the south like a thunderstorm, filling the capital with foreboding. While most despaired, some still clung to hope, the last refuge of the desperate.

Elizabeth nervously walked out onto the back portico of her home. A soft mist rose over the James River beyond the garden filled with fruit blossoms and dogwood blooms. Warm air spread over her. Across the horizon to the east a brilliant sun inched its way up through the orange hues of dawn. She took a turn around the green terraces and breathed in the scents of spring. Leaves encased in buds struggling to be free and an explosion of color stirred her senses. At once calmed and excited by the spectacle, she turned back to the house, determined to find out what was happening. Eliza sat in the parlor, her hands fretfully knotted together. Annie and little Eliza still slept the peaceful sleep of the innocent.

"I'm going to St. Paul's," she said. "If there's any news to be had, it'll be there. Davis will surely attend. He always does." Picking up yesterday's crumpled newspaper and tossing it down again, she added, "We'll get no news from these."

After breakfast Elizabeth set out for Capitol Square. She could not help noticing the warm breezes, exquisite beauty, and calm peacefulness of that day, the second day of April. As she approached the city center, the crowds grew, drawn by the same anxieties and desperate for news. As far as Elizabeth could determine, the impression prevailed that General Johnston was moving from the Carolinas to reinforce Lee's lines and that together they would mount an offensive against the enemy. People milled about the post office and the War Department asking anyone at hand for news, any news.

Inside the old brick building that had become the War Department, telegrams began to arrive around 9:30 a.m. from General Lee, the first reporting that his lines were broken in three places. The news was not shared with most. A second telegram told of Lee's losses being more serious than first thought.

As the telegrams trickled to War Department officials, the architects of the Confederacy left their homes to attend this or that church. One of them, Judah Benjamin, impeccably dressed and carrying a cane adorned with gold greeted Elizabeth warmly as they passed.

At the corner of Grace and Ninth Streets, St. Paul's Episcopal Church, with its magnificent spire rising 225 feet into the air, watched over the bustle in Capitol Square. Its church bells rang at 11:00 a.m., signaling the start of services and people walked up the stone steps and past the portico columns into church. Among those entering was a familiar, tall figure, Jefferson Davis, dressed in an immaculate gray uniform and carrying his hat, his pale face as impassive and inscrutable as always.

Elizabeth took a place in one of the rear pews in the elegantly simple church. Sprinkled through the congregation were a few officers and government officials. But women made up most of the people in church and of those more than half wore black mourning clothes, their gaunt faces full of sadness and worry. The rest of the few men present hobbled in on crutches or wore the look of illness. It tore at Elizabeth's heart to see them, and the image of Allen, wounded and feverish in her bed, crept into her thoughts.

As the Reverend Dr. Minnigerode walked in to begin the service for his communicants it suddenly struck him how like this Sunday was to the First Battle of Bull Run. His foreboding matched that of his congregation. Was it a premonition of good or bad to come?

Elizabeth impatiently watched from the rear as the service slowly progressed. How surreal, she thought, to be in this place of peace, surrounded by calm, when not far away chaos, destruction, and death stalked. And she pondered again, more in sadness than in anger, what she had felt so many times in the past five years. How strange that these people who considered themselves the best of Christians had gone to war for the cause of slavery. She thought of the biblical passage, "*Whatsoever you do to these, the least of my brethren, you do unto me.*" A flood of passages rolled in irony across her mind. "*For the first shall be last and the last shall be first. . . Blessed are they who hunger and thirst for justice, for they shall be satisfied . . . Love thy neighbor as thyself . . . Blessed are the peacemakers . . .*"

In the pulpit the pastor began to speak in a powerful voice of stirring things. Elizabeth had trouble focusing on the words. Suddenly, out of the corner of her eye, she saw someone move out of the vestibule behind her and down the aisle.

The church sexton, a tall, portly older man, wearing a faded blue suit with brass buttons marching down the front and an ostentatious, ruffled white shirt, walked down the center aisle with an air of self-importance. Stopping next to pew number sixty-three, halfway down on the right, he tapped President Davis on his shoulder, handed him a piece of paper, turned, and left.

Davis quickly glanced at the paper.

Petersburg, 2 April, 1865
  I see no prospect of holding our position here till night. I am not certain I can do that. I advise that all preparation be made for leaving Richmond to-night.

R. E. Lee

He folded the paper and tucked it in his pocket. Rising, his face unmoved, his posture straight and stiff, his demeanor calm, Jefferson Davis picked up his hat, left his pew, and walked down the aisle and out of the church as everyone watched. It had happened before. After all, he was president of a country at war and why should anyone be surprised, people thought to themselves.

Elizabeth did not for a moment think it an ordinary occurrence. As she pondered what transpired, the sexton came down the aisle again and whispered something to General Joseph Anderson who immediately rose and strode out of the church with an air of urgency. Heads began to turn and a restlessness rippled through the congregation.

Again the sexton walked down the aisle, this time stopping to whisper to Dr. Minnigerode's assistant, Reverend Kepler, who then rose and approached the pastor in his pulpit. A hush fell over the assemblage as Kepler murmured that Provost Marshal Isaac Carrington wished to speak with him. Minnigerode stepped down from the pulpit and walked back to the vestry behind the altar.

"General Lee's lines have been broken and Petersburg has fallen," Carrington said solemnly. "We must evacuate Richmond today."

By the time Minnigerode hurried back to the chancel, many people had begun leaving the church in alarm. The pastor tried to reassure those who remained. He told them calmly, "General Ewell asks the home guard to meet at three o'clock this afternoon to defend the city."

From the back Elizabeth immediately understood the significance of what he said. It could only mean that General Longstreet's divisions had left and that could only mean that Lee was in serious trouble. Her heart quickened as she hurried from the church. In other congregations the same thing had transpired, officials and generals called out, leaving a storm of questions swirling in their wake.

Stepping out of the church, Elizabeth found Capitol Square swarming with people. Reports of the fall of Petersburg, of the collapse of Lee's army, were already spreading with lightning speed through the city. Government reaction to the news came just as swiftly. Across the street from St. Paul's, in front of government buildings, civil servants began throwing mounds of paper on a bonfire, incriminating papers that documented a rebellion against a nation. As the flames flared and leapt to the sky, devouring government documents, they confirmed the worst, once and for all, for those who watched in despair.

But for Elizabeth there was still work to be done. So she rushed from the scene, angling her way through the milling crowds.

By the time Elizabeth got home, some of her neighbors from Church Hill had begun appearing at the mansion door, asking for help of one sort or another. People who had shunned and reproached the Van Lews, who had considered them traitors, who had spoken against them to Confederate authorities during the war years, now carried sacks of silver pieces, precious jewelry, and other valuables to them, imploring Eliza and her daughter to keep the pieces safe for them.

"Union troops will not trouble you when they enter the city," one woman affirmed, reflecting her understanding of the Van Lews' support for the Federal cause.

Elizabeth tried to console one of her neighbors, "The war will end now. The lives of many young men will be saved and your son will come home at last."

The woman answered in great distress, "I would rather have my son die than lose the war."

Eliza and her daughter exchanged stunned glances.

A few asked to stay at the mansion for a day or two when the troops arrived, fearing the wrath of Union soldiers and believing it to be the safest place on Church Hill. Still others implored Elizabeth to speak on their behalf when Federal forces took over the city. Elizabeth and her mother graciously accepted the personal items for storage and assured everyone they would do whatever they could.

Later, in the house alone, Eliza smiled at her daughter and recalling an old argument asked, "Your charitable duty to help your enemies . . . ?"

CHAPTER 14

OVERHEAD A SERENE BLUE SKY GUIDED A BRILLIANT SUN WEST OVER Richmond. The perfume of magnolia wove through the air and dogwood pinks and whites speckled the landscape. Tulips, daffodils, and hyacinths jutted through the ground, lazy in the warm sun. Around them blue bells, violets, trillium, and hepatica spread over the land. Trees sported the yellow-greens of spring as mourning doves, hummingbirds, and butter-flies flew from branch to branch. Over the trees osprey glided through the warm air, rising and diving.

From the south the distant din of cannon rumbled over the city, heedless of the quiet and peace of nature. Crowds of bewildered and anx-ious people roamed the streets, disoriented, set loose from their moorings, waiting to see what would happen next. An apocalypse? Or a setting right of an apocalypse?

In front of the railroad depot at the end of Mayo Bridge, crowds of people pressed to board one of the few remaining trains leaving for Dan-ville. A sentinel pushed them back, trying to reason with them. There was no room, he told them. There would likely be no room later. He urged them to go home, to try the packet boats on the canal, or to use the roads.

Over the confusion and pleading, two large, rattling farm wagons approached on the Old River Road. Crammed with human cargo, the wagons pulled up to the train station. Custis Lumpkin, slave dealer, sprang from one of the wagons, whip in hand, and began motioning forcefully and shouting at the slaves to get down. Black men and women of all ages, chained together at the ankles, tumbled out of the carts. Their faces etched with misery and privation, their ankles raw and bleeding, their clothes spare and worn, they stared at the commotion. Pushing and shoving through the crowd, Lumpkin herded the shuffling slaves toward the depot entrance.

One of the Confederate sentinels called out, "Where you think you're goin'?"

"I'm shipping my property to the Carolinas," Lumpkin barked back.

"Not today you ain't!" shouted the guard.

As the slave dealer began to argue and insist, the sentinel pushed him back. Furious, Lumpkin made a move to raise his whip.

"Outa my way, boy!"

The guard swiftly jammed his bayonet on his musket. Raising it to Lumpkin's throat, he snapped, "There's no room here for you or your gang."

Lumpkin thrashed about for a route of appeal, but a second guard moved up to support the demand that he leave.

Someone in the crowd shouted to the slave dealer, "Don't you know what's happenin' here?"

Another voice cried out, "We need these trains for people, not your property."

Lumpkin sputtered and looked about wildly. With no recourse, he backed off, his face red with rage. In front of him stood some fifty slaves manacled, bewildered, frightened. One of the men in the crowd stepped forward and spoke quietly to the angry man.

"Your selling days are over. They're free. Richmond will be in Yankee hands in a day or two. You best save yourself . . . now."

Lumpkin stared at the man, then at the chained blacks huddled together, his eyes flashing, his jaw clenched, his hands in fists. With a violent motion, he threw the whip to the ground and reaching into his pocket he pulled out a metal key on a thick ring. This he hurled at the feet of the slaves and turning briskly he stormed away.

For a few moments the captives froze in confusion. A hush had fallen over those in the crowd nearby. Then one of the blacks reached down, picked up the key, and began unlocking the manacles, one by one.

～

The streets of Richmond swarmed with people all afternoon. Soldiers rushing to find loved ones. People saying mournful goodbyes as if to the dead departing forever. Women searching for family. Crying children dragged along by anxious parents. People in transit without any idea where safety might be, leaving the city about to fall to the hated Yankees. Confederate troops marching through the city to Mayo Bridge, the chief escape route, heading west to join Lee. Army supply wagons rumbling through streets so clogged with people they inched and stopped, inched and stopped. Families, individuals trying to board canal boats, trains, carts to flee. People rushing to banks to exchange their worthless Confederate money for gold and silver. Government workers dashing about sending critical documents away, burning what remained. Treasury workers frantically packing gold and silver for shipment to safety, mindful it had once been confiscated from the United States government. Confederate officials, fearing the hangman's noose, hurrying to rail cars held in ready for them. Convalescent soldiers, the pallor of sickness sketched on their faces, pressed back into service and being marched out of the city. People wandering aimlessly like lost, purposeless spirits, unable to go back, unsure how to move forward, or where. Hungry people looking for food.

Among this shifting mass of humanity, an isolated figure moved, the president of the Confederacy. Jefferson Davis took time from the chaotic business of retreat to stop here and there, talk to people and make brief visits to friends before leaving the city. At one point he stopped at the African Church where a large crowd of blacks had gathered. William Brisby and Sylvanus Brown stood together in the church and exchanged startled glances when they spotted him entering their place of worship. At the sight of the Confederate president, the bewildered throng stepped back, opening a path down the center aisle as he moved through. Once at the front, he addressed the packed assembly.

"The disasters of today are temporary," he said, his voice calm, his tall frame erect. "There is nothing to fear, my friends. We will soon come back to establish the capital in this city. The ultimate success of the Southern Confederacy cannot be questioned. I urge you to have courage and fidelity in the midst of this momentary setback."

As Davis left the church, a murmur rose in the assembly. Brisby shook his head in puzzlement. "Can he really believe we fear the Union advance?"

"He sees us as his children," Brown answered simply, shrugging his shoulders.

Shortly after the strange visit, the congregation drifted out of church in high spirits, with an agenda far different than the president's. They moved about the streets, greeting other blacks happily, shaking hands, smiling in a celebratory mood.

—◦—

By late afternoon, a proclamation was read in Capitol Square. Since foodstuffs in the government commissaries could not be moved, the warehouses would be opened to the public and food distributed free of charge to any who needed it. The news swept through the starving city.

When Elizabeth heard, she immediately prepared to leave with Mary and Peter, sacks in hand. Eliza began to object, thinking it not fitting to "beg" for food, as she put it.

"We are all hungry, mother—the girls, the servants. Nothing could be more fitting than to feed the hungry. Besides, I feel sure we will have visitors, *many* visitors. The prisons will not stay sealed for very long . . . These people will need to be fed."

"Go, then," Eliza said, a look of worry on her face. "But be careful. There will be a terrible rush of hungry people."

When the three arrived at the Commissary Department, the great wooden doors had already been thrown open. People gaped at the rows and rows of hams, bacon, beef, rice, potatoes, flour, coffee, sugar . . . Here in the midst of starvation sat all this food.

A great diversity of humanity descended on the warehouses—poor and elite, frail and strong, old and young, white and black, women and men, even children, with outstretched hands, some of them crying. Elizabeth blinked, adjusting to the dim light of the commissary, as she jostled her way through the frantic crowd. She looked at the stacks of food and the hungry people around her and a wave of anger poured over her. All this time people have starved, she thought, soldiers have starved, while this food lay hoarded. Together with Mary and Peter, she filled her sacks as best she could and when they could carry no more they edged their way through the shoving crowds into the blinding light, stooped under their loads.

Outside the mood quickly began to turn rowdy and nasty as afternoon waned. A fistfight had broken out down the street amid shouts and screeches. Coarse, skulking mobs formed. Women of the night turned out in force in the light of day. For years the human residue of war, deserters and thieves, camp followers and profiteers, scoundrels and murderers had piled into Richmond, kept in check by military discipline. Now, with the troops leaving, they crawled into the sunshine, unbridled. Elizabeth saw looters smashing windows, breaking into shops. Even some soldiers still dressed in gray uniforms took part in the rampage. She hung back, staring in disbelief.

"Come along, Miss Lizzie," Mary urged gently.

But as they started to move, another spectacle caught their eyes. Government workers, charged by the municipal council with destroying all of the city's liquor to prevent drunkenness and civil unrest, were throwing cases of bottled liquor from windows and rolling barrels of whiskey from warehouses and stores into the streets. There they smashed the kegs with axes, and alcohol rushed in torrents down the city gullies. Enraged men tried to stop them, grabbing barrels and rolling them away. Elizabeth stared in alarm as men and women, even some soldiers and children, ran with pots, buckets, tin cups, and bowls to the gullies, scooping up the whiskey. Some guzzled it on the spot, others hurried away clutching their precious liquor.

"Come, Miss Lizzie," Mary said again firmly, tugging at her arm. "We best be home."

— ❦ —

The sounds of musket fire and cannon blasts drew nearer to Richmond. In the mansion on Church Hill, Elizabeth and her mother bustled about with preparations. Evening approached. Seeing that the city had shut down the gas works, servants hurried about with candles to light the rooms. Outside the day's warm sun hurried away from the city and the first colors of sunset streaked across the western sky.

Eliza stopped and listened. She heard a commotion outside.

"What's that? She said aloud.

Puzzled by the sounds that grew louder, Elizabeth stopped what she was doing. Shouts began to rise over the noise as it grew closer.

"Stay here," Elizabeth said to her mother as she turned and hurried to the front door.

Peter had already moved quickly to the door and was about to open it when Elizabeth motioned him to stop. She walked to the window and pulled back a corner of the drapes. Outside on the lawn in front of her home a menacing group of fifteen to twenty people, mostly men, stood shouting and gesturing angrily. Many carried burning wooden torches.

Standing behind her, Peter said, "Let me go out there, Miz Lizzie."

"No, Peter," she answered firmly. "I'll go."

By then Eliza and the girls had followed her into the room.

"No, Bet, you can't go out there," Eliza said in a panic as the shouts grew more menacing.

Elizabeth quickly moved to the door, opened it and stepped out, closing it behind her. A momentary hush fell over the mob when they saw her.

Then someone screamed, "Lincoln lover!"

"Traitor!" another cried.

"Nigger lover!"

Elizabeth stood on the porch facing the taunts, erect, unwavering, silent, buoyed by a powerful inner fury, long repressed, that robbed her of all fear and prudence. She stared, her eyes glaring and unflinching, her hands clenched at her sides. The shouts grew louder and the waving torches more threatening. Still Elizabeth faced them down without a word. Suddenly one of the men, threw his fiery torch at the house. It landed just shy of the wall in a thicket of rhododendron bushes. Immovable, she continued to glare at them.

A scruffy looking man dressed in a dirty coat and baggy pants, waving a burning piece of wood, stepped forward from the belligerent crowd. "Step aside. We intend to burn this Union house to the ground."

Elizabeth stood her ground. Then in a booming voice she shouted, "I know you . . . and you . . . and you . . ." She pointed to each in turn. "Grant will be here soon. Burn this house and your houses will burn with it." Her arm drew a wide arc in front of her.

Just then the door flew open and Annie ran out, rushing to her aunt and clutching her tightly. "Don't hurt my Aunt Lizzie," she cried out, tears streaming down her face.

On seeing the child, the startled man stood still, suddenly frozen. In the doorway Eliza appeared, her face full of alarm, and Peter behind her.

"You will have to kill me first," Elizabeth yelled, her angry voice firm and unwavering as she pushed Annie behind her.

A grumbling rose from the crowd, but for a moment no one moved. The eyes of the man before her darted about wildly for what seemed like a long time. Suddenly he took a small, tentative step backward. As if on signal, the others fell back, slowly, grudgingly, their faces tight with bitterness and venom.

Elizabeth made no move until the torches had disappeared into the growing darkness. Then, hugging Annie tightly, she turned and they walked back into the house.

A flurry of nervous activity overtook the prisons of Richmond that afternoon. In the midst of the chaos many thousands of Union prisoners of war still filled the city's jails. A critical question dogged Confederate authorities: what to do with them. Leave them behind and the Union Army moving against them would swell. Many still clung to the faint hope that the South could somehow regroup and hold out. Take them out of the city and deprive the North of thousands of soldiers. But take them where? No one knew for sure where the various enemy approaches were located. Confederate troops and officials were fleeing southwest through Danville to the Carolinas. That seemed the only option.

Prison officials scrambled to arrange for an orderly forced march south, not an easy assignment given the dearth of soldiers and guards for escort, lack of supplies, uncertainty about routes, and lack of transportation. Worst, they would have to move thousands of men in the darkness of night.

Among the prisoners to be transferred were Unionists Frederick Lohmann, William White, Lemuel Babcock, and others, who had languished for months in Castle Thunder, Libby, and elsewhere. Rumors spread through Castle Thunder of the evacuation of Richmond and the impending march. Immediately on hearing the news, feverish plans erupted and mushroomed among Lohmann and his friends to escape the march.

Another denizen of the prison system, Erasmus Ross, sweated over the news. As a Unionist in Elizabeth Van Lew's network, he had built a cover by acting the part of brutal, virulently pro-Confederate prison clerk at Libby. Now the prison doors would be flung open with completely inadequate security for controlling hoards of long-repressed, angry men. He entertained no illusions about what prisoners would do to him given the chance. So he too waited for his chance to escape.

In the streets, darkness settled over the tortured city, broken by flames of torches and bonfires that cast a brassy light over roaming crowds. At Castle Thunder prisoners were taken from their cells and given a chunk of corn bread each with the warning that it must last them for at least three days. Then guards marched the increasingly belligerent men into the yard. Sentries with rifles and bayonets herded them into a long formation and took positions along the sides of the line.

As the march began, Lohmann, White, and Babcock slowly fell back toward the rear of the line where only one guard walked. Once onto the streets, they saw crowds of people milling about. Guards in front shouted orders and cleared the way. Suddenly, someone in the line of prisoners shouted at the crowd.

"Hey Rebs, you're finished! We've won!"

Before the guards could figure out who hurled the insult, other prisoners began to taunt the crowd and yell more angry slurs. Some of the bystanders shouted back, raising their fists in the air. A rock was flung at the prisoners, who reacted with an uproar. As the shouting and throwing accelerated, Lohmann motioned his comrades. While guards struggled to bring order in the eerie moonlight, prisoners and onlookers surged against each other. The three men swiftly slipped out of the ranks one by one dissolving into the crowd. Within minutes they had slithered away into the night, mingling with the throngs of agitated and tawdry people, many of them staggering under their liquor.

Along the streets, gaslights had gone black as night. In their place bonfires burned. People carried flaming papers and sticks to light their way casting a garish light as they wove through the dangerous streets. Inside Richmond's homes, people huddled in fear behind locked doors, most of them women and children left behind.

Moving quickly the three men picked their way along the crowded, noisy streets. As Lohmann and his friends climbed Church Hill, the crowds began to thin. Then they saw it, the most beautiful sight in many months. Slipping around to the back of the dark mansion, they tapped on the door, softly at first, then more anxiously.

The door remained shut but a brusque male voice called out, "Who's there?"

"It's me. Frederick . . . Frederick Lohmann."

The door flew open and a smiling Peter greeted the men. "Come in. Come in. Miz Lizzie shor gonna be happy ta see you."

In the parlor, Elizabeth leapt from her seat in joy at the sight. Hugging the men in turn, she exclaimed, "My friends, I knew you would find a way."

As they spoke happily, more knocking came. Peter hurried to the back door again and called out, asking who was there.

"Rose . . ." the voice broke and hesitated. "Thomas Rose."

Peter froze, remembering the name and that day, that awful day when he learned he had turned away a desperate escaped prisoner. The door opened.

"It's you," he stammered. "Come in, please." He wanted to apologize, to tell this man how sorry he was. "Da other time . . . I didn't know . . ."

Just then Elizabeth entered the room. "Who is it, Peter?"

"Thomas Rose," the man answered extending his hand. He stared at the woman before him. A dim memory stirred.

"Dear God, Colonel Rose!" She hurried to him. "I'm Elizabeth. Elizabeth Van Lew," she said, taking his hand and holding it tightly.

He looked closely at the face, the mass of blond curls tumbling onto her forehead, and struggled to connect the face with . . . he didn't know what. Tears had begun to fall from her eyes.

"You cared for my Allen." She struggled to push back the tears and compose herself.

"Allen . . . ?" he said, puzzled.

"Allen Rockwell. Months ago. In Libby." Her voice cracked and the tears would not stop.

A rush of memories overcame him. "The woman in the brooch! That was you," he said in amazement. "I didn't know . . . I . . ."

"It was me," she interrupted, her heart heavy with grief and remorse. "The woman who failed you when you needed me most."

"It were my fault," Peter jumped in.

"No," Elizabeth said firmly, shaking her head. "Not Peter's fault. I was called away to help my brother in trouble. Peter knew nothing. He was protecting us."

"Dear lady," Rose said, overcome with emotion, squeezing her hand. "I always knew in my heart it was a terrible mistake. I never blamed you."

"Now you are here and that's all that matters. You've escaped again!"

"This time was much easier," he smiled.

"Come, I want you to meet my mother and the others," Elizabeth said, pulling him toward the parlor.

As they entered the candlelit room, Rose suddenly stopped. His face blanched and his body stiffened. In the corner stood the hated Confederate clerk of Libby Prison, Erasmus Ross. Rose instinctively stepped back through the doorway.

Elizabeth looked from Rose to Erasmus and back. It suddenly struck her what was happening and she quickly took Rose's hand again, "He's one of us," she reassured him. "Always has been."

Rose stood gaping, mystified. Ross a Unionist? Slowly the pieces began falling into place—the countless times during the dig that the clerk had failed to catch them when they took each other's places in the count, the relative ease with which they came and went from the cell to the kitchen to the basement, the escape of Lounsbury after being sent to Ross's office, the sudden removal of Rockwell to the infirmary . . .

He stepped back into the room as Eliza, Lohmann, and the others came forward to greet him. Last, young Ross stepped up and extended his hand with a nod.

"It's over," he said simply.

All through the night they came to the mansion on the hill—fugitives, fellow Unionists, friends.

◆

In the James River just south of the city the remnants of the Confederate Navy sat. Admiral Raphael Semmes, who once fought Union ships on the high seas, had only memories of glory left, of a time when he commanded the *Alabama,* the most feared ship on the great Atlantic. Now his worn and battered fleet of four ironclads and five wooden gunboats rested idly in river waters as he lingered over a late lunch in the gleaming, oak-paneled dining room of the *Virginia* on this Sunday afternoon. Oblivious to the dramatic events occurring around Petersburg and the capital, he was startled by a messenger with an unexpected letter from the Secretary of the Navy.

Admiral Semmes,
General Lee advises the Government to withdraw from this city and the officers will leave this evening . . . He withdraws upon his lines toward Danville, this night; and unless otherwise directed by General Lee, upon you is devolved the duty of destroying your ships, this night.

S. R. Mallory
Secretary of the Navy

Unbelieving, Semmes read the message again. Lee in retreat? The Confederate government fleeing the capital? Destroy all the ships? He rose, heartsick at the news. And angry. Why had there been no warning of this disaster in the making? He hurried to his signal man to communicate with Lee and Mallory. The frantic sailor rushed on shore to the signal station and tried for a full hour to get a response, but none came. So the stunned admiral called together his officers and began plans to destroy the remnants of the Confederate Navy. He decided to wait for the curtain of night to hide the deed and spare alarming the civilian population.

The men worked for hours setting the explosives and charges, positioning the ships to avoid damage to buildings along the shoreline and removing supplies for the sailors who would now trek after Lee. Long after darkness had crept over the city, Semmes gave the order to blow up the ships.

On Church Hill a busy Elizabeth heard the explosions one after another, like the sound of hundreds of cannon. Dashing onto the back portico followed by Eliza, the girls, their friends and fugitive guests, she saw the night sky light up with shooting flames over the river. The explosion of the magazines on the ships threw the loaded shells, with their fuses lit, across the sky in a blaze of flashing colors. The group on the great porch watched in awe as the fireworks erupted into an indescribable spectacle while their house shook around them.

Annie grabbed her aunt's arm in delight at the show and jumped up and down, exclaiming, "It's *so* pretty, Aunt Lizzie!"

Elizabeth, understanding at once that the Confederate Navy was headed for perdition, smiled. "Yes, Annie, *very* pretty."

<hr />

One officially ordained act remained for the troops before completing their flight from the doomed city—the order to destroy the tobacco and other large warehouses, the flour mills, and the huge public warehouse full of goods belonging to France and England. The mayor of Richmond and others frantically protested the military directive as misguided and threatening the whole business district of Richmond. After the middle of a night already filled with every imaginable calamity, they argued for over an hour with General Ewell and War Department staff, to no avail. The contents of the mills and warehouses would not be left to fall into Yankee hands.

Preparations having been made, General Ewell gave the order and torches quickly set the wooden structures to flames, a brisk southerly wind notwithstanding. One after another the burning buildings sent tongues of fire into the black night. As the blazes became visible, mobs rushed to the warehouse and, finding entrances away from the fire, began pillaging anew, dragging tobacco, flour, clothing, whatever they could find, out into the streets and away. A great confusion of shouts rose over the crackling and hissing infernos as the fires quickly spread beyond the targeted buildings.

At the Van Lew mansion, its residents and visitors still stood on the portico watching the pyrotechnics of the burning Confederate Navy.

Suddenly someone on the portico noticed the horizon over the city to the west lit up as well. Huge clouds of billowing smoke churned over the lower portion of the city near the river, where flames soared like mad demons. As it moved, the hungry fire lapped at the alcohol poured earlier into the gutters and potholes around the buildings. Fueled by the liquor clogging ditches along the roadways, flames flew down the streets, becoming a raging inferno.

Railroad trestles and bridges also blazed, all torched by retreating Confederate troops. The rear guard of the army, charged with destroying the last bridge, set fire to Mayo Bridge as the remaining troops crossed. The span from the rail depot to Old River Road burned as flames spewed dense black smoke in their wake.

"The city is burning!" Eliza gasped, pulling Annie and little Eliza to her.

They all stood transfixed by the sight. Charles Palmer, come to celebrate with the Van Lews, gasped when he saw the sight and rushed away in alarm. His office and home on the corner of Carey and Virginia Streets sat in the center of the business district that now appeared to be in flames.

No one slept that night as they huddled together anxiously waiting for sunrise. Before morning Palmer, who had already suffered reverses in his shipping business due to the blockade of Southern ports, dragged himself back to the Van Lew home to report that he had lost everything in the blaze that continued to ravage the center of Richmond.

"What will you do?" Elizabeth asked him uneasily.

"I may be forced to move in with my son." He shook his head despondently. "My Confederate son . . ."

Just before dawn a fantastic explosion, like an earthquake, startled the anxious group crowded into the Van Lew parlor. The house shook and seemed to roll like a ship on a stormy sea as a tremendous thundering sound cut through their ears. More than one person thought in that moment the end of the world must be at hand and surely the dead heard the horrific noise.

"The arsenal!" Lohmann said when he recovered. "It has to be the downtown arsenal."

Elizabeth jumped to her feet in alarm. The arsenal? Next to . . . "The almshouse . . . Emmie . . ." she shouted.

She immediately rushed from the room, men in tow. Down the hill they ran, gasping for air in the smoke-filled night as musket shells in the magazine continued to burst, sending lurid tongues of flame and shrapnel all around. Overhead countless eyes in the black sky quietly watched the chaotic spectacle and frantic rushing about. Images of sweet Emmie and the other bedridden residents followed Elizabeth while she raced down the slope, their mournful, lonely faces clinging to her, calling her, needing her, block after block after block.

As they approached, broken glass littered the streets, stabbing at their shoes and crunching in their ears. Ahead a fiery inferno and intense heat blocked their way. Breathless, they stopped, unable to move forward. Fire burned savagely everywhere. Distraught people milled about as choking dust swam in the unbearable heat. Behind the mountain of flames the whole of downtown and beyond lay consumed. Now only corpses of brick walls stood.

Elizabeth stared in horror and disbelief at the massive burning, smoking spectacle, her heart pounding, her head throbbing. In her frantic mind she peered into the flames, imagining the almshouse, where she had tended the elderly poor for so long, burning. She envisioned the horror of a fiery ruin, its roof gone, its floors collapsed onto the scorched earth. She could see in the chaos of her thoughts fire eating shards of mattresses, pieces of bedposts, bits of chairs, hunks of timber. And she imagined bodies lying strewn about. Elizabeth gasped and dropped to her knees, a crushing weight on her heart, an excruciating pain in her spirit, an unbearable image of feisty Emmie spinning through her dizzy mind.

Erasmus Ross kneeled beside Elizabeth and gently put his arm on her shoulders. No one spoke. The hurt lay too deep.

CHAPTER 15

THE MAYOR OF RICHMOND AND A SMALL DISHEARTENED ENTOURAGE rode out of the city in darkness. Behind them mobs of people milled about the littered streets in willful mayhem, while others hung about in dazed bewilderment. An inferno continued to devour the capital from its core, sending great black clouds of smoke into the dreadful night as flames leapt from building to building. The small group rode crowded together in a scruffy carriage with threadbare seats, slowly pulled by a horse as tired and hungry as the city's people. High above their shabby coach, a large white shirttail fluttered on a wooden pole as they rode past dark stands of battered pine trees and over earth hard packed by Confederate boots and horses' hooves. Along the road lay open fields, abandoned log fortifications, and spiked cannon. At intervals, brightly colored strips of cloth flapped on sticks pushed into the ground, warning of land mines.

About one mile from the Richmond docks on the southeastern outskirts of the city past Gillies Creek, a detachment of Union officers spotted the ragtag party with their white flag approaching the junction of New Market Road and Osborne Turnpike. A hush fell over the well-fed men dressed in tailored blue coats and spiffy boots. Only the sounds of creaking wagon wheels filled the eerie quiet where angry ghosts of the dead roamed the fields.

Streaks of morning light began to appear across the gray skies as Major Atherton Stevens of the Union detachment approached the carriage and asked, "Who is in charge of the flag of surrender."

"Joseph Mayo, mayor of the city of Richmond," came the answer.

269

Pulling a letter from the box he carried containing the city seal, the mayor handed the envelope to the major, who opened it.

To the General Commanding the United States Army in front of Richmond:

The Army of the Confederate Government having abandoned the City of Richmond, I respectfully request that you take possession of it with an organized force, to preserve order and protect women and children and property.

Respectfully,
Joseph Mayo, Mayor

"Mr. Mayo," Stevens addressed the man, "I can assure you that Union officers have strict orders to protect the city. I promise all of you that the city will be safe in our hands."

Within minutes Mayo and his colleagues proceeded back to Richmond with the officers. As they drew near the city in the early morning light, fires raged out of control and drunkenness, brawling, and looting continued unabated. With the last of the rebel troops gone, mobs made a demonic rush for the last unguarded government storehouses, ripping from shelves the goods so long deprived them. The dying Confederacy lay before the victorious Union army like a wounded animal turning on its own as it writhed in pain and despair.

❧

On Church Hill, Elizabeth sat alone in the library, struggling with an overwhelming grief after returning from the inferno, the crouching lion eyeing her suspiciously from his perch on the column, the wisdom of ages meaningless on the shelves around her. Here, at the moment of victory, oppressive feelings of anguish and turmoil paralyzed her, slithering through her veins, stinging her heart, shrouding her vision, throwing her thoughts in every direction. The chaos all around her in Richmond cast a deadly pall over everything. This was not what she imagined as the end of the Confederacy. Union victory should have come in joy and celebration.

"Is this what Allen died for, what our family has been torn apart for, what Emmie was sacrificed for," she agonized.

Her mind flew back, back to a lost world of innocence, to her childhood, to the peace and tranquillity of White Sulfur Springs in the days before secession fever fanned by those known as fire-eaters. What had these men brought to the South, with their cries of independence and the divine right to own slaves?

"Death. Only death," she answered herself. "Death has taken root in the South." She turned to the ever present phantom in the room. "Hundreds of thousands have died, Poppa." Her breath caught at the thought.

He listened and hoped to be spared another tongue lashing over slavery.

"Do I delude myself, Poppa? About a lost world of innocence?" Elizabeth asked silently.

Of course. The young are always deluded, he wanted to say. But he kept quiet.

"Yes," she answered herself. "A fabrication—that lost world of innocence. It *never* existed. It could never exist as long as slavery stood." She stared at the books lining the shelves around the room. "Innocence is only ignorance in the end."

Her torment pained him, but still he kept quiet.

"Death took root in the South long before the Civil War," she thought aloud. "Only the form of death changed. Blood washed away blood."

Dear Elizabeth. Wiser and better than your father.

"I fear, though, that blood will not be enough. Southerners will not reconcile easily to defeat—or to freedom for Negroes . . ."

Her sadness was more than he could bear. He rose up.

A sudden breeze swept over her in the still air of the library, a refreshing gust swirling around her, caressing her, rejuvenating her. Soft whispers from the dead spoke to her, prodded her, comforted her. Slowly, very slowly, a veil fell from her eyes, brushing away the rolling gray fog in her mind, lifting a terrible weight from her shoulders, draining the hurt from her aching heart. For a long while she sat, staring at nothing in the quiet peace of the room.

At last she rose from her chair and looked out the window at the garden teeming with life and color. How quickly spring came. It had not succumbed to the bleakness and desolation of winter after all. A weak smile broke across her lips. Turning, she walked out of the library and down the stairway to join the others.

"Peter, it's time to put up the flag."

As columns of Union soldiers marched into the city and made their way toward Capitol Square to raise the stars and stripes, a Federal flag had already been raised over the roof of a mansion on Church Hill.

The Federal troops entering the city of rebellion on Monday, April 3, watched in horror at the spectacle of raging fires consuming whole blocks in a large section of downtown. In front of government buildings they saw mounds and mounds of burning documents, the smoldering remnants of treasonous evidence. In turn, the sight of the armed men in blue began to sober the milling crowds who grudgingly fell back. In homes lining the streets, women and children, remembering warnings of rape and massacre, hovered anxiously together in windows, watching with trepidation as roadways below began to fill with Union soldiers.

The first cavalry regiment rode through the streets with pomp and noise, wagons and cannon rolling, banners flying, bands playing, first "Yankee Doodle," then the "Battle Cry of Freedom." As the troops moved in, blacks suddenly appeared from nowhere, flooding the sidewalks, cheering, weeping, falling to their knees, clutching the soldiers in gratitude. A few whites also welcomed them warmly. But for most, the enemy display was a requiem that banished all hope, tore hearts to shreds, and ripped sobs from their throats.

On reaching Capitol Square a heartrending sight greeted the cavalry. Desperate women and frightened children displaced by the fires sat and lay on the ground, the air around them thick with soot, the remnants of their worldly possessions piled at their sides, a few bits of furniture, blankets, a pillow here and there, clothes, small bundles. Their hungry, despairing faces, white and black, stared at the spectacle unfolding in the hot square. Moved by the tragic sight, Union soldiers walked about offering their rations of hardtack and meat.

Despite the desolation, the business of victory proceeded. An officer busily unbuckled a large flag from the front of his saddle. He and another officer made their way up to the roof of the capitol where the Confederate flag had already been removed. Unfurling the Stars and Stripes, which had flown over occupied New Orleans under General Butler, they lifted and proudly set it on the pole over the rebellious roof. At that instant, singing, led by the troops, rose through the air as the words of the national anthem, "The "Star-Spangled Banner," reached to the heavens. In the square below an immense cheering erupted from blacks and some whites, women, men, and children, even a few battered old men dressed in gray.

With those applauding in the square was Elizabeth Van Lew, tears streaming from her face, suddenly overcome by the vision she saw in the fluttering Stars and Stripes, a vision she had always known but forgotten in the blood of struggle. Liberty. The end of the cruelest of all human enterprises, slavery. The reunification of a great nation. Beside her, Annie and little Eliza, who had begged their aunt to take them along in the sleepless excitement of the early morning, watched with glee.

"Why are you crying, Aunt Lizzie," Annie asked when she noticed the tears.

"Because it's a wonderful day for the whole country, Annie. And for us. For everyone, especially the Negro people." She hugged the child tightly. "They will never be slaves again, Annie, never."

The girl looked at Elizabeth's face and thought it must be very good thing if her auntie said so, although she understood so little. "Does it mean daddy can come home to us now?" she asked.

"Yes, Annie, daddy can come home."

As the flag was being raised over the capitol, the officer in charge of the occupation of Richmond, formally accepted the surrender of the Confederate capital from the mayor at City Hall. He immediately sent a message to the Union high command.

3 April, 1865
General Ulysses S. Grant,
>*We took Richmond at a quarter past eight this morning.*
>>*Major General Godfrey Weitzel*

Stepping from the building into the intense heat fueled by the fires, Weitzel choked and squinted in the smoke and cinders. Before him stood an enormous cauldron of flames that continued making its destructive way toward Capitol Square. Overhead the Union flag flapped in the wind as fiery sparks from the spreading blaze angrily licked at the red, white, and blue set against a magnificent cloudless sky.

Weitzel moved quickly to fortify the city and stop further devastation. To his next in command, General Ripley, he said with urgency, "I wish this conflagration stopped, and this city saved if it is humanly possible, and you have carte blanche to do it."

Ripley looked again at the mass of billowing smoke and flames and mumbled to himself about the apparently hopeless task. But with military discipline and indomitable resolution he set to it, rallying his regiments. Confederate General Ewell's fleeing troops had cut the water hoses after torching the buildings, leaving nothing by way of firefighting equipment that worked. Ripley ordered that buildings in the fire's corridor be blown up, starving the hungry flames. The winds helped a bit by shifting toward the river away from residential areas.

With a determination that could not have been greater were they extinguishing flames in their own homes, Union soldiers battled the blaze, which spat and crackled, punctuated by the sound of falling timbers and exploding shells. Stripped to the waist, black soot covering their bodies, sweat pouring from every pore, the brave men of Ripley's First Brigade plunged into the searing heat. Joining them were many blacks and citizens of Richmond.

Even as they struggled to contain the flames, the fire reached Capitol Square, burning the State Courthouse and setting fire to a railing around the steeple of St. Paul's Church. The fire had reached the corner of Franklin and Twelfth Streets at the square's south end. Having consumed much of the business district, the blaze had also spread to private houses, spewing flames onto roofs and porches. Those who could rushed up and down pouring water on their roofs or laying wet blankets across them till the heat grew unbearable and they abandoned their homes to the licking tongues of fire. In one of the houses Mary Custis Lee, ailing wife of General Robert E. Lee, sat, refusing all pleas that she leave.

As Ripley's men worked, troops continued to pour into the city. Among them, lines of Negro cavalry rode, dressed in their blue finery and singing "John Brown's Body lies a moldering in his grave . . ." The effect of these Negro troops on the populace was tremendous—euphoric for Richmond's blacks, excruciating for most of the city's whites. For Union Colonel Charles Adams, Jr., descendant of two United States presidents and staunch abolitionist, leading his black troops into the fallen Capital of the Confederacy was the most glorious moment of his army career.

In his office, Colonel Ripley battled another onslaught—the women of Richmond. All day they poured into his office, convinced by years of tirades in the Confederate press that Yankees were beasts who would initiate a reign of terror and rape once they took hold of the city. So they came seeking protection and requiring multiple reassurances that they had nothing to fear. But Ripley made sure that everyone who asked got a guard for their homes.

The fires raged all day turning the sun black and covering the city with a shroud of smoke. By early afternoon the winds shifted again, coming from the south as the northwestern section of the city came under attack. Through it all Ripley's First Brigade endured, going so far as to rescue furniture from homes they could not save and putting a guard over it till it could be claimed by its owners. All day a stream of people, made homeless by the fire, carried what little they could save to the far end of Capitol Square and waited for salvation. From many homes, wounded Confederate soldiers left behind were carried out on stretchers into the furnace heat.

By evening the fire spent itself and only smoldering piles of rubble covered a large portion of the city. With a curfew in effect, the streets had fallen largely silent after a day of pandemonium. Only an occasional gunshot from a drunken Confederate soldier left behind, the clattering hooves of a sentry from the First Brigade passing, or a shouted order to a straggler violating curfew broke the ghostly silence.

Overhead a moon warily watched the smoking ruins of the Department of War of the Permanent Government of the Confederacy just off Capitol Square, where a darkened flag stood between earth and sky. Phantoms roamed the deserted streets surrounded by cadavers of buildings, searching for deceased promises of glory and independence. Behind closed doors, broken lives lay in fitful sleep, dreaming of breathless bodies given to the Cause. Quiet at last fell over the city of the dead.

—◆—

After the joyful raising of the United States flag that morning, Elizabeth made her way back home, stopping along the streets to greet Union soldiers and hug a Federal horse here and there. A bit of hope crept into her heart and slowly seeped into the dark corners of her soul. As she and the girls approached home they spotted horses in front and an armed guard.

Annie broke away in excitement and ran ahead up the hill with little Eliza close on her heels. After dashing into the house she quickly reemerged and ran back to Elizabeth.

"Aunt Lizzie, the soldiers are here! They're waiting for you."

With Annie tugging her hand, Elizabeth quickened her step. Inside a Union officer introduced himself as Lieutenant Colonel Ely Parker, military secretary to General Ulysses Grant.

"The general has given a specific order that on entering the city, we come immediately to you, Miss Van Lew," he said. "We have orders to protect you and your family."

Startled, Elizabeth stared at the officer with his dark hair, thick beard, prominent nose, and penetrating eyes, the son of a famous Seneca Indian chief from New York, she found out later. Eliza stood silently by, the slag heap of worry and fear, grown massive over the years, slowly lifting from her frail shoulders. Next to her mother, Mary Bowser and Eliza Carrington beamed in pride. Around the women in the crowded parlor stood the grateful fugitives from Castle Thunder and Libby Prison, liberated and about to be reunited with their comrades and families. Many of her Unionist friends, at last relieved of the label "traitor" and able to live again in the open, had also gathered.

"General Grant has asked that we see to it that all your wants be supplied. We are posting a guard for your family's protection. The Union owes you a debt that can never be repaid, Miss Van Lew," Parker continued kindly.

With that the room broke into applause. Embarrassed, Elizabeth gestured for them to stop.

"No, I cannot take credit for the work of so many. Those who suffered imprisonment . . ."

"But you were the master," Frederick Lohmann interrupted. "It was you who led us."

"You who inspired us," Charles Palmer said.

"You, whose iron heart never wavered," William Rowley added.

"And *your* charm that beguiled Winder, Benjamin, Davis, and who knows who else," joked Thomas McNiven, as the group broke into laughter.

Elizabeth smiled. Her eyes began to mist and the words "dear friends" caught in her throat and would not come out. She glanced from face to face in gratitude as the group relaxed and began to chat in earnest with each other. Behind the tears, after she looked into all the faces in the crowd, her eyes rested on the filmy image of a missing person, the visage of a lost love, the specter of Allen, bound to her forever.

The next day, Tuesday, west of Petersburg, General Robert E. Lee made his way to Amelia Courthouse, his hungry troops badly shrunken and dragging. The old man, still handsome, his brown eyes keenly searching, sat erect in his saddle. Behind him scattered rifle fire cut the air. Longstreet's men skirmished with Union cavalry, holding them back, and Grant was but hours away. The remnants of the commands under Longstreet, Gordon, Pickett, Mahone, and Anderson had arrived, but Ewell's men from Richmond were nowhere in sight. The remnants of Lee's army had been ordered to join together at the village.

The peaceful hamlet of Amelia Station on the Appomattox River looked picture-card perfect. Neat houses surrounded by picket fences, flowers and honeysuckle vines creeping over them, lined the unpaved streets. In the center of town a tavern and the courthouse stood along a square covered with newly mown grass, its scent spreading over the men as they rode in. Large oak trees, their leaves newly open, shaded the public areas.

Lee, dressed in an immaculate gray uniform, went immediately to the railroad depot. Days before he had ordered the remainder of the reserve food supplies in Richmond to be shipped immediately to Amelia Station to feed his retreating army, now near starvation and exhausted. The train from Richmond waited at the station when he arrived.

"I've come to get the food sent from Richmond for my troops," Lee said to the stationmaster. "On that train." He pointed.

"Food?" the puzzled stationmaster asked.

"Yes, the food sent from Richmond," Lee repeated, a sudden twinge of anxiety winding through his chest.

"Why, General, those rail cars are full of ammunition and government documents," the stationmaster nervously said. "There is no food."

A look of utter defeat spread across the face of the usually reserved general as he seemed to descend into a shadow. He stared in disbelief at the train, then turned and looked across the square to the fields beyond the village where his starving men camped, tattered, worn out, and demoralized. They broke his heart. The Confederate cause had come to this, the cause of secession and slavery that he had once bitterly opposed, the cause he joined because, in the end, he could not bear to take up arms against his own people in his beloved Virginia.

His troops would pick themselves up, he knew in his heart, and begin again. They would scavenge for food and continue their movement west toward Appomattox and Lynchburg.

But a different end had begun to seep into the dark corners of his mind.

Just one day after Union troops marched into Richmond, a strange apparition appeared on the James River. Through the smoke-filled skies over Richmond, a barge—a long rowboat really—could be seen making its way up the river. Twelve sailors manned the oars as they wove their way through the wreckage of sunken ships and debris clogging the waterway. Behind them lay the steamer, *Malvern,* that had safely brought them through the torpedoes mining the river's approach to the city—until it ran aground.

In the rowboat Admiral Porter sat chagrined at the frustration of his plan to escort his guest to Richmond in high style with a grand maritime entrance and hundreds of military men. Sensing the admiral's embarrassment, the man seated with him joked about how well it was to be humble. On land, smoke still rose over the smoldering ruins of the city.

As the sailors maneuvered their way to shore, Admiral Porter pointed to a stark brick building ahead that appeared to be a warehouse. "Libby Prison," he said simply.

The name sent a tremor through his guest. Libby Prison. For years the name horrified Northerners as a steady stream of newspaper accounts spoke of it as a shameful dungeon of sickness and death for captured husbands, sons, and brothers. Periodically, from those who escaped the prison, firsthand accounts of appalling conditions and treatment inflamed the North. Now here it stood before him.

On shore a group of black laborers—freed by the man now in their midst—glanced curiously at the unknown, tall, thin man dressed in black with a black stovepipe hat on his head. A Northern reporter happened to be on the dock when the barge arrived and gaped in disbelief at the sight.

Turning to the black men, he said, "Do you know who this is? This is the president of the United States."

For a moment bewildered blacks stared at the lanky man with the deeply furrowed face and the kind eyes. Then one of them, wild with joy, threw down his shovel and ran to Lincoln. Throwing himself down on the ground in front of the man, he kissed the president's feet.

Lincoln quickly reached down and lifted the man from the ground, putting his arm on the tearful man's shoulders. "Kiss the feet of no man," he said firmly. "Kneel only to God. You have your liberty and as long as I live, no one will put a shackle on your limbs."

The other workers rushed forward. "Glory Hallelujah" and "Thank you, dear Lord" flowed from their mouths as they wept and laughed in joy. In the crush of excitement, they pushed forward to touch the man they saw as savior. In an instant, an eruption of news that Abraham Lincoln had come to Richmond exploded over the city as word raced through the streets.

Admiral Porter tried to push the black men from Lincoln's path so he could move, but they clung to the president and continued to pour their gratitude, love, and tears over him. Other blacks began to flow onto the dock area and some broke out in song. Overwhelmed, Lincoln stood silently watching as more and more freed slaves came running down the hill as far as the eye could see. Porter's sailors surrounded the president with their bayonets mounted out of fear for his life, but the crowds could not be budged.

The president at last raised his hand to speak and a silence slowly descended over the mass of people. "My poor friends. You are free—free as air. You can cast off the name of slave and trample upon it; it will come to you no more. Liberty is your birthright. . ." He paused and looked into their faces. "It is a sin that you have been deprived of it for so many years. But you must try to deserve this priceless boom, as every person must. Let the world see that you merit it."

A hush had fallen over the crowd and only the waves lapping against the dock could be heard.

"There now," Lincoln said, his voice rising. "Let me pass on. I have but little time to spare. I want to see the capital."

Slowly the crowd began to step back, opening a passageway for the president to pass. Up the hill he strode in the hot sun, sweat pouring from his face, swarms of blacks in tow. As the great throng of people moved, dust rose from the ground as their feet kicked the dirt. All around, fruit trees and dogwoods bloomed in showy splendor. Overhead a brilliant blue sky covered the party moving through the streets of Richmond.

The admiral and his sailors anxiously scanned the crowd for signs of trouble as they moved along his side. A few whites had begun to appear in the crowd. Some of the white men seemed bad-featured, Porter thought uneasily.

When they reached Libby Prison, Lincoln stopped and a sadness spread over his face.

Some blacks in the crowd began to shout, "We'll tear it down, Massa Lincoln!"

The president quickly raised his hand, "No. Leave it as a monument."

From the windows of Libby, captured Confederate soldiers stared at the man in black who towered over the others. Looking up at the weary, sickly-looking faces behind bars, Lincoln sadly said to Porter, "We need to be done with this nasty business."

The heat of the afternoon grew oppressive, made worse by the smoke and dust in the air. Lincoln took off his jacket and lifted his hat to mop his sweaty forehead. As they prepared to move on, an ancient-looking black man, the care and wrinkles of epochs on his countenance, limped up to the president, removed his hat, and bowed deeply. Genuinely moved, Lincoln bowed to the old man in return. Those around him watched in stunned amazement. A white man bowing to a black man?

"Who can show us the way to Jefferson Davis's home?" Lincoln asked.

"I can," the Northern reporter following the group said.

"Lead on," the president said.

The jubilation of blacks continued as Lincoln's party walked away from the prison. All along the way freed slaves pushed forward to touch the man or shake his hand, to thank him or wish him well. One woman cried out on seeing him, "I know I am free, for I have seen Father Abraham." Another black woman shouted from the doorway of a house, "Thank you, dear Jesus." A mother pushed forward and thrust her baby to Lincoln who gently touched his head. A man fell to his feet before the tall apparition and began praying for the president. Out of respect, Lincoln stopped and removed his hat while the man prayed.

Here and there a few white folks approached the president as well. A small white girl ran up at one point and handed the lanky man a bunch of roses, a big smile on her face. Another girl said as he passed, "You are the best friend of the South." A white man in shirt sleeves rushed up and cried out, "Abraham Lincoln, God bless you. You are the poor man's friend." On one street corner a girl stood, wrapped in the stars and stripes. A few other women waved small flags or handkerchiefs as the president passed.

But mostly, white Richmonders glared in stony silence from their porches or peered in despair from behind their shuttered windows. In the houses along the streets people peered from their windows at the spectacle below. The admiral believed he saw more hatred than friendliness in those faces who for four years had heard a steady drumbeat of terrible references to the Northern president as a malignant monster. The finer the home, the more hostile the looks.

When at last they arrived at the home of Jefferson Davis, General Weitzel stepped forward to greet Lincoln. Having been misled about the time of arrival, he was embarrassed at not having been at the dock to meet the president. As Lincoln stepped onto the porch, a great cheer rose from the crowd. He turned and bowed to them. Then the doorway of the great mansion swallowed its unlikely visitor.

Inside Lincoln went first to the study of the man who had plagued him for four long years. Tired from the exhausting walk, he slumped into the comfortable chair behind the large desk and asked for a glass of water.

"I suppose this was Davis's chair," he said, smiling like a child who has found a long wanted toy.

"I am told it was, Mr. President," Weitzel said as Lincoln's eyes scanned the room, studying its contents and suddenly looking very serious and lost in thought.

After awhile Lincoln rose. "I would like to see the rest of the house."

So they took to poking about in the rooms. Upstairs Varina's trinkets still sat on dressers and tables and many of the family's clothes, left behind in the haste to leave, hung in closets and armoires. In the Davis bedroom the president spotted a photograph that had fallen unnoticed on the floor. He picked it up. The angelic face of a child, a small boy, stared back at him. He turned the photo over. The words "little Joe" were scrawled on the back. A pain pierced his heart as he remembered the news stories of little Joe's death in this very house. At the same time the ghost memory of his own son who died in the White House rose up to torment him. He struggled for a moment, then carefully placed the photograph on a table next to the bed and walked from the room.

On leaving the White House of the Confederacy, a carriage drawn by four horses waited to carry the president through the streets of Richmond. With a cavalry escort they headed toward Capitol Square, followed by many Union officers on horseback. Crowds of people, mostly black, lined the streets and ran alongside the coach, cheering and shouting for Lincoln and their newfound freedom. Army bands played as throngs followed the carriage onto the square.

Standing guard over Capitol Square, a towering George Washington looked down on the commotion. Someone had stuffed a small flag into his hand and he held it high in the air as a gentle wind blew the stars and stripes in flapping motions. The memory of a drenched Jefferson Davis being inaugurated as president of the Permanent Confederate States hovered about, but today the sun shone brightly.

Standing below Washington, Lincoln stared emotionally at the capitol with the Federal flag flying from its roof. From the great portico, he spoke to the throng of blacks packed into the square. He told them again that they were free and had no master now but God. After he finished speaking, the echo of the crowd's cheers rose, louder and louder, spreading far, reaching to the dead littered across the nation.

Inside the abandoned Confederate Congress, ghosts lingered in the legislative chambers. An eerie stillness met Lincoln in the disarray of abandonment. Furniture lay scattered around, victims of souvenir hunters who had already chopped off pieces. Looters had rummaged through desks and cabinets in the elegant room. Government documents and worthless Confederate dollars lay strewn across the floor. In the spittoons around the room charred papers, burned in haste, settled into ash and shards. Amidst the debris of failure, Lincoln could hear the silenced secessionist voices evaporating into the rafters.

After leaving the capitol, the carriage wound its way around the burned-out district where Weitzel pointed out that flames had eaten hundreds of buildings of every kind, old and new, simple and elegant, business and residential. The finest shops and the lowliest warehouses, he repeated to Lincoln as he had been told. The president stared numbly at the mindless waste before him, a mere fragment of the debris of war.

The carriage swung around for a closer look at the prisons—the infamous Libby, Castle Thunder, Castle Godwin . . . Weitzel pointed out an island in the James River.

"That is Belle Isle, Mr. President. It's where ordinary Union soldiers spent their captivity. Summer and winter they slept in the open, hungry and freezing, without bedding and adequate sanitation."

A deep sadness crept into Lincoln's eyes.

"Thousands died of exposure and disease in these prisons," Weitzel added. Before they left the prison area, he asked Lincoln, "What should we do with the captured Confederate soldiers now in these dungeons?"

"I don't want to give any orders on that, General. But if I were in your place, I'd let 'em up easy. Let 'em up easy," Lincoln said. "Now let me see where the people of Richmond live."

The carriage rode through the streets, escorted by a retinue of mounted officers. It snaked its way through humble, working-class sections where bewildered people gathered to watch as it passed. Richmond had fallen. Had the war ended? Then it twisted its way through the finer sections of the city, eventually climbing up Church Hill. Lincoln admired the grand homes and lush gardens, the dogwoods and fruit trees in bloom.

"The war has not touched these fine places, it seems," Lincoln said.

"That image is deceiving, Mr. President," Weitzel answered. "Many a secessionist comes from these fine homes. And a few Unionists, too."

Lincoln looked at him. "Unionists in these grand mansions?"

"Yes. Look there. See that beautiful mansion ahead." He pointed to a magnificent, three-story white building set in gardens lush with the colors of spring. "That is the home of Elizabeth Van Lew. She has been General Grant's spy here in Richmond."

"Ahh!" Lincoln exclaimed as a remembered phrase popped into his mind—"'Our lady in Richmond . . .' Yes, yes. Ulysses has spoken of her. Just last week at City Point."

"He refers to her as the person who has given him more helpful information than anyone during the war," Weitzel added.

"Then we must stop," Lincoln said excitedly.

The general quickly leaned out the carriage window and shouted to the driver, "Pull over, there." He pointed to the mansion.

The driver turned into the pathway leading to the front portico with its grand columns. As he did so, someone inside spotted the carriage. Before they had stopped, the door flung open and a small girl ran onto the porch, skipping down the steps past the guard posted there. The carriage door opened and Annie ran up to greet the visitors. When the tall man dressed in black stepped down, he took off his tall hat and bowed to the girl.

"I'm Annie," the animated child exclaimed. "Who are you?"

The flabbergasted guard suddenly realized who had stepped out of the carriage and hurried to Annie. "This is the president of the United States."

Annie looked at the man quizzically. On the porch a group of people began to spill out of the house.

"I've come to see Elizabeth Van Lew," Lincoln said, bending down to speak to the child.

"Aunt Lizzie?" Annie asked. Then grabbing his hand she led the smiling man up the porch stairs, General Weitzel in tow. "Aunt Lizzie," she called out.

As the president walked onto the portico, a passage opened as everyone stepped back in awe. A hush had fallen over them. In the doorway a petite blond, her hair falling in curls on her forehead, her crystal-clear blue eyes flashing, stood watching in amazement.

"Mr. President . . ." she said in disbelief as she extended her hand. "Is this a dream?"

"Miss Van Lew? Some would call me a nightmare," Lincoln replied with a laugh, taking her hand and kissing it. "I was passing by and General Weitzel here identified you as Grant's correspondent."

Eliza stepped forward at that moment and introduced herself, her daughter's speech seeming to have abandoned her. "Please, Mr. President. Come in. Come in."

"Only for a moment," Lincoln said as he was led into the grand parlor. Elizabeth had regained her composure and began to introduce her friends—Lohmann, Rowley, Palmer, McNiven, Ross, and the others. John Minor Botts, at last freed from house arrest, was present as well, having rushed back to Richmond to celebrate with his friends. She credited each of them in turn for their work on behalf of the Union.

"Don't forget my daddy," little Eliza jumped in. "He would not fight for the bad men."

"Good girl," Lincoln said to her, patting her shoulder, a broad grin on his face. "You have made us remember your daddy."

Next Elizabeth turned to the stately black woman who stood off to the side.

"And here, Mr. President, is our star, Mary Bowser."

Lincoln listened in amazement as Elizabeth explained Mary's Unionist activities in the home of Jefferson Davis.

"It was Miss Lizzie's idea to plant me there," Mary said as the president stepped up to her, bowed, and taking her hand, kissed it.

"But Mary who took all the risks," Elizabeth replied, immensely pleased by Lincoln's unprecedented gesture toward Mary. "There is another special person you must meet," and she turned to Peter Roane. "He has served us and your cause well for years."

Lincoln extended his hand to the brawny black man and put his arm on his shoulder in gratitude.

"You needs to know Mista President," Peter said shyly, "that Miz Eliza and Miz Lizzie done they own mancee'pation of slaves long before da war."

"Then all we did was follow the leaders in Richmond!" Lincoln said, beaming as the room broke into hearty laughter and a broad grin spread across Peter's face.

Eliza tried to convince the president to stay for dinner.

"Dear friends," he answered graciously, "there is no where I would rather be right now. But there is more work to be done and I must be off. The Union owes you all a debt of gratitude. Let's work now to heal the scars of war without delay."

And he was gone as quickly as he appeared.

That evening a brilliant sunset blazed across the west, etching crimson, orange, and yellow streaks over the fading blue sky. The sweet scents of spring rose from the garden as Elizabeth wandered alone over the terraces. The acrid smells of burning tobacco and charred wood had begun to grown faint. Fallen magnolia blossoms lay about on the grass, their pink petals spotting the lush green lawn. A small white rabbit twitched about, poking here and there for food.

In the hyacinth and tulip beds Elizabeth paused, and bent down to pick one of each. An earth-colored garden snake slithered away.

"These were your favorites, Poppa." Her thoughts drifted to the phantom seated in the purple and yellow clusters.

He nodded in agreement.

"You saw him? Lincoln?" she asked silently.

He had, but he didn't answer. He worried she'd bring up *the* subject again. Best to play dead.

"Such a simple, humble man. But so bright and kind," Elizabeth mused. "You would have liked meeting him."

He held his breath.

"It's over. Lee can't hold out much longer—his army decimated and Grant chasing him. It's only a matter of days," she said confidently. "The world can right itself again."

She sounds less hard somehow, he thought. *Winning does things to people.*

"You would have done the right thing, had you lived. I feel that now. I don't know why. Maybe my anger made me want to believe the worst."

He smiled for the first time in a long time. *My dear, beautiful Bet! How could I have stood up to the two of you? And your brother. Was there ever really a question what I would have done?*

But before he could ask her, she moved away from the tulips and hyacinths and strolled slowly toward the dogwood grove. Other ghost memories followed her as she ducked under the pink and white blossoms and breathed in the scented air.

"Dear Emmie, you're not in prison any more," she thought.

Overhead a yellowthroat warbler, back from his winter travels and singing loudly, fluttered from branch to branch. For a brief moment the world seemed different, less biting, more bearable somehow.

A gentle wisp of air brushed across her face in the evening stillness.

"Dearest Allen," Elizabeth whispered to him. "Your last months on earth were so horrible. The unbearable pain of a tormented mind that sees only the litter of life."

Except when we were together, he wanted to correct her.

"These last years the world has seemed so full of hate and meanness, selfishness and arrogance . . . and most of all, ignorance. That's what war is, after all—all those things. A mindless force. Pure rage." She reached up and picked a branch of pink blossoms from the dogwood overhead. "But you were love and gentleness . . ."

A stillness settled over her, a kind of peaceful calm. She saw the James River meandering past below the garden, making its way to City Point and out to sea, the brilliant colors of sunset skipping on its waters. As she stood watching the mesmerizing dance of being all around her, a gust of wind rustled her skirt and tousled her curls.

She smiled, remembering his fingers weaving through her hair.

Author's Note

I BEGAN MY SEARCH FOR THIS BOOK SOME YEARS AGO WHEN A COL-league, the late Dora Lee Dauma, collector of books and all things relating to women's history, suggested that my next historical novel should center on Mary Bowser, a former slave, who served in the home of Jefferson Davis and spied for the Union. Intrigued, I pursued Bowser, only to find that little information existed. Although she left a diary, it had apparently been tossed away by a descendant who failed to grasp its significance. But in that search I stumbled on Elizabeth Van Lew, who had planted Bowser, her former slave, in the Davis home. Happily, as it turned out, I was able to tell both women's stories.

In piecing together Elizabeth's life, I was fortunate that she left behind a diary, although almost half of it has been lost. During the war, in constant fear of being unmasked as a spy, Elizabeth took to burying the journal, unwittingly destroying some parts. She also kept a scrapbook with correspondence, newspaper accounts, and other materials. After the war she asked the War Department to return all correspondence and items relating to her Union work. Ultimately, she apparently destroyed most of these materials, likely out of fear of retaliation against herself and others in her network. Despite the losses, what remains is invaluable.

In addition, letters and other firsthand accounts of both her Unionist coconspirators and Confederate officials who dealt with her provide insights. Given her prominence in Richmond society, a number of newspaper reports from the period speak of her as well.

I am indebted to secondary studies by scholars like William Gilmore Beymer, David Ryan, and Elizabeth Varon, who, over the years since Elizabeth's death, have worked through the primary sources she, and those who knew her, left behind, making the details of her life accessible. Unfortunately these accounts often disagree in their details (for instance, whether or not Elizabeth was allowed into Libby Prison). In the end, I had to make choices to move the story forward and as a novelist I have, of course, taken liberties and imagined scenes to enhance dramatic effect.

Also helpful are accounts of Union prisoners who describe prison conditions and tell of Elizabeth's work among them. And of course, diaries of soldiers on both sides of the conflict provide a searing look at the war—its battles and horrors—that Unionists so vigorously fought against.

Biographies and other historical accounts of Confederate and Union figures (such as Jefferson Davis, Varina Davis, John Winder, and Ulysses S. Grant) fleshed out those characters and kept them from descending into caricatures.

Maps of Richmond and the surrounding region, as well as many photos and diagrams of Confederate sites (such as prisons and official buildings), helped immeasurably in understanding what Elizabeth and her coconspirators were up against. Photos and descriptions of her home, with its infamous fugitive room, also proved helpful. Likewise, my many travels to Civil War sites, North and South, provided indispensable context for the war.

The account of Elizabeth's Unionist and spying activities centered, of course, on Richmond and its environs. To me, that left an essential part of the story, the war itself and its horrors, untold. I grappled with how to include this since Elizabeth never ventured to the front lines of battle. Ultimately I settled on the introduction of a fictitious character, Major Allen Rockwell, a Union prisoner who becomes Elizabeth's love interest and eventually returns to battle. Rockwell enables us to follow the progress and dreadfulness of the war itself as Elizabeth and her Unionist network struggle to bring that fighting to an end. I trust that Elizabeth, in her place of rest, will forgive me this fabrication since it in no way affects the truth of her actual antislavery, pro-Union efforts in the book.

Historical fiction, after all, grants us the ability to use fiction to make the story more real for the reader—in a way that sometimes reality cannot.

Similarly, because the names and faces of so many of the people she helped are lost to us (like the slaves she helped escape and the poor she ministered to in Richmond's poverty-stricken neighborhoods), I have created characters who represent a composite picture of those lost individuals: the group of seven slaves escaping to Elizabeth in the wake of Dahlgren's attempted raid on Richmond and Emmie at the almshouse, who gives voice to Richmond's lower classes.

Finally, I want to address a most unfortunate myth that took hold in some quarters after Elizabeth died—that she was "crazy." The myth (begun by the speculation of John P. Reynolds, who wrote on her death that Elizabeth succeeded as a spy because she acted "crazy," making people think her harmless) has both benign and malicious motivations among those taking up this falsehood. One view grows from the feeling that she must have been crazy to expend her fortune and risk her life and reputation on antislavery and Unionist causes. No sane Southern lady would defy social custom in this way. These folks simply cannot grasp that one would rationally choose such a path. The other view is a deliberate attempt to undermine and trivialize Elizabeth to exonerate the incompetence of a Confederacy incapable of unmasking a serious threat—from a woman, no less. To treat her as a powerful person with extraordinary organizational skills, a rational force to be reckoned with, is to admit that she was smarter than the men she repeatedly outwitted. Elizabeth Varon, preeminent Van Lew scholar, argues that not a shard of evidence exists for the "crazy Bet" legend—quite the opposite. Elizabeth prided herself on her rationality and conducted herself as such. Among those who knew her best, her friend Eliza Carrington wrote a vindication of Van Lew's life (never published), referring to her as "possessed of a logical mind" and affirming, "I have never known as noble a woman."

Special thanks to my editors at Globe Pequot Press, Erin Turner, who believed in the book, and Meredith Dias, project editor; my colleagues,

Civil War historian Hiram Smith and literature instructor Janet Muir, who read the book and gave valuable feedback; Katherine Wilkins at the Virginia Historical Society and Hal Jespersen for map help; members of my reading group, Mary Krause, Renee Gadoua, Diana Putzer, and Jessica Christaldi, who allowed themselves to be turned into a focus group, especially Jessica, who suggested the title; and Joseph Agonito, historian and writer, who served as my endless sounding board.

Civil War and Richmond Chronology

Event	Date
John Brown's raid on Harper's Ferry	Oct. 16–18, 1859
Virginia Secession Convention begins	Feb. 13, 1861
Jefferson Davis inaugurated president of the Provisional Government of Confederate States in Montgomery, Alabama	Feb. 18, 1861
Abraham Lincoln inaugurated president of US	Mar. 4, 1861
Attack on Fort Sumter, SC, by Confederacy; War begins	Apr. 12, 1861
Lincoln forbids trade with seceded states	Apr. 16, 1861
Virginia leaves the Union	Apr. 17, 1861
Lincoln proclaims a blockade of Southern seaports	Apr. 19, 1861
Capital of the Confederacy moved to Richmond	May 29, 1861
Battle of Bull Run, Manassas	July 21, 1861
Jefferson Davis re-inaugurated as president of the Permanent Confederacy	Feb. 22, 1862
Richmond and ten-mile radius around the city put under martial law	Mar. 1, 1862
First wave of Unionist arrests in Richmond begins	Mar. 2, 1862
Peninsular Campaign to take Richmond under General McClellan	Apr.–June 1862
First Union spy—Timothy Webster—hanged in Richmond	Apr. 29, 1862
Emancipation Proclamation takes effect	Jan. 1, 1863
Bread riots in Richmond	Apr. 2, 1863
Battle of Chancellorsville	May 1, 1863
Battle of Gettysburg	July 1–3, 1863
Vicksburg falls to Grant, putting Union in control of Mississippi River	July 4, 1863

Event	Date
Dahlgren/Kilpatrick raid against Richmond begins	Feb. 28, 1864
General Grant named head of whole Union army	March 12, 1864
Wilderness Campaign under Grant begins	1st week of May, 1864
Spotsylvania battles	May 7–20, 1864
Cold Harbor battles	May 31–June 12, 1864
Siege of Petersburg begins	June 1864
Great crater explosion at Petersburg	July 30, 1864
General Sherman's Atlanta Campaign and march to the sea	Aug.–Dec. 1864
Lincoln reelected president of US	Nov. 1864
Fort Fisher, last Confederate seaport, falls	Jan. 15, 1865
Thirteenth Amendment to Constitution abolishing slavery passes	Jan. 31, 1865
Hampton Roads Conference	Feb. 3, 1865
Charleston, SC, falls to Sherman	Feb. 17, 1865
Lee attacks Fort Stedman and fails	Mar. 25, 1865
Lincoln goes to City Point to confer with generals	Mar. 26, 1865
Five Forks falls to General Sheridan	Apr. 1, 1865
Petersburg falls to General Grant	Apr. 2, 1865
Confederate government flees Richmond	Apr. 2, 1865
Union troops enter Richmond and occupy the city	Apr. 3, 1865
Lincoln comes to Richmond	Apr. 4, 1865
Lee surrenders at Appomattox	Apr. 9, 1865
Lincoln assassinated	Apr. 14, 1865

Selected Bibliography

Beymer, William Gilmore. *On Hazardous Service: Scouts and Spies of the North and South.* New York: Harper & Brothers, 1912.

Blakey, Arch Frederic. *General John H. Winder, C. S. A.* Gainesville: University of Florida Press, 1990.

Catton, Bruce. *The Centennial History of the Civil War.* 3 Volumes. New York: Doubleday, 1961.

Cox, Clinton. *Fiery Vision: The Life and Death of John Brown.* New York: Scholastic Press, 1997.

Davis, Burke. *To Appomattox: Nine April Days, 1865.* New York: Popular Library, 1959.

Davis, William C. *An Honorable Defeat: The Last Days of the Confederate Government.* San Diego: Harcourt, 2001.

Eaton, Clement. *Jefferson Davis.* New York: The Free Press, 1977.

Feis, William B. *Grant's Secret Service: The Intelligence War from Belmont to Appomattox.* Lincoln: University of Nebraska Press, 2002.

Fishel, Edwin C. The *Secret War for the Union: The Untold Story of Military Intelligence in the Civil War.* Boston: Houghton Mifflin, 1996.

Furgurson, Ernest B. *Ashes of Glory: Richmond at War.* New York: Alfred A. Knopf, 1996.

Grant, U. S. *Personal Memoirs of U. S. Grant.* New York: Charles L. Webster and Co., 1886.

Hamilton, Andrew G. "Tunnel Escape from Libby Prison." Chicago: 1893. Rare booklet. Library of Congress.

Hesseltine, William B., Ed. *Civil War Prisons.* Kent, OH: Kent State University Press, 1962.

Hoehling, A. A., and Mary Hoehling. *The Last Days of the Confederacy.* New York: Fairfax Press, 1981.

Horan, James D. *The Pinkertons: The Detective Dynasty That Made History.* New York: Crown, 1967.

Jones, Katharine M. *Ladies of Richmond.* Indianapolis: Bobbs-Merrill, 1962.

Lankford, Nelson. *Richmond Burning: The Last Days of the Confederate Capital.* New York: Penguin Books, 2002.

McPherson, James M. *The Atlas of the Civil War.* Philadelphia: Courage Books, 2005.

Moran, Captain Frank E. "Colonel Rose's Tunnel at Libby Prison," *Century Illustrated Monthly Magazine,* March 1888, pp. 770–790.

Oates, Stephen B. *To Purge This Land with Blood: A Biography of John Brown.* New York: Harper, 1970.

Parker, Sandra V. *Richmond's Civil War Prisons.* Lynchburg, VA: H. E. Howard, 1990.

Potter, David. *The Impending Crisis: 1848–1861.* New York: Harper, 1976.

"Richmond Spy: How Miss Van Lew and Other Richmond Citizens Aided General Grant," *Richmond Daily Dispatch,* July 17, 1883.

Rose, Colonel Thomas E. "Libby Tunnel," *National Tribune,* May 14, 1885.

Ross, Ishbel. *First Lady of the South: The Life of Mrs. Jefferson Davis.* Westport, CT: Greenwood Press, 1958.

Ryan, David D. *A Yankee Spy in Richmond: The Civil War Diary of "Crazy Bet" Van Lew.* Mechanicsburg, PA: Stackpole Books, 1996.

Schultz, Duane. *The Dahlgren Affair: Terror and Conspiracy in the Civil War.* New York: W. W. Norton, 1998.

Shrady, John. "Reminiscences of Libby Prison," *Magazine of American History with Notes and Queries,* Vol. XVI, July–December 1886.

Thomas, Emory M. *The Confederate Nation: 1861–1865.* New York: Harper and Row, 1979.

Varon, Elizabeth R. *Southern Lady, Yankee Spy: The True Story of Elizabeth Van Lew.* New York: Oxford University Press, 2003.

Wiley, Bell Irvin. *Confederate Women.* Westport, CT: Greenwood Press, 1975.

Winik, Jay. *April 1865: The Month That Saved America.* New York: Harper Collins, 2001.

Book Group Discussion Guide

1. We tend to think of Southerners in the Civil War as united in their thinking about secession, slavery, and the North. How does Elizabeth's story challenge this view?

2. What qualities did Elizabeth bring to her espionage work that helped her succeed?

3. Throughout the war, Elizabeth is suspected of aiding the enemy. How is it possible that, despite investigations, house surveillance, and arrests of her coconspirators, she was never charged?

4. How is Mary Bowser, a former slave, able to spy undetected in the home of Jefferson Davis?

5. Does Elizabeth bear any blame in the recapture of Col. Thomas Rose after he masterminded the great Libby Prison escape?

6. By all accounts Elizabeth was close to her father before his death. What do her "conversations" with her father's ghost add, if anything, to the story?

7. Elizabeth's mother, Eliza, certainly played a role in her daughter's Unionist network. How was Eliza's role different from Elizabeth's and was it any less important?

8. What does the character Emmie in the almshouse add to the story?

9. Perhaps one of the stranger things Elizabeth does with her coconspirators is the Ulric Dahlgren grave robbery. Why do you think she does this?

10. Elizabeth provides sanctuary and the means of escape to freedom for runaway slaves. What would have happened to Elijah, Holdy, Kriszy, Bula, and the children after Dahlgren abandons them if they had not found their way to Elizabeth?

11. Despite numerous expectations of victory, Elizabeth and her Unionist network are disappointed again and again by the Union's failure to bring the war to a conclusion. Given the Union's blockade of Southern ports, the Confederacy's lack of food, fuel, materials, and supplies, a crumbling infrastructure, a devalued currency, lack of manpower, a high rate of desertion among its soldiers, and enormous casualties, how does the Confederacy manage to keep the war going for four years?

12. Emmie says that starting wars is "a coward's game." Rockwell asserts that "war is madness." Elizabeth refers to war as a "mindless force." What does each mean and are they right?

ABOUT THE AUTHOR

ROSEMARY AGONITO, PhD, is an award-winning author whose first novel, also based on a true story, won the prestigious 2006 Western Heritage Award for the Outstanding Western Novel (previous winners include James Michener, Larry McMurtry, and Barbara Kingsolver). In addition to the award-winning *Buffalo Calf Road Woman: The Story of a Warrior of the Little Bighorn*, she has authored five non-fiction books and many articles. She has lectured widely on women's history and issues; appeared on national talk shows on CNN, NBC, MSNBC, CNBC, PBS, and others; and has been quoted in print media such as *People, Parents, USA Today, Christian Science Monitor, Marie Claire, Glamour, Mademoiselle, New Woman, Men's Health,* and *Human Resources Executive.* Visit Rosemary's website at www.rosemaryagonito.com.